Close-up

COMPANION A1+

Liz Gardiner

NATIONAL GEOGRAPHIC
LEARNING

Australia • Brazil • Mexico • Singapore • United Kingdom • United States

Close-up A1+ Companion
Liz Gardiner

Executive Editor: Sian Mavor

Editorial Manager: Claire Merchant

Commissioning Editor: Kayleigh Buller

Editor: Katie Foufouti

Head of Production: Celia Jones

Content Project Manager: Melissa Beavis

Manufacturing Manager: Eyvett Davis

Compositor: Wild Apple Design Ltd

For product information and technology assistance, contact us at
Cengage Learning Customer & Sales Support, cengage.com/contact
For permission to use material from this text or product,
submit all requests online at **cengage.com/permissions**
Further permissions questions can be emailed to
permissionrequest@cengage.com

ISBN: 978-1-4080-9830-1

National Geographic Learning
Cheriton House,
North Way, Andover,
Hampshire, SP10 5BE
United Kingdom

National Geographic Learning, a Cengage Learning Company, has a mission to bring the world to the classroom and the classroom to life. With our English language programs, students learn about their world by experiencing it. Through our partnerships with National Geographic and TED Talks, they develop the language and skills they need to be successful global citizens and leaders.

Locate your local office at **international.cengage.com/region**

Visit National Geographic Learning online at **NGL.Cengage.com/Closeup**
Visit our corporate website at **www.cengage.com**

Photo credits

Cover image: ©Filip Fuxa/Shutterstock Inc

Student Access: to access the Close-up A1+ Companion audio, please visit the Student Online Zone at **NGL.Cengage.com/closeup**

Teacher Access: to access the Grammar and Vocabulary Answer Keys, please visit the Teacher Online Zone at **NGL.Cengage.com/closeup** and use the password provided in the Teacher's Book

Printed in China by RR Donnelley
Print Number: 01 Print Year: 2017

Contents

Note to Teachers

Close-up A1+ Companion provides students with everything they need to understand the vocabulary and grammar in the *Close-up A1+ Student's Book*.

In the vocabulary section, words and phrases are listed in order of appearance together with their parts of speech and IPA. Each entry includes a clear explanation of the headword, an example sentence, derivatives (appropriate for the level) and the Greek translation of the word or phrase as it is used in the context of the Student's Book. For some entries there are special notes. These include antonyms, synonyms and expressions. At the end of the word lists for most sections, there are word sets that help students learn related words or phrases more easily. There are also *Look!* boxes with notes on usage. The vocabulary section ends with a variety of tasks that practise many of the new words and phrases of that unit.

In the grammar section, there are comprehensive grammar explanations in Greek with plenty of topic-related example sentences. The grammar section ends with tasks that practise the grammar of that unit.

At the back of the book, there is a complete list of all the words and phrases in the companion in alphabetical order with their entry number. This helps teachers and students to locate words easily, for example, if they want to refer to a word they learnt in another unit, or if they come across any difficulties.

Finally, *Close-up A1+ Companion* is accompanied by audio, which contains the accurate pronunciation of each headword. You can find the audio here: ngl.cengage.com

Terms & Abbreviations

Terms / Abbreviations		Όροι / Συντομεύσεις
n	noun	ουσιαστικό
v	verb	ρήμα
phr v	phrasal verb	περιφραστικό ρήμα
adj	adjective	επίθετο
adv	adverb	επίρρημα
det	determiner	προσδιοριστικό
pron	pronoun	αντωνυμία
prep	preposition	πρόθεση
conj	conjunction	σύνδεσμος
expr	expression	έκφραση
excl	exclamation	επιφώνημα
Opp	opposite	αντίθετο
Syn	synonym	συνώνυμο
abbr	abbreviation	συντόμευση

Key to pronunciation and phonetic symbols

Consonants					
p	pen	/pen/	tʃ	chain	/tʃeɪn/
b	bad	/bæd/	dʒ	jam	/dʒæm/
t	tea	/tiː/	f	fall	/fɔːl/
d	did	/dɪd/	v	van	/væn/
k	cat	/kæt/	θ	thin	/θɪn/
g	get	/get/	ð	this	/ðɪs/

Vowels and diphthongs					
iː	see	/siː/	ɜː	fur	/fɜː/
i	happy	/ˈhæpi/	ə	about	/əˈbaʊt/
ɪ	sit	/sɪt/	eɪ	say	/seɪ/
e	ten	/ten/	əʊ	go	/gəʊ/
æ	cat	/kæt/	aɪ	my	/maɪ/
ɑː	father	/ˈfɑːðə/	ɔɪ	boy	/bɔɪ/
ɒ	got	/gɒt/	aʊ	now	/naʊ/
ɔː	saw	/sɔː/	ɪə	near	/nɪə/
ʊ	put	/pʊt/	eə	hair	/heə/
u	actual	/ˈæktʃuəl/	ʊə	pure	/pjʊə/
uː	too	/tuː/	ʌ	cup	/kʌp/

1 This Is Me!

Page 5

1.1 **traditional** (adj) /trəˈdɪʃənl/
done in the same way for many years
• *Every year, the English do traditional dances on 1st May to welcome the summer.*
➣ tradition (n), traditionally (adv)
❖ παραδοσιακός

1.2 **clothing** (n) /ˈkləʊðɪŋ/
a type of clothes • *It's cold, so wear some warm clothing for the trip.* ➣ clothe (v)
❖ ντύσιμο, ένδυμα, ρουχισμός
✎ Syn: clothes

1.3 **bubble** (n) /ˈbʌbl/
a small ball made by filling chewing gum, liquid or other substance with air; a ball of liquid made from soap and water • *My little brother likes playing with bubbles in the bath.*
➣ bubble (v) ❖ φούσκα

1.4 **Papua New Guinea** (n) /ˌpæpuə njuː ˈgɪni/
❖ Παπούα Νέα Γουινέα

Reading
Page 6

1.5 **because** (conj) /bɪˈkɒz/
we use because to give the reason for sth
• *I'm making a sandwich because I'm hungry.*
❖ επειδή

1.6 **activity** (n) /æktˈɪvəti/
something that you do to have fun
• *My favourite activity is playing board games*
➣ act (v), active (adj), actively (adv)
❖ δραστηριότητα

1.7 **swimming** (n) /ˈswɪmɪŋ/
the activity of moving through water by moving your arms and legs • *It's a hot day. Let's go swimming in the pool.* ➣ swim (v), swimmer (n) ❖ κολύμπι

1.8 **noticeboard** (n) /ˈnəʊtɪsbɔːd/
a board on a wall where you can put notes or pictures, etc. • *The teacher put our drawings on the class noticeboard.* ❖ πίνακας ανακοινώσεων

1.9 **age** (n) /eɪdʒ/
how old sb/sth is • *I'm ten years old. What age are you?* ➣ age (v) ❖ ηλικία

1.10 **country** (n) /ˈkʌntri/
a place that has its own government, laws and way of life • *Australia is a very big country.*
❖ χώρα

1.11 **mountain biking** (n) /ˈmaʊntən baɪkɪŋ/
the sport of riding a special bike in the mountains • *Georgia goes mountain biking with her friends on Mount Parnitha.*
❖ ποδηλασία εκτός δρόμου (στο βουνό)

1.12 **mountain** (n) /ˈmaʊntən/
a very high area of land • *Olympus is the highest mountain in Greece.* ➣ mountainous (adj) ❖ βουνό

1.13 **karate** (n) /kəˈrɑːti/
a Japanese sport in which you use your hands and feet to fight • *Kostas has a black belt in karate.* ❖ καράτε

1.14 **watermelon** (n) /ˈwɔːtəmelən/
a large fruit that has a hard green skin and is red and juicy inside • *It's nice to eat a piece of watermelon after dinner in summer.*
❖ καρπούζι

1.15 **pizza** (n) /ˈpiːtsə/
a kind of food like flat bread cooked with cheese, tomato, etc. on top • *People in Italy often eat pizza for lunch.* ❖ πίτσα

1.16 **cheese** (n) /tʃiːz/
a hard round or square shaped food made from milk • *Greek farmers use sheep's milk to make cheese.* ❖ τυρί

1.17 **rabbit** (n) /ˈræbɪt/
a small animal that has got long ears and a short tail • *Susie has two white rabbits in her garden and they love carrots.* ❖ κουνέλι

1.18 **goldfish** (n) /ˈgəʊldfɪʃ/
a kind of small, yellow, orange or red fish
• *Our cat is watching the goldfish in the pool.*
❖ χρυσόψαρο

1.19 **tortoise** (n) /ˈtɔːtəs/
an animal with a hard shell on its back
• *Many tortoises sleep under the rocks and trees on Greek mountains.* ❖ (χερσαία) χελώνα

1.20 **Argentina** (n) /ˌɑːdʒənˈtiːnə/
➣ Argentinian (adj) ❖ Αργεντινή

1.21 **mountain bike** (n) /ˈmaʊntən baɪk/
a strong bicycle for riding off road in rocky places • *Be careful! Don't ride your mountain bike so fast down the hill.* ➣ mountain biking (n) ❖ ειδικό ποδήλατο για χρήση εκτός δρόμου

1.22 **reptile** (n) /ˈreptaɪl/
an animal that lays eggs and has cold blood
• *At the zoo, we saw crocodiles and other reptiles.* ❖ ερπετό

1.23 **kitten** (n) /ˈkɪtn/
a baby cat • *Mum found a little kitten last year and now it's a lovely big cat.* ❖ γατάκι

1.24 **snake** (n) /sneɪk/
an animal with a long thin body and no legs
• *I'm not afraid of snakes because they are more afraid of us.* ❖ φίδι

1.25 **of course** (expr) /əv kɔːs/
for sure; certainly ● *Of course Anna is Greek.
She's from Zakinthos.* ❖ φυσικά

Word Focus   Page 7

1.26 **farm** (n) /fɑːm/
a place where people grow plants for food or
have animals like cows or sheep
● *My grandpa worked on a potato farm in the
countryside.* ➤ farm (v), farmer (n)
❖ αγρόκτημα

1.27 **land** (n) /lænd/
an area of ground ● *My uncle has got some
land near the sea and he wants to build a hotel
on it.* ❖ γη, κτήμα

1.28 **grow** (v) /grəʊ/
make sth get bigger ● *Alice grows tomatoes in
her garden.* ➤ growth (n) ❖ καλλιεργώ

1.29 **plant** (n) /plɑːnt/
sth with leaves and roots that grows in the
earth ● *Harry hasn't got a garden, so he grows
plants on his balcony.* ➤ plant (v) ❖ φυτό

1.30 **keep (animals)** (expr) /kiːp ('ænɪmls)/
have and take care of farm animals ● *Nikos
and Maria keep chickens, so they have lots of
eggs every day.* ❖ εκτρέφω (ζώα)

1.31 **handloom** (n) /'hændluːm/
a machine that you use with your hands
to make material for clothes, carpets, etc.
● *People in this mountain village make
traditional clothes on handlooms.* ❖ αργαλειός

1.32 **simple** (adj) /'sɪmpl/
easy to use or understand; easy to make with
only a few parts ● *Football is a simple sport
that is easy to play.* ❖ απλός

1.33 **material** (n) /mə'tɪəriəl/
cloth we use to make clothes; sth that you can
make things from ● *Kate's dress is made of a
nice blue and white material.* ❖ ύφασμα

1.34 **only child** (n) /'oʊnli tʃaɪld/
a child who has no brothers or sisters
● *My dad is an only child, but my mum has
three sisters and one brother.* ❖ μοναχοπαίδι

1.35 **popular** (adj) /'pɒpjələ(r)/
liked by lots of people ● *Indian food is very
popular in Britain.* ➤ popularity (n)
❖ δημοφιλής
✎ Opp: unpopular ❖ μη δημοφιλής

1.36 **special** (adj) /'speʃl/
different from or better than what is usual
● *We wear special clothes to do karate.*
❖ ειδικός, ιδιαίτερος, ξεχωριστός

1.37 **important** (adj) /ɪm'pɔːtnt/
needed very much; of great value ● *It is
important to write your name correctly on the
test paper.* ➤ importance (n)
❖ σημαντικός
✎ Opp: unimportant ❖ ασήμαντος

Animals

chicken	pet	guard dog
goldfish	rabbit	guide dog
insect	reptile	police dog
kitten	snake	
mosquito	tortoise	

Reading   Page 7

1.38 **Peru** (n) /pə'ru/
❖ Περού

1.39 **enjoy** (v) /ɪn'dʒɔɪ/
like (doing sth) ● *Do you enjoy eating ice
cream in summer?* ➤ enjoyment (n), enjoyable
(adj) ❖ απολαμβάνω

1.40 **chicken** (n) /'tʃɪkɪn/
a bird often kept on a farm for its eggs or meat
● *Uncle Jerry has got eight chickens, so he
gives us eggs every day.* ❖ κότα, κοτόπουλο

1.41 **watch** (v) /wɒtʃ/
look at sb/sth for a short or long time to see
what they are doing ● *I watched Mum making
the pizza to learn how she does it.* ❖ κοιτάω,
παρακολουθώ

1.42 **collect** (v) /kə'lekt/
pick things up to put them together
● *Lucas collected his toy cars and put them in
a box.* ➤ collection (n) ❖ μαζεύω

1.43 **teenager** (n) /'tiːneɪdʒə(r)/
a boy or girl between thirteen and nineteen
years old ● *Now that she's a teenager, Lucy
doesn't want to play with her old toys.*
➤ teenage (adj) ❖ έφηβος, έφηβη

1.44 **parent** (n) /'peərənt/
a mother or father ● *Andrew lives with his
parents and his sister.* ❖ γονιός

1.45 **grandmother** (n) /'grænmʌðə(r)/
the mother of your mother or father ● *Nicola's
grandmother in Italy is her dad's mother.*
❖ γιαγιά

1.46 **kite** (n) /kaɪt/
a toy made of paper or cloth that you can fly
in the air ● *On a special day in spring, Greek
people fly kites in the parks.* ❖ χαρταετός

1.47 **great** (adj) /greɪt/
very good; wonderful ● *Let's go to the park.
We can have a great time there.* ❖ υπέροχος

1.48 **fun** (adj) /fʌn/
enjoyable ● *Playing with my dog is fun.*
➤ fun (n) ❖ διασκεδαστικός, ευχάριστος

1.49 **insect** (n) /'ɪnsekt/
a small animal that has six legs and usually
has wings ● *My favourite insects are bees
because I love honey.* ❖ έντομο

1.50 **interesting** (adj) /ˈɪntrəstɪŋ/
that you want to do or see because it is special or different ● *I'm reading an interesting book about animals.* ➤ interest (n), interested (adj) ❖ ενδιαφέρων

1.51 **hate** (v) /heɪt/
feel strongly that you don't like sth ● *Oscar hates doing tests at school.* ➤ hate (n) ❖ μισώ, σιχαίνομαι

1.52 **mosquito** (n) /məˈskiːtəʊ/
a small insect that bites people and animals ● *Mum always closes our windows at night to stop mosquitoes flying in.* ❖ κουνούπι

1.53 **use** (v) /juːz/
do an action with sth for a certain purpose ● *Use a pen to write your name.* ➤ use (n), useless (adj), useful (adj) ❖ χρησιμοποιώ

1.54 **information** (n) /ˌɪnfəˈmeɪʃn/
facts about sb/sth ● *Can you give me some information about your town? How many people live there?* ➤ inform (v) ❖ πληροφορία

1.55 **same** (adj) /seɪm/
not different; exactly like sth else ● *Leo and his friend, Vitalis are in the same class at school.* ❖ ίδιος

1.56 **both** (det, pron) /bəʊθ/
used to mean the one person/thing and also the other ● *Both Giorgio and Lucia are from Italy.* ❖ και οι/τα δυο

1.57 **broccoli** (n) /ˈbrɒkəli/
a green flower-shaped vegetable ● *My little brother hates eating broccoli, but it's my favourite vegetable.* ❖ μπρόκολο

1.58 **spinach** (n) /ˈspɪnɪtʃ/
a green leafy vegetable ● *Sometimes we have traditional spinach pie for lunch.* ❖ σπανάκι

Food

broccoli	pineapple	vanilla
cheese	pizza	watermelon
flavour	spinach	

1.59 **diary** (n) /ˈdaɪəri/
a notebook with spaces to write in for each day of the year ● *Helen writes down her family and friends' birthdays in her diary to remember them.* ❖ ημερολόγιο

1.60 **alarm clock** (n) /əˈlɑːm klɒk/
a special clock that makes a noise to wake you up in the morning ● *I hear my alarm clock at seven o'clock every morning on school days.* ❖ ξυπνητήρι

1.61 **agree** (v) /əˈɡriː/
say sth to show you think the same as sb else ● *I think India is a beautiful country. Do you agree?* ➤ agreement (n) ❖ συμφωνώ
✎ Opp: disagree ❖ διαφωνώ

Vocabulary
Pages 8–9

1.62 **cousin** (n) /ˈkʌzn/
a son or daughter of your aunt or uncle ● *Amanda's cousins live in Germany because her aunt and uncle are working there.* ❖ ξάδελφος, ξαδέλφη

1.64 **pound** (n) /paʊnd/
the main unit of money in the UK (= 100 pence) ● *An orange juice is one pound in this shop.* ❖ λίρα Αγγλίας

1.65 **school children** (n) /ˈskuːltʃɪldrən/
children who have lessons in a school ● *The school children are waiting in the classroom for their teacher.* ❖ μαθητές
✎ Singular: schoolchild, schoolboy, schoolgirl

1.66 **kilometre** (n) /ˈkɪləmiːtə(r)/
1,000 metres ● *Teresa's school is two kilometres from her house, so she takes the bus.* ❖ χιλιόμετρο

1.67 **metre** (n) /ˈmiːtə(r)/
a measure of how long or tall sth or sb is ● *Frank's dad is two metres tall.* ❖ μέτρο

1.68 **aunt** (n) /ɑːnt/
a sister of your parent; your uncle's wife ● *Aunt Tracy is my dad's oldest sister.* ❖ θεία

1.69 **uncle** (n) /ˈʌŋkl/
a brother of your parent; your aunt's husband ● *Basil is an uncle now because his sister has a baby.* ❖ θείος

1.70 **first** (det) /fɜːst/
before other things of the same kind ● *My cousin's first name is Oliver.* ➤ first (n), first (adv) ❖ πρώτος

1.71 **surname** (n) /ˈsɜːneɪm/
family name ● *My teacher's surname is Wilson, but I don't know his first name.* ❖ επίθετο, επώνυμο

1.72 **Rio de Janeiro** (n) /ˈriːəʊ də ˌdʒæˈniːrəʊ/ ❖ Ρίο ντε Τζανέιρο

1.73 **married** (adj) /ˈmærɪd/
having a husband or wife ● *Uncle Mark is married to my mum's sister, aunt Joanne.* ➤ marry (v), marriage (n) ❖ παντρεμένος

1.74 **husband** (n) /ˈhʌzbənd/
a man who is married ● *Sylvia's husband, Lee, is from China.* ❖ σύζυγος (άντρας)

1.75 **Brazilian** (adj) /brəˈzɪliən/ ➤ Brazil, Brazilian (n) ❖ βραζιλιάνικος

1.76 **boyfriend** (n) /ˈbɔɪfrend/
a boy that has a very close relationship with sb ● *My sister is going to the cinema with her boyfriend.* ❖ φίλος, σύντροφος

1.77 **football boot** (n) /ˈfʊtbɔːl buːt/
a special kind of shoe that you wear to play football ● *Please clean your football boots before you come into the house.* ❖ παπούτσι ποδοσφαίρου

7

1.78 **necklace** (n) /'nekləs/
a piece of jewellery that you wear around your
neck ● *I'm giving Mum a nice necklace for her
birthday.* ❖ κολιέ

1.79 **photograph** (n) /'fəʊtəgrɑːf/
a picture you make by using a camera
● *This is a photograph of me and my family.*
➢ photograph (v), photography, photographer
(n), photographic (adj) ❖ φωτογραφία

1.80 **poster** (n) /'pəʊstə(r)/
a big picture or notice that you put on a
wall ● *Irene has got posters of her favourite
basketball team on her wall.* ❖ αφίσα

1.81 **smartphone** (n) /'smɑːtfəʊn/
a phone that is like a small computer and
uses the Internet ● *My parents use their
smartphones to send photos and emails to
friends.* ❖ κινητό τηλέφωνο που λειτουργεί σαν
υπολογιστής με σύνδεση στο διαδίκτυο

1.82 **watch** (n) /wɒtʃ/
a small clock that you wear to see the time
● *Diane doesn't wear a watch because she
sees the time on her smartphone.*
❖ ρολόι (χειρός)

Look!

Να θυμάσαι ότι η λέξη **clock** σημαίνει ένα ρολόι
που βάζουμε στον τοίχο ή στο ράφι, ενώ η λέξη
watch σημαίνει ένα ρολόι που φοριέται στο χέρι.
*Aunt Millie is wearing her gold **watch**.*
*It's half past ten on the school **clock**.*

1.83 **gold** (n) /gəʊld/
a yellow metal often used to make jewellery
● *Grandad's watch is made of gold.* ➢ gold,
golden (adj) ❖χρυσάφι, χρυσός

1.84 **soft** (adj) /sɒft/
nice to touch and not hard ● *The baby's hair is
soft and curly.* ❖ μαλακός

1.85 **cute** (adj) /kjuːt/
pretty and nice ● *Look at the cute little
puppies!* ❖ χαριτωμένος

1.86 **be slow** (expr) /bi sləʊ/
used for a watch or clock that shows an earlier
time ● *The school clock is slow. It shows 11
o'clock, but the real time is 11.30.* ❖ πάει πίσω
(για ρολόι)

1.87 **slow** (adj) /sləʊ/
not fast ● *The slow train to London stops at
every town.* ➢ slowly (adv) ❖ αργός

1.88 **be late** (expr) /bi leɪt/
arrive at a time after the time you should
● *Why are you late for school today?*
❖ αργώ, καθυστερώ

1.89 **late** (adv) /leɪt/
at a time after sth should happen
● *I sometimes play basketball after school, so
I come home late.* ➢ late (adj)
❖ καθυστερημένος, αργά

1.90 **chat** (v) /tʃæt/
talk (or send texts) in a friendly way ● *Maria is
chatting with her boyfriend on the phone.*
➢ chat (n) ❖ κουβεντιάζω

Grammar
Pages 10–11

1.91 **possession** (n) /pə'zeʃn/
sth that is yours ● *We put all our possessions
into boxes to take to our new house.*
➢ possess (v) ❖ αυτό που έχω, υπάρχοντα

1.92 **relationship** (n) /rɪ'leɪʃnʃɪp/
the way that people are connected to each
other ● *What's George's relationship with
Theo? Are they brothers or cousins?* ➢ relate
(v), relative, relation (n) ❖ συγγένεια, σχέση

1.93 **pet** (n) /pet/
an animal that lives with you in your home
● *Granny's pets are two cats and a big dog.*
❖ κατοικίδιο ζώο

1.94 **French** (adj) /frentʃ/
❖ γαλλικός, Γάλλος

1.95 **Paris** (n) /'pærɪs/
❖ Παρίσι

1.96 **best friend** (n) /best frend/
the friend that you like spending time with most
● *Christina sits next to her best friend Sophie
in school.* ❖ καλύτερος φίλος

1.97 **vanilla** (n) /və'nɪlə/
juice from the beans of a vanilla plant that you
put in ice cream, cakes, etc. ● *Do you like
chocolate or vanilla ice cream?* ❖ βανίλια

1.98 **flavour** (n) /'fleɪvə(r)/
the taste of sth ● *These crisps have a cheese
flavour.* ❖ γεύση

1.99 **pineapple** (n) /'paɪnæpl/
a large, soft, juicy, yellow fruit that has very
hard skin ● *My favourite drink is pineapple
juice.* ❖ ανανάς

1.100 **caption** (n) /'kæpʃn/
a few words below a picture to say sth about
it ● *The captions on these photos say where
each place is.* ❖ λεζάντα

1.101 **called** (adj) /kɔːld/
having the name ● *My teacher is called
Mr Brown.* ➢ call (v) ❖ ονομάζομαι

1.102 **exam** (n) /ɪg'zæm/
a test in school ● *Please be quiet. The
children are doing a maths exam.* ➢ examine
(v), examination, examiner (n) ❖ εξέταση,
διαγώνισμα

1.103 **excuse me** (expr) /ɪkˈskjuːz miː/
You say this before a polite question, usually to sb you don't know. ● *Excuse me, is this your bag?* ❖ με συγχωρείτε, συγγνώμη

1.104 **belong to** (phr v) /bɪˈlɒŋ tuː/
be sb's possession; be owned by ● *This isn't my book. It belongs to John.* ❖ ανήκω σε

1.105 **wife** (n) /waɪf/
a woman who is married to sb ● *Aunt Fiona is my uncle's wife.* ❖ σύζυγος (γυναίκα)

1.106 **grandfather** (n) /ˈɡrænfaːðə(r)/
the father of your mother or father ● *My grandfather is sixty-two years old.* ❖ παππούς

Family & Friends

aunt	grandfather	parent
best friend	grandmother	teenager
boyfriend	grandparent	uncle
classmate	husband	wife
cousin	only child	

Listening

Page 12

1.107 **Malaysia** (n) /məˈleɪzə/
➤ Malaysian (adj) ❖ Μαλαισία

1.108 **grandparent** (n) /ˈɡrænpeərənt/
a grandmother or grandfather ● *Sometimes I stay with my grandparents in the school holidays.* ❖ παππούς ή γιαγιά

1.109 **wedding** (n) /ˈwedɪŋ/
an event when two people get married ● *We're going to my uncle's wedding on Saturday.* ❖ γάμος

1.110 **carefully** (adv) /ˈkeəfəli/
taking care of details to do sth correctly ● *She put the eggs carefully into the water to cook them.* ➤ care (v), care (n), careful (adj) ❖ προσεκτικά
✎ Opp: carelessly ❖ απερίσκεπτα

1.111 **similar** (adj) /ˈsɪmələ(r)/
almost the same as sth/sb else ● *Danae looks similar to her brother. They have the same colour of hair and eyes.* ➤ similarity (n) ❖ παρόμοιος

1.112 **actually** (adv) /ˈæktʃuəli/
in fact; used to show sth is true or stress a fact ● *They look like sisters, but they are actually cousins.* ➤ actual (adj) ❖ στην πραγματικότητα

1.113 **in fact** (expr) /ɪn fækt/
used to give more details, show sth is true or stress a fact ● *Barbara is from a big family. In fact, she's got three sisters, two brothers and twenty cousins.* ❖ πραγματικά, στην πραγματικότητα

1.114 **twice** (adv) /twaɪs/
two times ● *I play football twice a week – every Tuesday and Friday.* ❖ δυο φορές

1.115 **painting** (n) /ˈpeɪntɪŋ/
a picture that sb painted ● *It's a beautiful painting of the sea. I love the colours.* ➤ paint (v), painter (n) ❖ πίνακας

1.116 **photo album** (n) /ˈfəʊtəʊ ˈælbəm/
a book that you keep photos in ● *My grandmother keeps all her family photos in a photo album.* ❖ φωτογραφικό άλμπουμ

1.117 **camera** (n) /ˈkæmərə/
a small machine for taking photos or videos ● *My new phone has a good camera. Look at these pictures.* ❖ φωτογραφική μηχανή

1.118 **towel** (n) /ˈtaʊəl/
a piece of cloth that you use to dry yourself or other things ● *John goes swimming after school, so he carries a towel in his bag.* ❖ πετσέτα

Possessions

alarm clock	gold	poster
camera	necklace	smartphone
diary	photo album	watch
football boots	photograph	

Speaking

Page 13

1.119 **each other** (expr) /iːtʃ ˈʌðə(r)/
used to show that both of two people do sth to the other ● *We looked at each other and laughed because we were wearing the same clothes.* ❖ ο ένας τον άλλο, η μια την άλλη

1.120 **I'm good, thanks.** (expr) /aɪm ɡʊd θæŋks/
I'm okay/fine, thanks. ● *'How are you, Laura?' 'I'm good, thanks.'* ❖ Ειμαι καλά, ευχαριστώ.

1.121 **meet** (v) /miːt/
get together with sb ● *Where do you meet your friends after school?* ➤ meeting (n) ❖ συναντώ

1.122 **Pleased to meet you.** (expr) /pliːzd tə miːt juː/
You say this when you meet sb new. ● *'Hi, I'm Martha.' 'Pleased to meet you, Martha. I'm Jill.'* ❖ χαίρω πολύ, χάρηκα για τη γνωριμία

1.123 **personal** (adj) /ˈpɜːsənl/
about you and nobody else ● *I never give any personal information on the phone.* ➤ personality (n), personally (adv) ❖ προσωπικός

1.124 **Chile** (n) /ˈtʃɪli/
➤ Chilean (adj) ❖ Χιλή

1.125 **Quebec** (n) /kwɪˈbek/
❖ Κεμπέκ

1.126 **classmate** (n) /ˈklɑːsmeɪt/
a person in your class at school ● *Some of my classmates are coming to my birthday party.*
❖ συμμαθητής, συμμαθήτρια

1.127 **hobby** (n) /ˈhɒbi/
something that you do to have fun
● *Dad's favourite hobby is reading.*
❖ χόμπι, ενασχόληση

1.128 **free time** (n) /friː taɪm/
the time when you don't have to work or study
● *We don't have much free time this month because we've got exams at school.*
❖ ελεύθερος χρόνος

1.129 **idea** (n) /aɪˈdɪə/
a thought or plan about what to do ● *I've got an idea. Let's go for a picnic.* ❖ ιδέα

Expressions

I'm good, thanks.	at least
Pleased to meet you.	in fact
best wishes	of course
excuse me	

Writing
Pages 14–15

1.130 **different** (adj) /ˈdɪfrənt/
not the same ● *My teacher's hair is a different colour every month! This month it's red.*
➣ difference (n) ❖ διαφορετικός

1.131 **description** (n) /dɪˈskrɪpʃn/
words that tell you what sb/sth is like
● *Can you write a description of your home?*
➣ describe (v) ❖ περιγραφή

1.132 **contrast** (n) /ˈkɒntrɑːst/
a clear difference between two things
● *There is a big contrast between living on a farm and living in a city.* ➣ contrast (v)
❖ αντίθεση

1.133 **Sweden** (n) /ˈswiːdn/
➣ Swedish (adj) ❖ Σουηδία

1.134 **capital** (n) /ˈkæpɪtl/
the most important city of a country
● *Edinburgh is the capital of Scotland, but Glasgow is the biggest city.* ❖ πρωτεύουσα

1.135 **Norway** (n) /ˈnɔːweɪ/
➣ Norwegian (adj) ❖ Νορβηγία

1.136 **like** (prep) /laɪk/
similar to; in the same way as ● *There's a big old hotel, like a castle, next to the lake.* ❖ σαν

1.137 **rap music** (n) /ræp ˈmjuːzɪk/
a kind of music in which the singer says words fast in a rhythm without singing ● *Mum hates listening to rap music because she doesn't like the words.* ➣ rap (v), rapper (n)
❖ ραπ μουσική

1.138 **hip hop** (n) /ˈhɪp hɒp/
a kind of music with spoken words, a fast electronic beat and a modern dance style
● *Our class is doing a hip hop dance for the school show.* ❖ χιπ χοπ

1.139 **classical music** (n) /ˈklæsɪkl ˈmjuːzɪk/
a traditional kind of music, usually without words ● *Sonia likes playing classical music on the piano.* ❖ κλασική μουσική

1.140 **strange** (adj) /streɪndʒ/
unusual ● *Some traditional clothes from other countries look strange to us.* ➣ stranger (n), strangely (adv) ❖ περίεργος, παράξενος

1.141 **imagination** (n) /ɪˌmædʒɪˈneɪʃn/
the ability to think of new ideas or make pictures of sth in your mind ● *Brian has a good imagination and he writes beautiful stories.*
➣ imagine (v) ❖ φαντασία

1.142 **at least** (expr) /ət liːst/
not less or fewer than ● *All my friends have got at least two pets and my family has got four.* ❖ τουλάχιστον

1.143 **include** (v) /ɪnˈkluːd/
put sth in as part of sth else; have sth as part of sth else ● *Does the hotel price include food?* ❖ περιλαμβάνω, περιέχω

1.144 **spelling** (n) /ˈspelɪŋ/
the letters in the correct order that make a word ● *We have a spelling test in our English lesson once a week.* ➣ spell (v) ❖ ορθογραφία

1.145 **tutor** (n) /ˈtjuːtə(r)/
a teacher, often for a small group of students or personal lessons ● *Hilde is going to work in France, so she has a tutor to teach her French.* ❖ καθηγητής, καθηγήτρια

1.146 **best wishes** (expr) /best wɪʃɪz/
You use this to end a friendly letter or card.
● *In the birthday card, I wrote 'love and best wishes.'* ❖ (τα) χαιρετίσματα (μου), τις καλύτερες ευχές

1.147 **fantastic** (adj) /fænˈtæstɪk/
really good ● *This song is fantastic! I love it.*
❖ φανταστικός, υπέροχος

Hobbies & Activities

classical music	mountain biking
fly a kite	painting
free time	rap music
hip hop	swimming
karate	training

Video 1
Super Dogs Page 16

1.148 human (n) /ˈhjuːmən/
a person ● *Humans can live together happily with animals.* ➣ human (adj) ❖ άνθρωπος

1.149 police dog (n) /pəˈliːs dɒg/
a dog that helps the police find people or things ● *The police dog found the children who got lost in the forest.* ❖ αστυνομικός σκύλος

1.150 carer (n) /ˈkeərə(r)/
sb who takes care of sb who is ill or old at home ● *Mrs Jones is my grandma's carer.* ➣ care (v), caring (adj) ❖ αυτός που φροντίζει κάποιον που είναι ηλικιωμένος ή άρρωστος στο σπίτι

1.151 guide (n) /gaɪd/
sb who shows you or takes you on the way to somewhere ● *Your guide will tell you about the things in the museum.* ➣ guide (v), guidance (n), guided (adj) ❖ οδηγός

1.152 guide dog (n) /ˈgaɪd dɒg/
a dog that guides sb who can't see ● *That guide dog is helping the man to find his way home.* ❖ σκύλος-οδηγός τυφλών

1.153 guard (n) /gaːd/
sb who stops people hurting sb or stops people going into a place ● *There are always guards in front of the Queen's home.* ➣ guard (v) ❖ φύλακας, φρουρός

1.154 guard dog (n) /ˈgaːd dɒg/
a dog that stops people going into a place ● *Our old Labrador is too friendly to be a guard dog. She likes everybody she sees.* ❖ σκύλος φύλακας

1.155 rescue (n) /ˈreskjuː/
the act of helping sb out of a dangerous place or position ● *The island's rescue team helps people when they have problems in the sea.* ➣ rescue (v), rescuer (n) ❖ διάσωση

1.156 switch on (phr v) /swɪtʃ ɒn/
make a machine or light start working by pressing sth ● *Please switch on the TV. I want to watch a film.* ❖ ανάβω, ανοίγω
✎ Opp: switch off ❖ σβήνω, κλείνω

1.158 press (v) /pres/
push your finger on sth ● *Press the doorbell to see if anyone is at home.* ➣ pressure (n) ❖ πατάω, πιέζω

1.159 button (n) /ˈbʌtn/
a small part of a machine that you press to make it start; a small hard piece of plastic, etc., on a shirt (or other clothes) to close it together ● *Press the green button to start the video.* ❖ πλήκτρο, κουμπί

1.160 carry (v) /ˈkæri/
hold sth to take it from one place to another ● *I carry my books to school in my bag.* ❖ κουβαλάω, μεταφέρω

1.161 owner (n) /ˈəʊnə(r)/
sb that sth belongs to ● *Who is the owner of that car? Is it your uncle's?* ➣ own (v), own (adj) ❖ ιδιοκτήτης

1.162 object (n) /ˈɒbdʒɪkt/
a thing you can see ● *What is that strange object in the sky? It doesn't look like a plane.* ❖ πράγμα, αντικείμενο

1.163 airport (n) /ˈeəpɔːt/
a place where people get on and off planes to travel ● *We live near the airport, so we hear planes above our house every day.* ❖ αεροδρόμιο

1.164 camp (n) /kæmp/
a place people go for a short time to do special activities; a place where people go to stay for a short time in tents or small buildings ● *Steve goes to a sports camp for four weeks every summer.* ➣ camp (v), camper, camping (n) ❖ κατασκήνωση

1.165 body (n) /ˈbɒdi/
the main part of a living thing ● *Put on more clothes to keep your body warm.* ❖ σώμα

1.166 supermarket (n) /ˈsuːpəmaːkɪt/
a very big shop that has food, drinks, and things to use in the home ● *Mum and Dad go to the supermarket every week to get food.* ❖ σουπερμάρκετ

1.167 trainer (n) /ˈtreɪnə(r)/
sb who teaches animals to do things ● *The trainer is teaching the police dogs to catch people.* ➣ train (v), training (n) ❖ εκπαιδευτής, προπονητής

1.168 train (v) /treɪn/
teach a person or animal how to do sth ● *Sarah is training her dog to sit.* ➣ training, trainer (n) ❖ εκπαιδεύω, προπονούμαι

1.169 look after (phr v) /lʊk ˈaːftə(r)/
take care of ● *Mike looks after his little brother when his parents aren't at home.* ❖ φροντίζω, προσέχω

1.170 disability (n) /ˌdɪsəˈbɪləti/
a condition that means it is difficult or not possible to use part of your body, or learn easily ● *Aunt Katie walks with a stick because of her disability.* ➣ disable (v), disabled (adj) ❖ ειδικές ανάγκες, αναπηρία

1.171 training (n) /ˈtreɪnɪŋ/
learning to do sth ● *Roberto is getting specific training to become a teacher.* ➣ train (v), trainer (n) ❖ εκπαίδευση

1.172 **brain** (n) /breɪn/
the part of your body that you think, feel and
remember with ● *You need to use your brain
to learn new things.* ❖ μυαλό, εγκέφαλος

1.173 **trip** (n) /trɪp/
a short journey to a place and back again
● *Our school trips are always fun.* ❖ εκδρομή

1.174 **amazing** (adj) /əˈmeɪzɪŋ/
very surprising, fantastic ● *This painting is
amazing. I really like the colours.* ➢ amaze (v),
amazement (n) ❖ εκπληκτικός, καταπληκτικός

1.175 **save** (v) /seɪv/
get sb/sth out of a dangerous place or situation
● *Rolf took the cat home from the street and
saved its life.* ➢ safety, saviour (n), safe (adj),
safely (adv) ❖ σώζω, διασώζω

Places	**Countries & Cities**
airport	Argentina
camp	Chile
farm	Malaysia
land	Peru
mountain	Quebec
supermarket	

Phrasal Verbs
belong to
switch on/off
look after

Vocabulary Exercises

A Match.

1	alarm	☐	**a** friend
2	best	☐	**b** album
3	football	☐	**c** hop
4	guard	☐	**d** biking
5	photo	☐	**e** music
6	mountain	☐	**f** clock
7	classical	☐	**g** boots
8	hip	☐	**h** dog

B Circle the correct words.

1 I have a good **relationship** / **age** with my cousin.
2 My uncle's **husband** / **wife** is Aunt Dora.
3 Mark has no brothers or sisters, so he's an only **child** / **parent**.
4 The children are having great **fun** / **time** at the party.
5 Please don't be **late** / **slow** for the wedding!
6 The old woman is using a **capital** / **handloom** to make material for clothes.
7 Tom's favourite fruit is **spinach** / **watermelon**.
8 In the photograph, Sandra is wearing a gold **necklace** / **towel**.

C Read the meanings and complete the words.

1 a person between 13 and 19 years old   t _ _ _ _ _ _ _
2 my mum's mother and father   g _ _ _ _ _ _ _ _ _ _ _
3 a teacher, often for small groups of students   t _ _ _ _
4 facts about sb/sth   i _ _ _ _ _ _ _ _ _ _
5 my aunt's son or daughter   c _ _ _ _ _
6 a person's last name   s _ _ _ _ _ _
7 my dad's brother   u _ _ _ _
8 something that belongs to you   p _ _ _ _ _ _ _ _ _

D Complete the sentences with these words.

exam   fantastic   flavour   free   grandmother   imagination   interesting   married
owner   personal   pineapple   popular   similar   swimming   trainer   wedding

1 Use your _____ to write an _____ description.
2 Betsy's mother looks very _____ to her _____.
3 We're all having a _____ time at Sue and Peter's _____. It's great fun!
4 My brother has a music _____ soon, so his _____ tutor is helping him.
5 I enjoy _____ in the sea in my _____ time.
6 This drink has a strange _____. Is it _____ or vanilla?
7 My dad's sister is getting _____ to a guide dog _____.
8 The _____ of the painting is a _____ hip hop singer.

E Find ten animal words and write them on the lines.

M	O	S	Q	U	I	T	O	L	E	M	P
F	L	D	F	E	C	O	T	V	R	K	H
O	I	Y	G	U	A	R	A	B	B	I	T
S	T	M	O	S	Q	T	Y	E	C	T	E
E	P	T	L	C	H	O	C	R	E	T	P
C	A	K	D	G	O	I	N	E	K	E	F
Q	K	E	F	U	Y	S	M	P	R	N	I
U	E	N	I	N	S	E	C	T	I	L	U
T	R	C	S	E	N	L	A	I	T	N	G
I	M	H	H	V	A	G	O	L	O	R	M
L	P	E	K	T	K	I	P	E	T	S	H
C	H	I	C	K	E	N	I	K	C	T	H

1 _____   6 _____
2 _____   7 _____
3 _____   8 _____
4 _____   9 _____
5 _____   10 _____

1 Grammar

1.1 *Be*

Κατάφαση
I am ('m).
We/you/they **are** ('re).
He/she/it **is** ('s).

Άρνηση
I am not ('m not).
We/you/they **are not (aren't)**.
He/she/it **is not (isn't)**.

Ερώτηση
Am I?
Are we/you/they?
Is he/she/it?

Σύντομες απαντήσεις	
Yes, I am.	**No**, I'm not.
Yes, we/you/they **are**.	**No**, we/you/they **are not (aren't/'re not)**.
Yes, he/she/it **is**.	**No**, he/she/it **is not (isn't)**.

Χρησιμοποιούμε το ρήμα *to be*:
με επίθετα.
→ *I am tall.*
→ *It is blue.*
→ *They are strange.*
με ουσιαστικά.
→ *We are friends.*
για να μιλήσουμε για την ηλικία ή εθνικότητα μας.
→ *She is 12 years old.*
→ *It is from Spain.*
→ *They're English.*
για μια τοποθεσία.
→ *It's in the park.*
→ *The pens are on my desk.*
ως βοηθητικό ρήμα για να σχηματίσουμε άλλους χρόνους.
→ *I am swimming.*
→ *We are playing football.*
→ *His boots are made in China.*

Σημείωση: Σε σύντομες απαντήσεις, δεν υπάρχει συστολή: *'Is she from Paris?'* – *'Yes, she is.'* **NOT** *'Yes, she's.'*

1.2 *Have got*

Κατάφαση
I/we/you/they **have got**.
He/she/it **has got**.

Άρνηση
I/we/you/they **haven't got**.
He/she/it **hasn't got**.

Ερώτηση
Have I/we/you/they **got**?
Has he/she/it **got**?

Σύντομες απαντήσεις	
Yes, I/we/you/they **have**.	**No**, I/we/you/they **haven't**.
Yes, he/she/it **has**.	**No**, he/she/it **hasn't**.

Χρησιμοποιούμε *have got* για:
τα υπάρχοντα.
→ *They've got a kite.*
→ *I've got a bike.*
τις σχέσεις.
→ *I've got three cousins.*
→ *Theo has got a sister.*

1.3 *This, That, These, Those*

Χρησιμοποιούμε *this* και *these* για να δείξουμε ότι κάτι είναι *κοντά* μας στο χώρο ή στο χρόνο.
Χρησιμοποιούμε *this* + ουσιαστικό στον ενικό.
→ *This is my desk. I sit here.*
→ *This colour is nice. I like blue.*
Χρησιμοποιούμε *these* + ένα ουσιαστικό στον πληθυντικό.
→ *These photographs are nice.*

Χρησιμοποιούμε *that* και *those* για να δείξουμε ότι κάτι δεν είναι τόσο κοντά μας στο χώρο ή στο χρόνο.
Χρησιμοποιούμε *that* + ουσιαστικό στον ενικό.
→ *That camera over there is Japanese.*
Χρησιμοποιούμε *those* + ένα ουσιαστικό στον πληθυντικό.
→ *Those paintings on the wall are beautiful.*

Μπορούμε να χρησιμοποιήσουμε *this, that, these, those* χωρίς ουσιαστικό.
→ *This is my brother, James.*
→ *Are these your books?*
→ *That is a nice colour.*
→ *Those are my football boots.*

1.4 Possessive adjectives

Personal pronouns	Possessive adjectives
I	my
you	your
he	his
she	her
it	its
we	our
you	your
they	their

Χρησιμοποιούμε possessive adjectives (κτητικά επίθετα) πριν από ουσιαστικά για να δείξουμε κυριότητα.
→ *It's my brother's birthday and these are his presents.*
→ *We live here. This is our house.*

1 Grammar

1.5 Possessive 's

Χρησιμοποιούμε 's για να δείξουμε ότι:
κάτι ανήκει σε κάποιον.
→ *Mum's car is black.*
κάτι έχει μια συγκεκριμένη σχέση με κάποιον ή κάτι άλλο
→ *Paul is Tracy's cousin.*

Χρησιμοποιούμε 's μετά από ενικά ουσιαστικά.
→ *That's my friend's house.*
→ *The girl's bag is under the table.*
Χρησιμοποιούμε 's μετά από ουσιαστικά που έχουν ανώμαλο πληθυντικό.
→ *People's hobbies are all different.*
→ *The children's kite is red.*

Χρησιμοποιούμε s' μετά από ουσιαστικά που έχουν ομαλό πληθυντικό.
→ *The dogs' ears were very long.*
→ *My cats' names are Rose and Toby.*

Grammar Exercises

A Choose the correct answer.

1 My bedroom _____ very big.
   a aren't   **b** isn't

2 Yessica's dad _____ a farm in Peru.
   a is   **b** has got

3 _____ a pet cat?
   a Are you   **b** Have you got

4 I _____ 11 years old.
   a 'm   **b** 've got

5 She _____ my best friend.
   a 's   **b** 're

6 They _____ from Italy, they're from Greece.
   a aren't   **b** am not

B Write the words in the correct order to make questions.

1 ? / friends / are / who / Tom's

   _____

2 ? / Jim / got / what / in / his / bedroom / has

   _____

3 ? / she / has / how / pets / many / got

   _____

4 ? / where / from / is / Maria

   _____

5 ? / why / basketball / favourite / is / sport / his

   _____

6 ? / your / have / got / football boots / you

   _____

C Complete the sentences with these words.

my your its her his our their this that these those

1 We've got _____ swimming competition today.
2 _____ kittens in the teacher's garden are funny.
3 The children enjoy playing with _____ friends.
4 I'm Helen and these are _____ parents.
5 I don't like _____ broccoli. It's not nice!
6 Grandma likes writing in _____ diary.
7 I like _____ poster over there.
8 The dog loves playing with _____ ball.
9 Is that you in the photo with _____ cat?
10 Mike's brother has got _____ guitar.
11 _____ are beautiful photographs in this book.

D Complete the sentences using 's or s'.

1 Mark is the uncle of Pauline.
Mark is _____.
2 This watch belongs to my brother.
This is _____.
3 Those books belong to the children.
Those are _____.
4 That house belongs to my grandparents.
That's _____.
5 Is Janice my cousin?
Am I _____?
6 These clothes belong to the man.
These are _____.

2 Friends & Fun

2.1 **take part in** (phr v) /teɪk pɑːt ɪn/
be active in sth with other people
● *Are you taking part in the school sports day?*
❖ συμμετέχω

2.2 **native** (adj) /ˈneɪtɪv/
belonging or relating to the people who are
from a particular area ● *Egypt is Maya's native
country, but now she's living in Sweden.*
➢ native (n) ❖ ντόπιος, ιθαγενής

2.3 **blanket** (n) /ˈblæŋkɪt/
a thick cover for a bed ● *It's cold tonight. Put
another blanket on your bed.*❖ κουβέρτα

2.4 **toss** (n) /tɒs/
a throw ● *With a quick toss from Jackie, the
basketball went into the net.* ➢ toss (v)
❖ βολή, ρίψη

Reading

2.5 **Wednesday** (n) /ˈwenzdeɪ/
❖ Τετάρτη

2.6 **drama** (n) /ˈdrɑːmə/
acting; theatre plays ● *Nick enjoys his drama
class and he wants to be an actor.* ➢ dramatic
(adj) ❖ θεατρικό, υποκριτική

2.7 **theatre** (n) /ˈθɪətər/
a building or area where people go to watch
people acting, playing music or singing, etc.
● *Our ballet class is doing a show in the
school theatre on Friday.* ➢ theatrical (adj)
❖ θέατρο

2.8 **club** (n) /klʌb/
a place where people meet to take part in a
common activity or interest ● *Marinos goes to
a swimming club three times a week.*
❖ όμιλος, σύλλογος, λέσχη

2.9 **Tuesday** (n) /ˈtjuːzdeɪ/
❖ Τρίτη

2.10 **Friday** (n) /ˈfraɪdeɪ/
❖ Παρασκευή

2.11 **running** (n) /ˈrʌnɪŋ/
the sport of running on a track, etc. ● *Aunt Eva
goes running in the park before work every
day.* ➢ run (v), runner (n) ❖ τρέξιμο

2.12 **chess** (n) /tʃes/
a board game for two players who follow
special rules to move pieces across black and
white squares ● *Adrianna plays chess as a
hobby in the school club.* ❖ σκάκι

2.13 **Monday** (n) /ˈmʌndeɪ/
❖ Δευτέρα

2.14 **bhangra** (n) /ˈbɑːŋgrə/
a kind of aerobic dance style from India
● *Marina is teaching us to do bhangra dancing
at the gym.* ❖ είδος γυμναστικής με ινδικό
χορό

2.15 **Thursday** (n) /ˈθɜːzdeɪ/
❖ Πέμπτη

2.16 **street dance** (n) /ˈstriːt ˌdɑːns/
a kind of modern dance like hip hop
● *A group of boys did a street dance outside
the supermarket and everyone stopped to
watch them.* ❖ χορός στο δρόμο (σαν χιπ χοπ)

2.17 **Saturday** (n) /ˈsætədeɪ/
❖ Σάββατο

2.18 **missing** (adj) /ˈmɪsɪŋ/
not included; not in the place where it usually
is ● *We can't do this puzzle because half of
the pieces are missing.* ➢ miss (v) ❖ που
λείπει, απών

2.19 **Sunday** (n) /ˈsʌndeɪ/
❖ Κυριακή

Days of the Week

Monday	Friday
Tuesday	Saturday
Wednesday	Sunday
Thursday	

Word Focus

2.20 **patient** (adj) /ˈpeɪʃnt/
able to stay calm and not get angry easily
● *Olga is very patient with children, so she's a
good teacher.* ➢ patience (n) ❖ υπομονετικός

2.21 **wait** (v) /weɪt/
stay somewhere until sth happens or sb/sth
comes ● *We're waiting for the film to start.*
➢ wait (n) ❖ περιμένω

2.22 **shy** (adj) /ʃaɪ/
quiet and not easily able to talk to new people
● *Don't be shy – my friends want to talk to you.*
➢ shyness (n) ❖ ντροπαλός

2.23 **difficult** (adj) /ˈdɪfɪkəlt/
not easy; hard ● *Chess is a difficult game, but
it's fun.* ➢ difficulty (n) ❖ δύσκολος

2.24 **smile** (v) /smaɪl/
use your mouth to show you are happy
● *Look at the camera and smile, please!*
➢ smile (n) ❖ χαμογελάω

2.25 **homework** (n) /ˈhəʊmwɜːk/
work that your teacher gives you to do at home
● *I do my homework after dinner every day.*
❖ εργασία για το σπίτι, μαθήματα

2.26 **sociable** (adj) /ˈsəʊʃəbl/
sb who likes talking to other people ● *The Browns are a very sociable family and they like having parties in their garden.* ❖ κοινωνικός

2.27 **friendly** (adj) /ˈfrendli/
kind and sociable ● *Frank's dog is very friendly with children.* ➣ friend, friendship (n) ❖ φιλικός

2.28 **creative** (adj) /kriˈeɪtɪv/
good at making things or having new ideas
● *Gary is really creative and he enjoys writing songs.* ➣ create (v), creation, creativity (n)
❖ δημιουργικός

Reading
Pages 18–19

2.29 **play** (n) /pleɪ/
a show performed by actors in a theatre
● *There's a great play on at the theatre on Thursday. Let's go and see it.* ➣ play (v), player (n) ❖ θεατρικό έργο, παράσταση

2.30 **musical** (adj) /ˈmjuːzɪkl/
a show with music and singing ● *I never go to watch musicals, but I like plays.*
➣ musical, music (n) ❖ μουσική παράσταση, μιούζικαλ

2.31 **show** (n) /ʃəʊ/
a theatre play or musical; a programme on the radio or TV. ● *My favourite TV show is on at eight o'clock.* ❖ παράσταση

2.32 **repeat** (v) /rɪˈpiːt/
say or do the same thing again ● *Can you repeat that? I didn't hear you.* ➣ repetition (n)
❖ επαναλαμβάνω

2.33 **again and again** (expr) /əˈgen ənd əˈgen/
many times ● *We need to do our dance again and again to get it right.* ❖ ξανά και ξανά

2.34 **stage** (n) /steɪdʒ/
an area at the front of a theatre where people stand to do a show ● *The singer is coming on to the stage now.* ➣ stage (v) ❖ σκηνή

Theatre

drama	play
instrument	show
lines	stage
musical	

2.35 **laugh** (v) /lɑːf/
make a sound with your mouth to show you are happy or sth is funny ● *The play is very funny, so everyone is laughing a lot.*
➣ laugh, laughter (n) ❖ γελάω

2.36 **boring** (adj) /ˈbɔːrɪŋ/
not interesting ● *I like playing chess, but watching other people play is boring.*
➣ bore (v), bore (n), bored (adj) ❖ βαρετός

2.37 **style** (n) /staɪl/
way of doing sth ● *What's your favourite dance style? Do you like hip hop?* ➣ stylish (adj)
❖ είδος, στιλ, τρόπος

2.38 **energetic** (adj) /ˌenəˈdʒetɪk/
with lots of energy; that doesn't get tired easily
● *Marilyn isn't very energetic today because she is ill.* ➣ energy (n) ❖ ενεργητικός

2.39 **sporty** (adj) /ˈspɔːti/
good at or liking sports ● *I'm not a sporty person, but I enjoy dancing.* ➣ sport (n)
❖ αθλητικός

2.40 **extra** (adj) /ˈekstrə/
more than usual ● *We've got extra homework today because we have an exam next week.*
❖ επιπλέον

2.41 **probably** (adv) /ˈprɒbəbli/
that might happen ● *We're probably going for a walk on Saturday, but I'm not sure yet.*
➣ probable (adj) ❖ πιθανώς, ίσως, μάλλον

2.42 **date** (n) /deɪt/
the day of the month ● *What date is your party? Is it on the third or fourth of May?*
❖ ημερομηνία

2.43 **cheesecake** (n) /ˈtʃiːzkeɪk/
a kind of sweet pie made from soft biscuits covered with a soft cream cheese mixture and fruit on top ● *Norah is making a big cherry cheesecake.* ❖ τσιζκέικ

2.44 **tired** (adj) /ˈtaɪəd/
needing to sleep or relax ● *I'm tired, so I'm going to bed now.* ➣ tire (v), tiring (adj)
❖ κουρασμένος

2.45 **active** (adj) /ˈæktɪv/
always doing a lot of activities, like sport
● *David doesn't go to a sports club, but he's very active and goes walking and running in the park.* ➣ act (v), action, activity (n)
❖ δραστήριος

Vocabulary
Pages 20–21

2.46 **sock** (n) /sɒk/
an item of clothing that you wear on your foot
● *I usually wear a pair of long socks to keep my feet warm.* ❖ κάλτσα

2.47 **shorts** (n) /ʃɔːts/
short trousers that end on or above your knee ● *The children are wearing shorts today because it's hot and sunny.* ❖ σορτς, σορτσάκι

2.48 **T-shirt** (n) /ˈtiː ʃɜːt/
a kind of shirt without buttons that has short sleeves ● *Ted wears a T-shirt and shorts to play tennis.* ❖ μπλουζάκι, κοντομάνικο

2.49 **skirt** (n) /skɜːt/
an item of clothing that hangs down and
covers the legs, for a girl or woman • *Kay is
wearing a nice blue skirt with her white T-shirt.*
❖ φούστα

2.50 **trousers** (n) /ˈtraʊzəz/
an item of clothing that covers your legs
• *Does your sister wear a skirt or trousers to
school?* ❖ παντελόνι

2.51 **jeans** (n) /dʒiːnz/
a style of trousers made of strong material
• *My teacher wears jeans at the weekend,
but she has to wear a skirt or other trousers at
school.* ❖ τζιν παντελόνι

2.52 **boot** (n) /buːt/
a shoe that covers your foot and part of your
leg • *Wear your boots today. It's raining.*
❖ μπότα

2.53 **hoody** (n) /ˈhʊdi/
a kind of jacket or sweatshirt with a hood
that covers the top of your head • *Thomas's
favourite clothes are his blue hoody and jeans.*
➤ hood (n) ❖ φούτερ με κουκούλα
✎ Also: hoodie

2.54 **shirt** (n) /ʃɜːt/
an item of clothing for the top part of the body,
with sleeves and a collar and with buttons on
front • *Dad has to wear a shirt when he goes
to work at the bank.* ❖ πουκάμισο

2.55 **trainers** (n) /ˈtreɪnəz/
shoes you wear for sports • *Lynne has got a
new pair of trainers to wear for volleyball.*
❖ αθλητικά παπούτσια

2.56 **sweatshirt** (n) /ˈswetʃɜːt/
an item of clothing made of soft material,
with long sleeves, for the top part of your
body • *It's cold today, so I'm wearing a warm
sweatshirt.* ❖ φούτερ

2.57 **judo** (n) /ˈdʒuːdəʊ/
a kind of fighting sport for two people who try
to throw or push each other down • *My cousin
has got a black belt in judo.* ❖ τζούντο

2.58 **skateboarding** (n) /ˈskeɪtbɔːdɪŋ/
the sport of riding on a skateboard • *I never
go skateboarding on roads with lots of cars.*
❖ σκέιτμπορντ

2.59 **tracksuit** (n) /ˈtræksuːt/
a pair of trousers and sweatshirt or jacket that
you wear for sports • *We wear our tracksuits
to go to the sports centre.* ❖ αθλητική φόρμα

2.60 **tracksuit bottoms** (n) /ˈtræksuːt ˈbɒtəmz/
the trousers that are part of a tracksuit
• *Pauline is wearing her tracksuit bottoms and
a T-shirt to go walking.* ❖ παντελόνι αθλητικής
φόρμας

Clothes

boot	sweatshirt
hoody	tracksuit
shirt	tracksuit bottoms
shorts	trainers
skirt	trousers
sock	T-shirt

2.61 **go out** (phr v) /gəʊ aʊt/
go somewhere to have fun, usually with other
people • *We've got a maths exam tomorrow,
so I'm not going out with my friends today.*
❖ βγαίνω

2.62 **lines** (n) /laɪnz/
the words an actor says in a play or film; words
of a song • *Do you know all your lines for the
school play?* ❖ λόγια, στίχοι

2.63 **origami** (n) /ˌɒrɪˈgɑːmi/
the art of folding paper to make interesting
shapes • *Helena is learning to do origami to
make things with paper in her art class.*
❖ οριγκάμι

2.64 **organised** (adj) /ˈɔːgənaɪzd/
good at planning your activities and work, etc.
• *Duncan always tidies his room because
he's a very organised person.* ➤ organise (v),
organiser, organisation (n) ❖ οργανωμένος
✎ Opp: disorganised ❖ ανοργάνωτος

2.65 **suggestion** (n) /səˈdʒestʃən/
an idea you say to sb about sth • *I want
to read a new book. Have you got any
suggestions?* ➤ suggest (v) ❖ πρόταση

2.66 **recommend** (v) /ˌrekəˈmend/
tell sb that sth is good for sth • *This is a really
good film. I recommend it for teenagers.*
➤ recommendation (n) ❖ προτείνω

2.67 **instrument** (n) /ˈɪnstrəmənt/
sth that you play music with, e.g. piano, guitar
• *My sister plays the guitar, but I don't play
any instruments.* ❖ (μουσικό) όργανο

2.68 **board game** (n) /ˈbɔːd geɪm/
a game played on a board, usually with small
pieces and a dice • *Is chess your favourite
board game?* ❖ επιτραπέζιο παιχνίδι

2.69 **join** (v) /dʒɔɪn/
become a member of; start taking part in
• *You like drawing. Why don't you join an art
club?* ❖ γίνομαι μέλος

2.70 **comfortable** (adj) /ˈkʌmftəbl/
nice to wear or sit on, etc. • *I love my new
trainers – they're really comfortable.*
➤ comfort (n) ❖ άνετος, αναπαυτικός
✎ Opp: uncomfortable ❖ άβολος

2.71 **colourful** (adj) /ˈkʌləfl/
with many different colours • *Becky is wearing
a colourful red and orange T-shirt and blue
jeans.* ➤ colour (v), colour (n) ❖ πολύχρωμος

2.72 **hang out with** (phr v) /hæŋ aʊt wɪθ/
spend time with • *Carol hangs out with her best friend at weekends.* ❖ κάνω παρέα με

2.73 **get on with** (phr v) /get ɒn wɪθ/
be friends with; have a relationship with • *Ursula and Mary like the same hobbies and they get on well with each other.* ❖ έχω (καλή) σχέση, τα πάω καλά με

2.74 **meet up** (phr v) /miːt ʌp/
get together in the same place • *Let's meet up at the café this evening.* ➤ meeting (n) ❖ συναντώ, έχω ραντεβού

Phrasal Verbs

get on with	look forward to
go out	meet up
hang out with	take part in

Grammar
Pages 22–23

2.75 **cycle** (v) /ˈsaɪkl/
ride a bicycle • *Do you cycle to school or do you walk?* ➤ cycle, cycling, cyclist (n) ❖ κάνω ποδήλατο, πάω με ποδήλατο

2.76 **Portuguese** (n) /ˌpɔːtʃʊˈgiːz/
➤ Portugal (n) ❖ πορτογαλικός

2.77 **visit** (v) /ˈvɪzɪt/
go to see sb/sth for a short time • *Peter is visiting his uncle in Canada.* ➤ visit, visitor (n) ❖ επισκέπτομαι

2.78 **hardly ever** (adv) /ˈhɑːdli ˈevə(r)/
almost never • *We hardly ever see our American cousins.* ❖ σχεδόν ποτέ

2.79 **girlfriend** (n) /ˈgɜːlfrend/
a girl or woman that sb is close friends with • *Steven is going to the theatre with his girlfriend.* ❖ φιλενάδα, κορίτσι

2.80 **frequency** (n) /ˈfriːkwənsi/
how often sth happens • *Look at the timetable to see the frequency of the dance classes. I think they're on twice a week.* ➤ frequent (adj), frequently (adv) ❖ συχνότητα

2.81 **match** (n) /mætʃ/
a game between two sports teams or players • *I enjoy watching football matches on TV.* ❖ αγώνας, ματς

2.82 **shell** (n) /ʃel/
a hard cover that a small animal lives in • *Mum collects pretty shells from the sea.* ❖ κοχύλι

2.83 **beach** (n) /biːtʃ/
a flat area of land with sand or stones next to the sea • *We're having a picnic on the beach.* ❖ παραλία

2.84 **message** (n) /ˈmesɪdʒ/
sth that you write or say for sb when you can't talk to them • *There's a message from Dad on the phone. He's at the tennis club.* ❖ μήνυμα

2.85 **once** (adv) /wʌns/
one time • *Anita cleans her bicycle once a month.* ❖ μία φορά

2.86 **shopping** (n) /ˈʃɒpɪŋ/
the activity of going to shops to buy things • *Sometimes I go shopping with my parents, but it's really boring!* ➤ shop (v), shopper (n) (adv) ❖ ψώνια

2.87 **cycling** (n) /ˈsaɪklɪŋ/
riding a bicycle • *Lee has got a new bike and he goes cycling every Sunday.* ➤ cycle (v), cyclist (n) ❖ ποδηλασία

2.88 **volleyball** (n) /ˈvɒlibɔːl/
a sport for two teams of six players who hit a ball over a net with their hands to score points • *Do you play volleyball on the beach?* ❖ βόλεϊ

Listening
Page 24

2.89 **horse-riding** (n) /ˈhɔːs raɪdɪŋ/
the activity of riding a horse • *We live in a big city, so we never go horse-riding.* ❖ ιππασία

2.90 **climbing** (n) /ˈklaɪmɪŋ/
the activity of going up rocks or mountains, etc. • *Ed wants to go climbing in the mountains of France.* ➤ climb (v), climber (n) ❖ ορειβασία, αναρρίχηση

2.91 **scrapbooking** (n) /ˈskræpbʊkɪŋ/
the hobby of collecting pictures or news stories, etc. and putting them in a notebook • *Katherine likes scrapbooking to keep her drawings and notes about her trips.* ➤ scrapbook (n) ❖ ενασχόληση με λευκώματα

2.92 **making models** (n) /ˈmeɪkɪŋ ˈmɒdlz/
the activity of making small copies of different objects • *Simon likes making models of old ships and planes.* ❖ κατασκευή μοντέλων/μακέτας

2.93 **photography** (n) /fəˈtɒgrəfi/
the activity of taking photos • *Irene is great at photography and she's taking photos at my aunt's wedding.* ➤ photograph (v), photograph, photographer (n), photographic (adj) ❖ φωτογραφία

2.94 **Zumba** (n) /ˈzuːmbə/
a kind of aerobics with Latin dance music • *Liz goes to Zumba classes once a week at the gym.* ❖ Zumba, είδος γυμναστικής με λάτιν χορό

Activities

bhangra	origami
board game	photography
camping	pick (fruit)
chess	running
climbing	scrapbooking
club	shopping
cycling	skateboarding
homework	street dance
horse-riding	take photos
judo	volleyball
making models	yarn bombing
match	Zumba

2.95 **arrange** (v) /əˈreɪndʒ/
plan for sth to happen • *Panos is arranging the music for the party.* ➣ arrangement (n) ❖ κανονίζω, σχεδιάζω

2.96 **share** (v) /ʃeə(r)/
have or use the same thing as sb else • *Terry and Ken share the same hobbies – they both like cycling and photography.* ➣ share (n) ❖ μοιράζομαι

Speaking　　　Page 25

2.97 **yarn bombing** (n) /ˈjɑːn bɒmɪŋ/
the activity of decorating things in the street with pieces of knitting • *Granny thinks yarn bombing is a creative kind of graffiti.* ❖ πράξη διακόσμησης αντικειμένων στο δρόμο με πλεκτά

2.98 **personality** (n) /ˌpɜːsəˈnæləti/
the things about sb's character that make them different from others • *My brother has a different personality from me. He's shy and I'm very sociable.* ➣ person (n), personal (adj), personally (adv) ❖ προσωπικότητα

2.99 **camping** (n) /ˈkæmpɪŋ/
the activity of staying in a tent, usually for a short time • *I love camping next to the beach, so I can swim all day.* ➣ camp (v), camp, camper (n) ❖ κατασκήνωση, κάμπινγκ

2.100 **adventurous** (adj) /ədˈventʃərəs/
sb who enjoys doing new and exciting things • *Emily isn't very adventurous and she doesn't want to go camping or climbing.* ➣ adventure (n) ❖ περιπετειώδης

2.101 **confident** (adj) /ˈkɒnfɪdənt/
sure that you are able to do sth well • *Douglas is not confident about singing on stage. He's very shy.* ➣ confidence (n) ❖ σίγουρος, πεπεισμένος

2.102 **kind** (adj) /kaɪnd/
friendly and caring • *The teachers at the camp are kind and friendly.* ➣ kindness (n) ❖ ευγενικός, καλός

2.103 **national park** (n) /ˌnæʃnəl ˈpɑːk/
an area that is protected because it's important to nature or a country's history • *We are visiting the Lake District National Park in the north of England.* ❖ εθνικός δρυμός, εθνικό πάρκο

2.104 **camp** (v) /kæmp/
stay in a tent, usually for a short time • *My friends often camp in a forest at weekends.* ➣ camping, camp, camper (n) ❖ κατασκηνώνω, κάνω κατασκήνωση

2.105 **outside** (adv) /ˌaʊtˈsaɪd/
not in a building • *When it's hot in summer, some people in villages sleep outside in their gardens.* ➣ outside (n), outside (adj) ❖ έξω

2.106 **understand** (v) /ˌʌndəˈstænd/
know what sth means • *I don't understand this word. Please tell me what it means.* ➣ understanding (n), understandable (adj) ❖ καταλαβαίνω

2.107 **swap** (v) /swɒp/
give sth to sb and get sth from them in return • *My friend and I often swap books with each other when we finish reading them.* ➣ swap (n) ❖ ανταλλάσσω

2.108 **repetition** (n) /ˌrepəˈtɪʃn/
saying or doing sth again and again • *Sometimes, repetition of phrases helps me learn new words in English.* ➣ repeat (v), repetitive (adj) ❖ επανάληψη

2.109 **(I'm) sorry** (excl) /aɪm ˈsɒri/
You say this when you want to ask sb to do sth or when you want to say you feel bad about sth you have done. • *I'm sorry, can you say your name again slowly?* ❖ με συγχωρείτε, συγγνώμη

Personality

active	energetic	shy
adventurous	friendly	sociable
boring	kind	sporty
confident	organised	tired
creative	patient	

Writing　　　Pages 26–27

2.110 **respond** (v) /rɪˈspɒnd/
write or say sth in answer to sth you read or hear • *Alison has got a lot of emails and she's responding to the important ones.* ➣ response (n) ❖ απαντώ

2.111 **advert** (n) /ˈædvɜːt/
an advertisement; a sign with writing and/ or pictures or a film telling people about sth they can buy or do, etc. • *I don't like watching adverts on TV.* ➣ advertise (v), advertiser (n) ❖ διαφήμιση, αγγελία

2.112 **advertisement** (n) /əd'vɜ:tɪsmənt/
a sign with writing and/or pictures or a film telling people about sth they can buy or do, etc. ● *There's an advertisement for a cycling club on the school noticeboard.* ➢ advertise (v), advertiser (n) ❖ διαφήμιση, αγγελία
✎ Short forms: ad, advert

2.113 **product** (n) /'prɒdʌkt/
sth that sb makes or grows usually to sell
● *You can find many products, like food or clothes, in the shopping centre.* ➢ produce (v), producer, production (n) ❖ προϊόν

2.114 **detailed** (adj) /'di:teɪld/
with a lot of information describing sth ● *Billy is writing a detailed description of his camping trip.* ➢ detail (v), detail (n) ❖ λεπτομερής

2.115 **website** (n) /'websaɪt/
a place on the Internet with information about a person, company, school, etc. ● *Our teacher always puts a note about our homework and tests on the school website.* ❖ ιστοσελίδα

2.116 **contact** (v) /'kɒntækt/
talk to or write to (sb) ● *Please contact Mr Jones to ask about the school camp.* ➢ contact (n) ❖ επικοινωνώ με, απευθύνομαι σε

2.117 **company** (n) /'kʌmpəni/
an organisation that makes money by making or selling products or other things ● *Jurgen works for a big company in Stockholm that makes shoes.* ❖ εταιρεία

2.118 **for sale** (expr) /fə seɪl/
that is ready for sb to buy ● *Are these skateboards for sale? I need a new one.* ➢ sell (v) ❖ προς πώληση, πωλείται

2.119 **cost** (n) /kɒst/
price; the money you need to buy or do sth
● *The cost of the dance classes is £20 a month.* ➢ cost (v) ❖ τιμή, κόστος

2.120 **free** (adj) /fri:/
not costing anything ● *You get a free T-shirt when you join our sports club.* ❖ δωρεάν

2.121 **take photos** (expr) /teɪk 'fəʊtəʊz/
make a picture using a camera
● *Nadia likes taking photos of animals.*
❖ βγάζω φωτογραφία, τραβάω φωτογραφία

2.122 **discover** (v) /dɪ'skʌvə(r)/
find out about sth new ● *Read the advertisement again to discover when the class starts.* ➢ discovery (n) ❖ ανακαλύπτω, μαθαίνω

2.123 **side** (n) /saɪd/
a part of sb's personality ● *Grandpa shows his sporty side by going swimming every morning.* ❖ πλευρά, όψη

2.124 **location** (n) /ləʊ'keɪʃn/
a place where sth is or sth happens ● *Where is the location of the camp? Is it near the river?* ➢ locate (v) ❖ τοποθεσία

2.125 **beginner** (n) /bɪ'gɪnə(r)/
sb who is new at doing or learning sth
● *I don't know any Spanish, so I'm joining the beginners' class.* ➢ begin (v), beginning (n) ❖ αρχάριος

2.126 **look forward to** (phr v) /lʊk 'fɔ:wəd tu/
feel happy because of sth that is going to happen ● *I'm looking forward to seeing the play.* ❖ ανυπομονώ να

2.127 **regards** (n) /rɪ'gɑ:d/
good wishes ● *Please give my regards to your family.* ➢ regard (v) ❖ (με) εκτίμηση, χαιρετισμούς, χαιρετισμοί

2.128 **cost** (v) /kɒst/
have as a price ● *How much does the trip cost?* ➢ cost (n) ❖ στοιχίζω, κοστίζω

2.129 **beginning** (n) /bɪ'gɪnɪŋ/
the start of sth ● *At the beginning of the book, Harry is starting his new school.* ➢ begin (v), beginner (n) ❖ αρχή

2.130 **ending** (n) /'endɪŋ/
the end of a story, letter, film etc. ● *The beginning of the story is a bit boring, but I love the happy ending.* ➢ end (v), end (n) ❖ τέλος

2.131 **interested** (adj) /'ɪntrəstɪd/
showing you like an activity or idea ● *What kind of hobbies are you interested in doing?* ➢ interest (v), interest (n) ❖ ενδιαφέρομαι, ενδιαφερόμενος

2.132 **course** (n) /kɔ:s/
an organised programme of classes on one subject ● *There's a one-week course in photography at the art school.* ❖ μάθημα, σειρά μαθημάτων

2.133 **handwriting** (n) /'hændraɪtɪŋ/
writing that you do with a pen or pencil, not on a computer, etc. ● *What is this word in Granny's letter? I can't read her handwriting.* ❖ χειρόγραφο, γράψιμο

2.134 **formal** (adj) /'fɔ:ml/
the correct style for writing or speaking to important people that you usually don't know
● *Dad often ends formal emails about his work with 'Kind regards.'* ❖ επίσημος
✎ Opp: informal ❖ ανεπίσημος, καθημερινός

2.135 **yours faithfully** (expr) /jɔ:z 'feɪθfəli/
a very formal way to sign off before your name at the end of a letter ● *This letter from the company ends with 'yours faithfully.'*
❖ μετά τιμής, με εκτίμηση

2.136 **single** (adj) /'sɪŋgl/
not married ● *Mum's brother and sisters are single. They don't want to get married.*
❖ ανύπαντρος, ελεύθερος

2.137 **show** (v) /ʃəʊ/
make sth clear for others to see ● *Dogs show that they're happy by moving their tails.* ➢ show (n) ❖ δείχνω

2.138 **interest** (n) /ˈɪntrəst/
the feeling that you want to know more about sth/sb ● *Roger likes doing sports, but he has no interest in watching football.* ➢ interest (v), interesting, interested (adj) ❖ ενδιαφέρον

Video 2
Yoro, the Fulani Boy

Page 28

2.139 **connected** (adj) /kəˈnektɪd/
having sth that links with another person/thing ● *The kind of plants we can grow on our farm is connected to the weather.* ➢ connect (v), connection (n) ❖ σχετικός, που έχει σχέση, που συνδέεται

2.140 **desert** (n) /ˈdezət/
a big area of land where there is not much water and not many plants or trees, often with a lot of sand and rocks ● *The Sahara is one of the biggest deserts in the world.* ❖ έρημος

2.141 **cross** (v) /krɒs/
go across from one side of sth to the other ● *Be careful when you cross the road.* ➢ crossing (n) ❖ διασχίζω, περνάω

2.142 **village** (n) /ˈvɪlɪdʒ/
a very small town ● *Lucia's grandmother is from a small mountain village in Lefkada.* ❖ χωριό

2.143 **Mali** (n) /ˈmɑːli/
➢ Malian (adj) ❖ Μάλι

2.144 **dry** (adj) /draɪ/
without much rain; without water ● *In summer, the weather is usually hot and dry in Cyprus.* ➢ dry (v) ❖ ξερός, στεγνός

2.145 **wet** (adj) /wet/
with a lot of rain; not dry ● *Take your umbrella – it's wet outside.* ➢ wet (v) ❖ βροχερός, υγρός

2.146 **season** (n) /ˈsiːzn/
a part of the year ● *Camping isn't much fun in the wet season.* ❖ εποχή

2.147 **almost** (adv) /ˈɔːlməʊst/
nearly, but not exactly ● *Almost all my friends like football.* ❖ σχεδόν

2.148 **pick (fruit)** (v) /pɪk fruːt/
take (fruit, etc.) from the trees ● *We're picking oranges to make juice.* ❖ μαζεύω (φρούτα)

2.149 **Egypt** (n) /ˈidʒɪpt/
➢ Egyptian (adj) ❖ Αίγυπτος

2.150 **Mauritania** (n) /ˌmɒrəˈteɪniə/
➢ Mauritanian (adj) ❖ Μαυριτανία

2.151 **return** (v) /rɪˈtɜːn/
come back ● *What time do you return home from school every day?* ➢ return (n) ❖ επιστρέφω

2.152 **celebrate** (v) /ˈselɪbreɪt/
do sth special and fun to show that sth is important ● *Are you having a party to celebrate the end of the school year?* ➢ celebration (n) ❖ γιορτάζω, εορτάζω

2.153 **get married** (expr) /get ˈmærid/
become the wife or husband of sb ● *Robin and Marian are getting married on Saturday. Are you coming to their wedding?* ❖ παντρεύομαι

2.154 **move** (v) /muːv/
go from one place to another; change (position) ● *The cat is moving slowly so the bird doesn't see it.* ➢ move, movement (n) ❖ κινούμαι

2.155 **responsibility** (n) /rɪˌspɒnsəˈbɪləti/
sth that you must do because it's your job or because of what you are ● *It's your responsibility to tidy your room.* ➢ responsible (adj) ❖ ευθύνη, υποχρέωση

Vocabulary Exercises

A Complete the days of the week.

1 M _ _ _ _ _
2 T _ _ _ _ _ _
3 W _ _ _ _ _ _ _ _
4 T _ _ _ _ _ _ _
5 F _ _ _ _ _
6 S _ _ _ _ _ _ _
7 S _ _ _ _ _

B Circle the odd one out.

1 boot   sock   village
2 bhangra   chess   Zumba
3 beginning   climbing   cycling
4 blanket   beach   desert
5 play   photography   show
6 match   stage   theatre

C Circle the correct words.

1 Are you going to take **place / part** in the school musical?
2 Tom is learning his **models / lines** for the play.
3 Who do you **hang / meet** out with at weekends?
4 Come and **join / share** the volleyball club.
5 Nina is **boring / tired** because she's got a lot of difficult homework.
6 I'm really **looking forward to / getting on with** seeing you again.
7 Oscar enjoys writing plays. He's very **active / creative**.
8 My feet hurt because my new trainers aren't **comfortable / colourful**.

D Complete the description with these words.

adventurous   beach   beginner   camping   climbing   interested   outside   photos   probably   shells   show   understand

You ^{1} _____ know that my family often goes ^{2} _____. We love it because it's great being ^{3} _____.
My favourite camp is near a ^{4} _____. My sisters like ^{5} _____ the rocks. I'm not so ^{6} _____! I enjoy
collecting ^{7} _____ and taking ^{8} _____ of the sea. I'm really ^{9} _____ in photography. My camera is new
and I'm a ^{10} _____. My parents usually ^{11} _____ me how to take good pictures. I don't ^{12} _____ what
buttons to press!

E Do the crossword.

Across

1 a kind of fighting sport for two people
5 the sport of riding on a kind of board
7 the art of folding paper to make interesting shapes
8 the activity of riding a horse
9 the activity of decorating things in the street with pieces of knitting

Down

2 acting or theatre plays
3 riding a bicycle
4 a game played on a board, usually with small pieces and a dice
5 the activity of going somewhere to buy things
6 the sport of moving fast on a track, etc.

2 Grammar

2.1 Present Simple

Κατάφαση
I/we/you/they play.   He/she/it play**s**.

Άρνηση
I/we/you/they **don't** play.   He/she/it **doesn't** play.

Ερώτηση
Do I/we/you/they play?   **Does** he/she/it play?

Σύντομες απαντήσεις	
Yes, I/we/you/they **do**. **Yes**, he/she/it **does**.	**No**, I/we/you/they **don't**. **No**, he/she/it **doesn't**.

Χρησιμοποιούμε τον Present Simple για:
γεγονότα.
→ Fish **swim** in the sea.
ρουτίνες ή συνήθειες (συχνά με επιρρήματα συχνότητας).
→ I **get up** at 7 o'clock every morning.
μόνιμες καταστάσεις.
→ My dad **works** in a sports centre.

Σημείωση: Χρονικές εκφράσεις που αφορούν επαναλαμβανόμενες πράξεις χρησιμοποιούνται συχνά με τον Present Simple. Για παράδειγμα, every day/week/month, once a week, twice a year, at weekends, at night, in the morning κλπ.

2.2 Question Words

Χρησιμοποιούμε:
who για ανθρώπους.
→ Who is your best friend?
what για πράγματα ή ιδέες.
→ What do you do in your free time?
when για χρόνο γενικά.
→ When do you play basketball?
where για μέρη.
→ Where do your grandparents live?
why για λόγους.
→ Why does he like painting?
how για να ρωτήσουμε με ποιον τρόπο γίνεται κάτι.
→ How do you travel to school?
Σημείωση: η σειρά των λέξεων για να σχηματίσουμε μια ερώτηση είναι η εξής:
Question word + do/does + υποκείμενο + ρήμα ...?

2 Grammar

2.3 Adverbs of Frequency

Χρησιμοποιούμε adverbs of frequency για να πούμε πόσο συχνά συμβαίνει κάτι. Μπαίνουν **πριν από** το κύριο ρήμα, αλλά **μετά από** το ρήμα *be*.

Διαφορετικά επιρρήματα δείχνουν διαφορετική συχνότητα.

100% ●━━━━━●━━━━━●━━━━━●━━━━━●━━━━━● 0%
always   usually   often   sometimes   rarely   never

→ *We **often watch** films on TV.*
→ *The teacher is **never** late for school.*
→ *Our grandparents **are always** happy to see us.*

Grammar Exercises

A Match the questions to the short answers.

1 Do your friends play chess? ☐
2 Does Kelly's brother do judo? ☐
3 Do I take good photos? ☐
4 Does the chess club meet on Sundays? ☐
5 Do you and your family go camping? ☐
6 Does your mum wear jeans? ☐
7 Do you like painting? ☐

a Yes, she does.
b No, we don't.
c No, it doesn't.
d Yes, I do.
e Yes, they do.
f No, you don't.
g No, he doesn't.

B Circle the correct words.

1 Why **do** / **does** your cousin like singing?
2 My best friend **play** / **plays** the guitar every day.
3 My classmates **don't** / **doesn't** read books often.
4 **What** / **Where** do you live?
5 We **go** / **goes** shopping once a week.
6 **When** / **What** does the sports centre open?
7 I chat on the phone **in** / **on** the afternoon.
8 Do your friends like music? Yes, they **do** / **like**.
9 They don't go out late **at** / **in** night.
10 My mum hardly ever **watch** / **watches** sport on TV.

C Complete the sentences with the frequency adverb and the correct form of the verb in brackets.

1 John _____ (usually / go) cycling at weekends.
2 Our school bus _____ (sometimes / be) late.
3 My grandparents _____ (never / read) comics.
4 How _____ you _____ (often / play) tennis?
5 I _____ (always / do) my homework before I go to bed.
6 My dad _____ (hardly ever / have) free time.
7 We _____ (often / not fly) our kites.
8 My teachers _____ (usually / not be) late for school.

3 My Home Town

3.1 **common** (adj) /ˈkɒmən/
usual; often seen or used by many people
● *It's common to see sheep crossing the road near our village.* ❖ κοινός, συνηθισμένος

3.2 **road sign** (n) /ˈrəʊd saɪn/
a notice near a road that shows information for drivers ● *Many of the road signs in Spain show place names in Spanish and English.*
❖ ταμπέλα, πινακίδα (στο δρόμο)

Word Focus   Page 32

3.3 **miniature** (adj) /ˈmɪnətʃə(r)/
very small; that looks like sth else, but a lot smaller ● *For our school project, I'm making a miniature farm with small plants and toy animals.* ➢ miniature (n) ❖ μινιατούρα, μικρού μεγέθους

3.4 **inhabitant** (n) /ɪnˈhæbɪtənt/
sb who usually lives in a place ● *The UK has more than 65 million inhabitants.* ➢ inhabit (v)
❖ κάτοικος

3.5 **windmill** (n) /ˈwɪndmɪl/
a tall building with parts that turn around in the wind ● *Marios is taking photos of the old white windmills on Mykonos.* ❖ ανεμόμυλος

3.6 **grind** (v) /ɡraɪnd/
break sth into very small pieces ● *The café has a machine that grinds coffee beans.*
➢ ground (adj) ❖ αλέθω, τρίβω
✎ Past Simple: ground

3.7 **grain** (n) /ɡreɪn/
the seeds of a plant like rice, corn, etc. ● *You can cook some grains of corn to make a plate of popcorn.* ❖ σπόρος, κόκκος, δημητριακά

3.8 **flour** (n) /ˈflaʊə(r)/
a soft white or brown substance used for making bread, cakes, etc. ● *How much flour do you need to make biscuits?* ❖ αλεύρι

3.9 **harbour** (n) /ˈhɑːbə(r)/
a place in the sea next to the land where ships can stop safely and people get on or off them
● *The ship from Samos is coming into the harbour now.* ❖ λιμάνι

3.10 **coast** (n) /kəʊst/
the land next to the sea ● *The island of Gozo is near the coast of Malta.* ➢ coastal (adj)
❖ ακτή

3.11 **racecourse** (n) /ˈreɪskɔːs/
a track where people race horses ● *There's a big racecourse in my town and you can see the horses running on Saturdays.*
❖ ιππόδρομος, ιπποδρόμιο

3.12 **observe** (v) /əbˈzɜːv/
watch (sth) carefully ● *Alistair enjoys observing the birds in the garden outside his window.*
➢ observant (n) ❖ παρακολουθώ, παρατηρώ

Reading   Pages 32–33

3.13 **leaflet** (n) /ˈliːflət/
a page with words and pictures that give information about sth ● *Every day people bring us leaflets with adverts for different restaurants, but I don't often read them.*
❖ φυλλάδιο

3.14 **make up** (phr v) /meɪk ʌp/
form the parts of sth ● *One old building and four new classrooms make up our school.*
❖ αποτελούμαι (από)

3.15 **building** (n) /ˈbɪldɪŋ/
a structure that has a roof and walls
● *The building next to my school is a theatre.*
➢ build (v), builder (n) ❖ κτίριο

3.16 **several** (det) /ˈsevrəl/
some, a lot of ● *Christine has got several cousins in Australia.* ❖ μερικοί, αρκετοί

3.17 **form** (n) /fɔːm/
type; kind ● *Fred is good at different forms of art, including model making.* ➢ form (v)
❖ μορφή, είδος

3.18 **transport** (n) /ˈtrænspɔːt/
a way to take people from place to place
● *Trains are my favourite form of transport.*
➢ transport (v) ❖ μεταφορά, μέσο μεταφοράς

3.19 **railway** (n) /ˈreɪlweɪ/
a system of tracks that trains move on
● *We live near the railway line, so we often hear trains.* ❖ σιδηρόδρομος

3.20 **connect** (v) /kəˈnekt/
make one thing join together with another
● *They're making a new road to connect the city to the airport.* ➢ connection (n), connected (adj) ❖ ενώνω, συνδέω

3.21 **zoo** (n) /zuː/
a place where people keep wild animals to look after or study them and for others to look at ● *The boys are watching the lions in the zoo.* ❖ ζωολογικός κήπος

3.22 **castle** (n) /ˈkɑːsl/
a very big building with high walls where important people like kings or queens live
● *Some parts of Edinburgh Castle are about 900 years old.* ❖ κάστρο, πύργος

3.23 **penguin** (n) /ˈpeŋgwɪn/
a black and white bird that is native to Antarctica • *Penguins can swim well, but they can't fly like other birds.* ❖ πιγκουίνος

3.24 **church** (n) /tʃɜːtʃ/
a building where Christians meet together and do things connected with their religion • *Tom's sister is getting married in the village church.* ❖ εκκλησία

3.25 **cinema** (n) /ˈsɪnəmə/
a building where people go to watch films • *I like going to the cinema to watch films with my friend.* ❖ κινηματογράφος, σινεμά

3.26 **fire station** (n) /ˈfaɪə steɪʃn/
a building where firefighters have their trucks and other things to stop fires • *The school children are visiting the fire station to learn about how to stop fires.* ❖ πυροσβεστικός σταθμός

3.27 **police station** (n) /pəˈliːs steɪʃn/
a building where police officers work • *Kelly is going to the police station to ask about her missing bag.* ❖ αστυνομικό τμήμα

3.28 **bridge** (n) /brɪdʒ/
sth that is built over a road or river, etc. for people to go across • *There are lots of bridges for cars and people to cross the River Clyde in Glasgow.* ❖ γέφυρα

3.29 **sports club** (n) /spɔːts klʌb/
a place where you can do different sports • *We play table tennis at the sports club every Thursday after school.* ❖ αθλητικός όμιλος

3.30 **swimming pool** (n) /ˈswɪmɪŋ puːl/
an area of water made for people to swim in • *Martin lives in a big house with a swimming pool in the garden.* ❖ πισίνα, κολυμβητήριο

3.31 **hospital** (n) /ˈhɒspɪtl/
a building where people go when they are very ill or hurt • *Dennis is in hospital because he's got a broken arm and leg.* ❖ νοσοκομείο

3.32 **ambulance** (n) /ˈæmbjələns/
a kind of vehicle for taking sick people to hospital • *Call an ambulance! This woman is very ill.* ❖ ασθενοφόρο

3.33 **tractor** (n) /ˈtræktə(r)/
a strong vehicle with big back tyres that you use on a farm • *Tony is learning to drive a tractor on his grandparents' farm.* ❖ τρακτέρ

3.34 **everyday** (adj) /ˈevrideɪ/
sth that happens every day; usual • *We live near the pool, so swimming is part of our everyday lives.* ❖ καθημερινός, συνηθισμένος

3.35 **routine** (n) /ruːˈtiːn/
the way you usually do things • *Runnng in the park is part of Tricia's morning routine.* ❖ ρουτίνα

3.36 **couple** (n) /ˈkʌpl/
two people who are together • *A young couple are moving into the house next door to us.* ❖ ζευγάρι, αντρόγυνο

3.37 **firefighter** (n) /ˈfaɪəfaɪtə(r)/
sb who tries to stop fires as a job • *The firefighters are throwing water on the burning trees.* ❖ πυροσβέστης

3.38 **put out** (phr v) /pʊt aʊt/
stop a fire or sth else that is burning • *You can put a blanket over a small fire to put it out.* ❖ σβήνω

3.39 **fair** (n) /feə(r)/
a place where you can go on rides and play games to have fun or win sth • *Dad's taking us to the fair to have fun.* ❖ λούνα παρκ, πανηγύρι
✎ Syn: funfair, fairground

3.40 **lady** (n) /ˈleɪdi/
a woman (used formally); sometimes used to talk about/to a woman that you don't know • *This shop sells ladies' hats and bags.* ❖ κυρία, γυναίκα

3.41 **gentleman** (n) /ˈdʒentlmən/
a man (used formally); sometimes used to talk about/to a man that you don't know • *There's an old gentleman waiting for the bus.* ❖ κύριος, τζέντλεμαν

3.42 **fisherman** (n) /ˈfɪʃəmən/
a man who catches fish as a job • *The fishermen are sailing their boats into the harbour.* ❖ ψαράς

3.43 **spend** (v) /spend/
use (time, money, energy, etc.) • *Diane spends two hours a day doing her homework.* ➤ spending (n) ❖ ξοδεύω (χρόνο, χρήματα), περνάω (χρόνο)

3.44 **giant** (n) /ˈdʒaɪənt/
sb or sth that is unusually big • *The story is about a friendly giant that lives in a really big castle.* ➤ giant (adj) ❖ γίγαντας

3.45 **opening times** (n) /ˈəʊpnɪŋ taɪmz/
the hours when a building or other place is open for people to come in • *The swimming pool's opening times are from 7 a.m. to 9 p.m. on Monday to Saturday.* ❖ ώρες λειτουργίας

3.46 **open** (adj) /ˈəʊpən/
ready for people to come in • *Some supermarkets in the UK are open 24 hours a day.* ➢ open (v), opening (n) ❖ ανοιχτός

3.47 **a.m.** (abbrev) /ˌeɪ ˈem/
the time after 12 o'clock midnight until 12 o'clock midday; used after a number for the time in the morning • *I get up at 7.30 a.m.* ❖ π.μ. (προ μεσημβρίας)

3.48 **p.m.** (abbrev) /ˌpiː ˈem/
the time after 12 o'clock midday until 12 o'clock midnight; used after a number for the time in the afternoon or evening up to midnight • *Our school classes finish at 3.30 p.m.* ❖ μ.μ. (μετά μεσημβρίας)

3.49 **price** (n) /praɪs/
the money that sth costs to buy • *The ticket price is £1.50 for children.* ➢ pricey (adj) ❖ τιμή

3.50 **adult** (n) /ˈædʌlt/
sb over 18 years old • *Young children can't go into the zoo without an adult.* ➢ adult (adj) ❖ ενήλικας

3.51 **picnic area** (n) /ˈpɪknɪk ˈeəriə/
a place outside with tables, etc. where you can have a picnic • *After their walk, the girls are having their sandwiches at the picnic area next to the lake.* ❖ χώρος για πικ νικ

3.52 **ice-cream van** (n) /ˌaɪs ˈkriːm væn/
a large van that opens at one side where sb sells ice cream to people in the street • *We sometimes get sweets from the ice-cream van that comes to our street in the evening.* ❖ παγωτατζίδικο (όχημα)

3.53 **facilities** (n) /fəˈsɪlətiz/
buildings and other things that people can use for different activities • *The hotel has very good facilities, including a swimming pool and tennis courts.* ❖ εγκαταστάσεις, ευκολίες

3.54 **only** (adv) /ˈəʊnli/
just; no more than • *Only six children want to go to the castle.* ➢ only (adj) ❖ μόνο, απλά

3.55 **minute** (n) /ˈmɪnɪt/
a measure of time that is a small part of an hour; 60 seconds • *The film is starting in ten minutes.* ❖ λεπτό

3.56 **frequent** (adj) /ˈfriːkwənt/
that happens often • *Trains to the city are frequent from here. There's one every 15 minutes.* ➢ frequency (n), frequently (adv) ❖ τακτικός, συχνός

Time

a.m.	hour
p.m.	later
constantly	minute
frequent	opening times
half an hour	

3.57 **car park** (n) /ˈkɑː pɑːk/
a place for people to leave their cars • *There is a big car park near the shops and cinema.* ❖ χώρος στάθμευσης, πάρκινγκ

3.58 **for hire** (expr) /fə ˈhaɪə(r)/
sth that you can have to use for a short time when you pay money • *There are bicycles for hire outside the station.* ❖ προς ενοικίαση

3.59 **supervise** (v) /ˈsuːpəvaɪz/
watch sb/sth to make sure that everything is alright • *Sotiria supervises the children on the school bus.* ➢ supervisor, supervision (n) ❖ επιβλέπω, προσέχω

3.60 **feed** (v) /fiːd/
give food to sb/sth • *Terry feeds his pet rabbits twice a day.* ➢ food (n) ❖ ταΐζω

3.61 **switch off** (phr v) /swɪtʃ ɒf/
press a button to stop sth working • *Please switch off the TV and do your homework.* ❖ σβήνω, κλείνω
✎ Opp: switch on ❖ ανάβω, ανοίγω

3.62 **mobile phone** (n) /ˌməʊbaɪl ˈfəʊn/
a phone that you can carry and use any place you go • *Switch off your mobile phone in the class.* ❖ κινητό τηλέφωνο

3.63 **shut** (adj) /ʃʌt/
not open; closed • *Please keep the window shut. It's cold outside.* ➢ shut (v) ❖ κλειστός

3.64 **graze** (v) /greɪz/
eat grass or other plants • *The cows are grazing in the field.* ❖ βόσκω

3.65 **direction** (n) /dəˈrekʃn/
the way you go to arrive at a place • *Which direction is the hospital? Left or right?* ➢ direct (v), direct (adj), directly (adv) ❖ κατεύθυνση

3.66 **worry** (v) /ˈwʌri/
think about sth bad that might happen • *Don't worry about the cost of the bus – it's free for school children.* ➢ worry (n), worried (adj) ❖ ανησυχώ

3.67 **compare** (v) /kəmˈpeə(r)/
look at what things are the same or different between people or things • *How can I compare my village with Athens? Everything is very different.* ➢ comparison (n) ❖ συγκρίνω

3.68 **one way** (adj) /ˌwʌn ˈweɪ/
where cars should only go in one direction
• *You can't drive up this road, you can only go down because it's one way.* ❖ (για δρόμους) μονόδρομος

3.69 **litter** (v) /ˈlɪtə(r)/
drop pieces of rubbish • *Don't litter the forest. Take your rubbish away with you.* ➢ litter (n)
❖ ρίχνω σκουπίδια

3.70 **closed** (adj) /kləʊzd/
not open; shut • *British schools are closed for two months in summer.* ➢ close (v) ❖ κλειστός

3.71 **allow** (v) /əˈlaʊ/
let sb do sth • *You're not allowed to go fishing in the lake.* ❖ επιτρέπω

3.72 **pay** (v) /peɪ/
give money for sth • *How much do you pay to go to the the theatre?* ➢ pay, payment (n)
❖ πληρώνω

3.73 **pedestrian** (n) /pəˈdestriən/
sb who is walking and not going by car or bus, etc. • *This bridge is for pedestrians and cyclists to cross the river, so cars are not allowed on it.* ❖ πεζός

3.74 **pedestrian crossing** (n) /pəˈdestriən ˈkrɒsɪŋ/
a part of the street where cars have to stop to let people go across • *I always cross the road at the pedestrian crossing in front of my school.* ❖ διάβαση πεζών

Vocabulary   Pages 34–35

3.75 **library** (n) /ˈlaɪbrəri/
a building where you can read, study books or take them home to read for a short time before returning them • *There is a good library in our town, so we don't need to buy many books.*
❖ βιβλιοθήκη

3.76 **restaurant** (n) /ˈrestrɒnt/
a place where you can sit down and buy food to eat • *We're eating lunch at a fish restaurant near the beach.* ❖ εστιατόριο

3.77 **stadium** (n) /ˈsteɪdiəm/
a place with a large space to do sports and seats around where people can watch
• *Thousands of people are watching the races in the stadium.* ❖ στάδιο

3.78 **police officer** (n) /pəˈliːs ɒfɪsə(r)/
a man or woman who works in the police force to help stop people who do sth bad • *Police officers are looking for the missing car.*
❖ αστυνομικός, αστυνόμος

3.79 **waiter** (n) /ˈweɪtə(r)/
sb who brings food and drinks to people in a restaurant • *The waiter is bringing our salad now.* ❖ σερβιτόρος, γκαρσόν
✎ Also: waitress (female)

3.80 **actor** (n) /ˈæktə(r)/
sb who plays a part in a play, film or musical
• *Who is your favourite actor? Do you like Ryan Gosling?* ➢ act (v), acting (n)
❖ ηθοποιός ✎ Also: actress (female)

3.81 **spectator** (n) /spekˈteɪtə(r)/
sb watching a sports event • *It's a goal and the spectators look very happy.* ➢ spectate (v)
❖ θεατής

3.82 **nurse** (n) /nɜːs/
sb who helps people that aren't well in a hospital or health centre • *Tania is a nurse in the children's hospital. She enjoys helping people.* ➢ nurse (v), nursing (n)
❖ νοσοκόμος, -α

3.83 **librarian** (n) /laɪˈbreəriən/
sb who looks after the books in a library
• *Ask the librarian to help you find an interesting book to read.* ❖ βιβλιοθηκάριος, βιβλιοθηκονόμος

3.84 **shop assistant** (n) /ˈʃɒp əsɪstənt/
sb who works in a shop and serves people who want to buy sth • *Barry works as a shop assistant in the supermarket.* ❖ πωλητής

3.85 **emergency** (n) /iˈmɜːdʒənsi/
sth bad that happens, like an accident that needs sb to do sth quickly to help • *It's good to have a mobile phone to call for help in an emergency.* ❖ έκτακτη ανάγκη, επείγον περιστατικό

3.86 **sick** (adj) /sɪk/
ill • *Emily isn't playing tennis today because she's sick.* ➢ sickness (n) ❖ άρρωστος

3.87 **criminal** (n) /ˈkrɪmɪnl/
sb who does sth bad, like stealing sth or hurting sb • *Call the police to catch that criminal! He's taking our car!* ➢ crime (n), criminal (adj) ❖ εγκληματίας

3.88 **chemist** (n) /ˈkemɪst/
sb who works in a shop that sells medicine and other things to make you feel well • *Ask the chemist for some cream to help with your skin problem.* ❖ φαρμακοποιός

3.89 **pharmacy** (n) /ˈfɑːməsi/
a shop where you can buy medicine, etc.
• *Is the pharmacy open? I need to get some medicine.* ➢ pharmacist (n) ❖ φαρμακείο
✎ Syn: chemist's

3.90 **greengrocer** (n) /ˈgriːngrəʊsə(r)/
sb who has or works in a shop that sells fruit and vegetables • *Please buy some potatoes and apples from the greengrocer.* ❖ μανάβης, μανάβικο

3.91 **bookshop** (n) /ˈbʊkʃɒp/
a shop where you can buy books • *Neil is in the bookshop. He's buying a book for his mum's birthday.* ❖ βιβλιοπωλείο

3.92 butcher (n) /ˈbʊtʃə(r)/
sb who sells meat; a shop where people buy meat • *You can buy fresh chicken at the butcher's shop.* ❖ χασάπης, χασάπικο, κρεοπωλείο

3.93 fishmonger (n) /ˈfɪʃmʌŋgə(r)/
sb who sells fish; a shop where people buy fish to eat • *Our village fishmonger gets fish from the boats in the harbour every morning.* ❖ ιχθυοπώλης, ιχθυοπωλείο

3.94 bakery (n) /ˈbeɪkəri/
a shop where people buy bread, cakes or biscuits; a place where bread, etc. is made • *Nicky always buys lovely biscuits from the bakery.* ➢ bake (v), baker (n) ❖ φούρνος, αρτοποιείο, ζαχαροπλαστείο

3.95 catch (**a bus/train**) (v) /kætʃ (ə bʌs/treɪn)/
go by bus/train • *We're going to catch a bus home after the cinema.* ❖ παίρνω/πηγαίνω με το λεωφορείο/τρένο

3.96 drive (v) /draɪv/
control a car, bus, etc. to make it move • *Georgina drives her car to work because there aren't many buses from her village.* ➢ drive, driver (n) ❖ οδηγώ

3.97 turn (v) /tɜːn/
change the way you are going and go in a different direction • *Go down this street and turn right at the police station.* ➢ turn, turning (n) ❖ στρίβω

3.98 get off (phr v) /get ɒf/
get out of a bus, train, etc. • *The children are getting off the school bus to go to their classes.* ❖ κατεβαίνω από, αποβιβάζομαι από

3.99 get on (phr v) /get ɒn/
go into a bus, train, etc. • *You can pay for your ticket when you get on the bus.* ❖ ανεβαίνω σε, επιβιβάζομαι σε

3.100 miss (v) /mɪs/
be too late for sth • *I don't want to miss the start of the film. Let's catch the bus now.* ❖ χάνω, δεν προλαβαίνω

3.101 travel (v) /ˈtrævl/
go to another place • *Sylvia wants to travel to South America.* ➢ travel, traveller (n) ❖ ταξιδεύω

3.102 half an hour (expr) /ˌhaːf ˈaʊə(r)/
30 minutes • *I can walk to my school in half an hour.* ❖ μισή ώρα, ένα μισάωρο

3.103 hour (n) /ˈaʊə(r)/
a period of 60 minutes • *They're waiting for the plane to New York, but it's two hours late.* ➢ hourly (adj) ❖ ώρα

3.104 later (adv) /ˈleɪtə(r)/
at a time after now in the future • *I'm doing my homework now, so please phone me later.* ➢ late (adj) ❖ αργότερα, μετά, έπειτα

3.105 cook (n) /kʊk/
sb who makes food ready to eat as a job • *Samantha is a good cook. She makes great pizza.* ➢ cook (v), cooker (n), cooked (adj) ❖ μάγειρας

3.106 town centre (n) /ˌtaʊn ˈsentə(r)/
the middle of a town where the shops and other facilities are • *There are always lots of people shopping in the town centre on Saturdays.* ❖ κέντρο της πόλης

3.107 far (adv) /faː(r)/
in a place not near • *There's a good fish restaurant not far from the beach.* ❖ μακριά

3.108 left (adv) /left/
to or on the left side of sth • *Turn left at the library and the park is there.* ➢ left (n), left (adj) ❖ αριστερά

3.109 straight on (adv) /streɪt ɒn/
in the same direction without turning • *Drive straight on for five kilometres and the station is on the left.* ❖ ευθεία

Transport

ambulance	connect
direction	drive
ice-cream van	explore
	leave
Nouns	miss
one-way ticket	skate
pedestrian crossing	travel
railway	turn
return ticket	
taxi	**Adverbs**
ticket	far
tractor	left
	on foot
Verbs	opposite
catch (a bus/train)	straight on

Phrasal verbs

get off	put out
get on	switch off
make up	

3.110 define (v) /dɪˈfaɪn/
give the meaning of sth • *It's easy to define simple words with pictures.* ➢ definition (n) ❖ εξηγώ, ορίζω

3.111 review (v) /rɪˈvjuː/
read sth again to check it • *Paul reviews his emails to check his spelling before he sends them.* ➢ review (n) ❖ ξανακοιτάζω, τσεκάρω

3.112 definition (n) /ˌdefɪˈnɪʃn/
meaning (of a word/phrase) • *The definition of 'librarian' is a person who works in a library.* ➢ define (v) ❖ ορισμός

3.113 **constantly** (adv) /ˈkɒnstəntli/
all the time; without stopping • *My sister talks constantly on her mobile phone.* ➣ constant (adj) ❖ συνεχώς, συνέχεια

3.114 **borrow** (v) /ˈbɒrəʊ/
take sth from sb else to use it and return it later • *Can I borrow your phone for a minute?* ❖ δανείζομαι

3.115 **railway station** (n) /ˈreɪlweɪ ˈsteɪʃn/
a place where trains stop for people to get on or off • *Where is the railway station? I want to catch a train.* ❖ σιδηροδρομικός σταθμός
✎ Syn: train station

3.116 **serve** (v) /sɜːv/
bring food or drinks to sb • *We're having dinner with our friends and Dad is serving the food.* ➣ service (n) ❖ σερβίρω

Grammar — Pages 36–37

3.117 **opposite** (adv) /ˈɒpəzɪt/
on the other side of sth • *Our house is opposite the bakery, so we can buy bread any time.* ➣ opposite (n), opposite (adj) ❖ απέναντι, στην άλλη πλευρά

3.118 **bus stop** (n) /ˈbʌs stɒp/
a place on the street where a bus stops for people to get on or off • *Get off at the bus stop after the hospital.* ❖ στάση λεωφορείου

3.119 **famous** (adj) /ˈfeɪməs/
sb/sth that a lot of people know about • *John's uncle is a famous football player. He plays for Real Madrid.* ➣ fame (n) ❖ διάσημος

3.120 **ice-skating** (n) /ˈaɪs skeɪtɪŋ/
the sport of moving across ice on skates • *My Canadian friends sometimes go ice-skating on a lake in winter.* ➣ ice-skate (v) ❖ πατινάζ

3.121 **painter** (n) /ˈpeɪntə(r)/
sb who paints pictures as a job • *This is a picture by the famous painter, Picasso.* ➣ paint (v), painting (n) ❖ ζωγράφος

Jobs

actor	librarian
butcher	nurse
cook	painter
firefighter	police officer
fisherman	receptionist
fishmonger	shop assistant
greengrocer	waiter

Other People

adult	lady
couple	pedestrian
criminal	spectator
gentleman	tourist
inhabitant	

3.122 **frozen** (adj) /ˈfrəʊzn/
so cold that sth has ice on it • *It's very cold outside and you can't drive on the frozen snow.* ➣ freeze (v) ❖ παγωμένος

3.123 **scene** (n) /siːn/
the things you can see in a place/picture • *The flowers in the garden make a very colourful scene.* ➣ scenic (adj) ❖ σκηνή

3.124 **quiet** (adj) /ˈkwaɪət/
without noise • *Our hotel is in a quiet place near the harbour.* ➣ quietly (adv) ❖ ήσυχος

3.125 **wooden** (adj) /ˈwʊdn/
made of wood • *There are two small wooden boats on the river.* ➣ wood (n) ❖ ξύλινος

3.126 **background** (n) /ˈbækɡraʊnd/
the part of a picture that is behind the main subject • *This is a photo of my family with our house in the background.* ❖ φόντο, βάθος (σε μια εικόνα ή φωτογραφία)

3.127 **skate** (v) /skeɪt/
move on skates across ice; move on roller skates • *My brother is showing me how to skate on the ice.* ➣ skating, skater (n) ❖ κάνω πατίνι/πατινάζ

Listening — Page 38

3.128 **taxi** (n) /ˈtæksi/
a car with a driver that people pay to drive them somewhere • *Your taxi is waiting to take you to the station.* ❖ ταξί

3.129 **selfie** (n) /ˈselfiː/
a photo that you take of yourself • *I don't understand why some people put a new selfie on Facebook every week.* ❖ selfie, σέλφι

3.130 **ticket** (n) /ˈtɪkɪt/
a piece of paper or card that sb buys to travel on sth or go into a place • *Have you got our train tickets?* ❖ εισιτήριο

3.131 **tourist** (n) /ˈtʊərɪst/
sb who is visiting a place for fun • *Hundreds of tourists visit Delphi every week.* ➣ tour (v), tour (n) ❖ τουρίστας, τουρίστρια

3.132 **tour** (n) /tʊə(r)/
an organised trip • *Ian and Tracy are enjoying their tour of Las Vegas.* ➣ tour (v), tourist (n) ❖ οργανωμένη εκδρομή, ξενάγηση

3.133 office (n) /ˈɒfɪs/
a room where sb works at a desk; a building or room where you can get information from a company ● *The woman in the office gives tourists information about things to do in the city.* ❖ γραφείο

Speaking
Page 39

3.134 leave (v) /liːv/
go away; start a journey ● *What time does the next bus leave?* ❖ φεύγω, αναχωρώ

3.135 return ticket (n) /rɪˌtɜːn ˈtɪkɪt/
a ticket for sb to travel to a place and come back again ● *We've got return tickets for the boat that leaves today and comes back on Sunday night.* ❖ εισιτήριο με επιστροφή

3.136 one-way ticket (n) /ˌwʌn ˈweɪ ˈtɪkɪt/
a ticket for sb to travel to a place, but not to come back again ● *Jane has a one-way ticket to France because she's going to work there.* ❖ απλό εισιτήριο, χωρίς επιστροφή

3.137 receptionist (n) /rɪˈsepʃənɪst/
sb who works in the front office of a building and helps people when they arrive ● *The hotel receptionist is showing us where our rooms are.* ➣ reception (n) ❖ ρεσεψιονίστ, υπάλληλος υποδοχής

3.138 San Francisco (n) /ˈsan fræn'sɪskʊ/
❖ Σαν Φρανσίσκο

3.139 bus station (n) /ˈbʌs steɪʃn/
a building where buses leave and arrive ● T*he first bus leaves the bus station at 6 a.m.* ❖ σταθμός λεωφορείων

3.140 Christmas (n) /ˈkrɪsməs/
25th December; the day that Christians celebrate as the birthday of Christ
● *At Christmas, we usually have a big meal with a few friends and family members and give each other presents.* ❖ Χριστούγεννα

Writing
Pages 40–41

3.141 notice (n) /ˈnəʊtɪs/
● *There was a big notice on the wall about the school fair.* ➣ notice (v), noticeable (adj) ❖ ανακοίνωση

3.142 recognise (v) /ˈrekəgnaɪz/
know what sth is or who sb is because you've seen them before ● *I don't recognise this street. I think we're lost.* ➣ recognition (n) ❖ αναγνωρίζω

3.143 pattern (n) /ˈpætn/
sth that happens or appears often in the same way ● *His stories all have the same pattern, so I always know the ending.* ❖ σχέδιο, μοτίβο

3.144 similarity (n) /ˌsɪməˈlærəti/
sth that is almost the same about two things/people ● *Tom's house in the city has no similarity with his cousin's farm.* ➣ similar (adj) ❖ ομοιότητα

3.145 Dublin (n) /ˈdʌblɪn/
❖ Δουβλίνο

3.146 explore (v) /ɪkˈsplɔː(r)/
go around a place to find out about it ● *We're going for a walk to explore the mountain.* ➣ explorer, exploration (n) ❖ εξερευνώ

3.147 on foot (expr) /ɒn fʊt/
by walking ● *Owen never goes to school on foot because it's five kilometres from home. He goes by bus.* ❖ με τα πόδια

3.148 incredible (adj) /ɪnˈkredəbl/
very good or big; hard to believe ● *The food at Luigi's is incredible! I love their pizza.* ❖ απίστευτος, φοβερός

3.149 museum (n) /mjuˈziːəm/
a building where there are very old objects, paintings, etc. for people to look at ● *The castle is a museum now and nobody lives there.* ❖ μουσείο

3.150 art gallery (n) /ˈɑːt gæləri/
a building where you can see paintings and other kinds of art ● *We're on a school trip to the art gallery and we can see lots of beautiful paintings here.* ❖ πινακοθήκη, μουσείο τέχνης

3.151 bar (n) /bɑː(r)/
a building or part of a building where sb can go to buy drinks ● *You can buy some juice or an ice cream at the beach bar.* ❖ μπαρ

3.152 delicious (adj) /dɪˈlɪʃəs/
with a very nice taste ● *The eggs from my uncle's farm are delicious.* ❖ νοστιμότατος

3.153 doughnut (n) /ˈdəʊnʌt/
a small round cake usually with a hole in the middle ● *I want to get a delicious jam doughnut from the bakery.* ❖ λουκουμάς, ντόνατ

3.154 hundred (n) /ˈhʌndrəd/
100 ● *Mum's aunt is almost one hundred years old. She's 99 this year.* ❖ εκατό

3.155 problem (n) /ˈprɒbləm/
sth that is difficult ● *There isn't a bus stop near our house, so transport is a problem.* ❖ πρόβλημα

3.156 Berlin (n) /bɜːˈlɪn/
❖ Βερολίνο

3.157 shopping centre (n) /ˈʃɒpɪŋ sentə(r)/
a place or building that has a lot of different shops together ● *Mum is taking us to the shopping centre to buy some new clothes.* ❖ εμπορικό κέντρο

3.158 **clue** (n) /kluː/
a piece of information that helps sb find out about sth • *The mountain rescue team are looking for clues to find the missing people.*
❖ στοιχείο, ένδειξη

3.159 **content** (n) /ˈkɒntent/
the things or ideas that are in sth • *Before writing your email, think about how much information you need in the content.*
➤ contain (v) ❖ περιεχόμενο

Places

art gallery	hospital
background	library
bakery	museum
bar	office
bookshop	pharmacy
bridge	picnic area
building	police station
bus station	racecourse
bus stop	railway station
burrow	restaurant
car park	seashore
castle	shopping centre
church	sports club
cinema	stadium
cliff	swimming pool
coast	town centre
fire station	windmill
harbour	zoo

Video 3
Town Rescue
Page 42

3.160 **puffin** (n) /ˈpʌfɪn/
a large black and white sea bird with a small coloured beak, like a parrot's • *On the boat trip around the island, we can see puffins flying above the rocks and looking for fish.*
❖ θαλάσσιος παπαγάλος, θαλασσοψιττακός

3.161 **burrow** (n) /ˈbʌrəʊ/
a hole in the ground that an animal makes for its home • *The rabbit is running into its burrow with some food for its babies.* ➤ burrow (v)
❖ λαγούμι, φωλιά

3.162 **cliff** (n) /klɪf/
a rocky place with a high straight side usually next to the sea • *The castle is on top of a high cliff above the beach.* ❖ γκρεμός

3.163 **puffling** (n) /ˈpʌflɪŋ/
a young puffin • *The puffin is carrying some food to feed its baby pufflings.* ❖ νεοσσός θαλάσσιου παπαγάλου ή θαλασσοψιττακού

3.164 **puffy** (adj) /ˈpʌfi/
looking bigger or rounder than usual • *Do you like these big puffy doughnuts?* ➤ puff (v), puff (n) ❖ πρησμένος, φουσκωτός

3.165 **confuse** (v) /kənˈfjuːz/
make sb feel mixed up • *All the streets in the town look the same and this confuses tourists.* ➤ confusion (n), confusing, confused (adj) ❖ μπερδεύω

3.166 **flashlight** (n) /ˈflæʃlaɪt/
a small light that you can carry • *When I go camping, I always take my flashlight to see at night.* ❖ φακός
✎ Syn: torch

3.167 **throw** (v) /θrəʊ/
make sth move from your hand through the air • *Throw the ball to Jason.* ➤ throw (n)
❖ ρίχνω, πετάω

3.168 **seashore** (n) /ˈsiːʃɔː(r)/
a beach or rocky area next to the sea • *It's nice to go for a walk along the seashore in the evening.* ❖ ακτή

3.169 **tradition** (n) /trəˈdɪʃn/
sth that people have done in the same way for many years • *It's a family tradition for us to meet for dinner together on Sunday afternoons.* ➤ tradition (adj) ❖ παράδοση

3.170 **enough** (adv) /ɪˈnʌf/
as much as sth needs to be • *Is the sea warm enough to go swimming?* ➤ enough (pron), enough (det) ❖ αρκετά

3.171 **confused** (adj) /kənˈfjuːzd/
not able to understand sth easily • *I'm confused – where can I catch a bus to the swimming pool?* ➤ confuse (v), confusion (n) ❖ μπερδεμένος, σαστισμένος

3.172 **towards** (adv) /təˈwɔːdz/
in the direction of • *The boat is sailing towards the island.* ❖ προς

3.173 **patrol** (n) /pəˈtrəʊl/
a small group that moves around an area to find sth/sb or watch out for problems • *The rescue patrol is looking for the missing boat.* ➤ patrol (v) ❖ περίπολος, περιφρούρηση

3.174 **protect** (v) /prəˈtekt/
look after sb/sth to keep them safe • *The mother cat is chasing the dog to protect her kittens.* ➤ protection (n) ❖ προστατεύω

3.175 **wildlife** (n) /ˈwaɪldlaɪf/
animals and plants that live or grow in nature • *I enjoy taking photos of wildlife when we go camping.* ❖ άγρια ζωή

Vocabulary Exercises

A Match to make sentences.

1 You can see beautiful paintings at the art ☐
2 They stopped at a picnic ☐
3 Cross the road at the pedestrian ☐
4 We're going to the shopping ☐
5 I can hear the ice-cream ☐
6 The hotel has a swimming ☐

a van. Let's get some sweets.
b area to have a snack.
c gallery beside the museum.
d pool outside the restaurant.
e centre to buys some clothes.
f crossing in front of the school.

B Circle the correct words.

1 Theodore is taking a **tractor / taxi** to the airport.
2 The library isn't **far / left** from our house. It's very close.
3 Kate is a shop **assistant / officer** in the supermarket.
4 Can I **turn / connect** my phone to your computer?
5 The tickets are £3.00 for **adults / pedestrians** and it's free for children.
6 Two people are waiting in the street at the **bus station / bus stop** outside the museum.
7 I get up at **7.30 a.m / 7.30 p.m.** in the morning.
8 You can **borrow / burrow** books to read from the library.

C Choose the correct words (A, B or C).

1 Please ___ the lights before you go out.
   A get off   B get on   C switch off
2 I want a return ___ from Brighton to London.
   A crossing   B ticket   C direction
3 Hurry up! The bus ___ in ten minutes.
   A misses   B leaves   C drives
4 Ladies and ___, welcome to our tour of the city.
   A tourists   B fishermen   C gentlemen
5 The ___ is making lunch in the hotel kitchen. It smells good!
   A cook   B bakery   C greengrocer
6 People are ice skating on the ___ river.
   A frozen   B common   C delicious
7 The police officers are trying to catch the ___.
   A spectator   B inhabitant   C criminal
8 We're waiting at the ___ to catch the boat to Mykonos.
   A church   B bridge   C harbour

D Unjumble the words to find the jobs.

1 urnes   _____

2 bralirani   _____

3 carto   _____

4 hercutb   _____

5 reitwa   _____

6 stoneceptiri   _____

7 gherefitfir   _____

8 monfigersh   _____

E Match the meanings a–h to the words 1–8 from D.

☐ a This person looks after the books in a library.

☐ b This person tries to put out fires.

☐ c This person helps people that aren't well in a hospital or health centre.

☐ d This person works in the front office of a building and helps people when they arrive.

☐ e This person plays a part in a play, film or musical.

☐ f This person sells fish.

☐ g This person brings food and drinks to people in a restaurant.

☐ h This person sells meat.

3 Grammar

3.1 *There is / There are*

Κατάφαση	
There **is**. There **are**.	
Άρνηση	
There **is not (isn't)**. There **are not (aren't)**.	
Ερώτηση	
Is there? **Are** there?	
Σύντομες απαντήσεις	
Yes, there **is**. **Yes**, there **are**.	**No**, there **is not** / there **isn't**. **No**, there **are not** / there **aren't**.

Χρησιμοποιούμε *there is / there are* για να:
περιγράψουμε ένα μέρος.
→ **There's** a bridge.
→ **There are** cars on the bridge.
περιγράψουμε που βρίσκονται πράγματα.
→ **There is** a new bakery next to the school.
μιλήσουμε για αριθμούς και ποσότητες.
→ **There are** two cafes in this street.
→ **There is** a lot of ice cream in the fridge.
ξεκινήσουμε ένα νέο θέμα.
→ **There's** a show on at the theatre.

Σημείωση: χρησιμοποιούμε *there is* και με μη μετρήσιμα ουσιαστικά.
→ **There is** food on the table.

3.2 Prepositions of place

Χρησιμοποιούμε *at* με:
τους χώρους γενικά.
→ *at the cinema/theatre*
→ *at a cafe*
→ *at the bank*
→ *at the shops*
→ *at home*
→ *at school*
→ *at work*

Χρησιμοποιούμε *in* με:
τα δοχεία.
→ *in his bag*
→ *in a box*
→ *in the fridge*

δωμάτια, κτίρια, χώρες, πόλεις, σημεία με όρια.
→ *in the living room*
→ *in the library*
→ *in hospital*
→ *in France*
→ *in London*
→ *in the town*

Χρησιμοποιούμε *on* με:
τις επιφάνειες.
→ *on the floor/wall*
→ *on the road*

τα μέσα μεταφοράς.
→ *on a bus/plane/boat/ship*

right (δεξιά) και *left* (αριστερά).
→ *on the right*
→ *on the left*

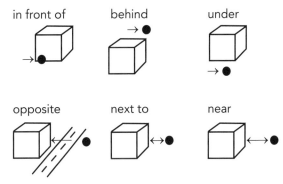

3.3 Present Continuous

Κατάφαση
I am ('m) play**ing**. He/she/it **is ('s)** play**ing**. We/you/they **are ('re)** play**ing**.

Άρνηση
I am ('m) not play**ing**. He/she/it **is not (isn't)** play**ing**. We/you/they **are not (aren't)** play**ing**.

Ερώτηση
Am I play**ing**? **Is** he/she/it play**ing**? **Are** we/you/they play**ing**?

Σύντομες απαντήσεις	
Yes, I **am**. **Yes**, he/she/it **is**. **Yes**, we/you/they **are**.	**No**, I'm **not**. **No**, he/she/it **isn't**. **No**, we/you/they **aren't**.

Ορθογραφία:

live → liv**ing**   stop → sto**pping**   cry → cry**ing**

Χρησιμοποιούμε τον Present Continuous για:

πράξεις που συμβαίνουν τώρα, την ώρα που μιλάμε.

→ *They **are walking** to school now.*

πράξεις που συμβαίνουν γύρω από την ώρα που μιλάμε.

→ *I **am learning** to ride a bike.*

προσωρινές καταστάσεις.

→ *He **is working** in a restaurant this summer.*

Σημείωση: Χρησιμοποιούμε συχνά εκφράσεις όπως: *now, nowadays, these days, this week, this month* και *at the moment, today* κλπ. με τον Present Continuous.

Σημείωση: Δεν χρησιμοποιούμε τον Present Continuous με ρήματα όπως: *have, like, love, believe, know, think.*

Grammar Exercises

A Circle the correct words.

1 **It's / There's** a new student in my class.
2 There **isn't / aren't** a library in the village.
3 Where's your house? **Is it / Is there** next to the school?
4 **There / They** are two restaurants near the theatre.
5 **There is / Is there** a cinema in your town?
6 **There / They** are delicious! Where are these biscuits from?
7 I'm going to the chemist's. Where is **there / it**?
8 **Are / Is** there supermarkets near your house?

B Choose the correct answer (A, B or C).

1 There's a painting of a beach ___ the wall.
  A in   **B** at   **C** on
2 A family is sitting ___ the right.
  A behind   **B** in   **C** on
3 They're having a picnic ___ the rocks.
  A next to   **B** front of   **C** under
4 In the sea, ___ is a small boat.
  A it   **B** there   **C** they
5 That boat ___ near the beach.
  A sail   **B** sails   **C** is sailing
6 A fisherman is ___ work and he's catching a fish.
  A at   **B** in   **C** on
7 The scene is somewhere ___ Greece.
  A at   **B** in   **C** on
8 It's on an island ___ the coast of Athens.
  A in   **B** opposite   **C** under

C Complete the sentences with the Present Continuous form of the verbs in brackets.

1 We _____ (watch) a film in the cinema.
2 The children _____ (not skate) now.
3 Mum _____ (talk) to the receptionist at the moment.
4 I _____ (wait) for the bus.
5 What _____ you _____ (do) outside the theatre.
6 The criminal _____ (not stop) and the police officer is angry.
7 _____ the boats _____ (move) on the river?
8 The birds _____ (fly) in the park.

4 Celebrate!

Page 43

4.1 **perform** (v) /pə'fɔːm/
act, dance or sing, etc. for others to watch
• *Martha and her friends are performing
a traditional dance in the school concert.*
➣ performance, performer (n) ❖ δίνω
παράσταση, παίζω

4.2 **hula hoop** (n) /'huːlə huːp/
a large ring that you put around your waist and
move your body to make the hoop go round
• *How many times can you make a hula hoop
go round without stopping?* ❖ χούλα χουπ

4.3 **treasure** (n) /'treʒə(r)/
sth that is worth a lot of money • *The museum
is full of treasures from Ancient Greece and
Rome.* ❖ θησαυρός

4.4 **island** (n) /'aɪlənd/
an area of land that has water all around it
• *Arran is a large island near the coast of
Scotland.* ❖ νησί

Reading
Page 44

4.5 **New Year** (n) /ˌnjuː 'jɪə(r)/
the celebration of the first day of the year
• *We're having dinner with our friends to
celebrate New Year.* ❖ πρωτοχρονιά

4.6 **celebration** (n) /ˌselɪ'breɪʃn/
an event to celebrate for a special reason
• *It's my brother's name day and we're having
a big family celebration.* ➣ celebrate (v)
❖ γιορτή

4.7 **typical** (adj) /'tɪpɪkl/
usual as an example of sth • *The photo shows
a typical British garden with colourful flowers.*
➣ typically (adv) ❖ τυπικός, συνηθισμένος

4.8 **Singapore** (n) /ˌsɪŋə'pɔː(r)/
❖ Σιγκαπούρη

4.9 **December** (n) /dɪ'sembə(r)/
❖ Δεκέμβριος, Δεκέμβρης

4.10 **before** (prep) /bɪ'fɔr/
earlier than sth • *David always gets up before
seven o'clock.* ➣ before (conj), before (adv)
❖ πριν, πριν από

4.11 **midnight** (n) /'mɪdnaɪt/
12 o'clock at night • *Our plane arrives in Paris
at midnight, so we can catch the 1 a.m. train
from the airport.* ❖ μεσάνυχτα

4.12 **hold hands** (expr) /həʊld hændz/
hold sb's hand, often to show that you are
together • *For some of our traditional dances,
everyone holds hands and moves around in a
circle.* ❖ κρατιέμαι χέρι-χέρι

Word Focus Page 44

4.13 **fireworks** (n) /'faɪəwɜːks/
a small thing that burns to make a loud noise
with coloured lights used outside at some
celebrations • *It's a big celebration on the
island and we can watch the fireworks going
up in the harbour tonight.* ❖ πυροτεχνήματα

4.14 **explode** (v) /ɪk'spləʊd/
burst making a loud noise • *Stand back – that
car is exploding!* ➣ explosion (n)
❖ εκρήγνυμαι, σκάω

4.15 **display** (n) /dɪ'spleɪ/
a show of things or sth happening for people to
watch • *There's a firework display tomorrow.*
➣ display (v) ❖ επίδειξη

4.16 **confetti** (n) /kən'feti/
small pieces of coloured paper that people
throw during celebrations like weddings
• *Take some confetti to throw on Jim and
Louise when they get married.* ❖ κομφέτι

4.17 **rubber** (adj) /'rʌbə(r)/
made of a strong material that can bend easily
• *Granny wears rubber gloves to protect her
hands when she washes the dishes.*
➣ rubber (n) ❖ πλαστικός, από καουτσούκ

4.18 **fill** (v) /fɪl/
make sth full • *Can you fill my glass with
water, please?* ❖ γεμίζω

4.19 **procession** (n) /prə'seʃn/
a line of people or cars, etc. moving together
one after the other • *We're watching a
procession of people in funny clothes walking
through the town streets.* ❖ πορεία, πομπή

4.20 **lantern** (n) /'læntən/
a lamp in a kind of box that you can carry
and use outside • *Sometimes we eat on our
balcony in the evening with light from lanterns
on the table.* ❖ φανάρι, καντήλι

4.21 **container** (n) /kən'teɪnə(r)/
sth that you can put sth inside to keep it or
carry • *Helen puts her lunch in a container to
take to work.* ➣ contain (v) ❖ δοχείο

Reading
Pages 44–45

4.22 **New York** (n) /ˌnjuː 'jɔːk/
❖ Νέα Υόρκη

4.23 **job** (n) /dʒɒb/
work that sb does, usually for money • *Janice
has got a job in a supermarket. She's a shop
assistant.* ❖ δουλειά, εργασία

4.24　**work** (v) /wɜːk/
have/do a job ● *Lee is a cook and he works in a hotel restaurant.* ➣ work, worker (n)
❖ δουλεύω, εργάζομαι

4.25　**New Year's Eve** (n) /ˌnjuː ˈjɪəz iːv/
❖ παραμονή πρωτοχρονιάς

4.26　**weather** (n) /ˈweðə(r)/
the state of the air outside, e.g. rainy, sunny, windy ● *How is the weather in your country? Is it hot in summer?* ❖ καιρός

4.27　**count** (v) /kaʊnt/
say the numbers in order ● *Can you count from one to a hundred in English?* ❖ μετράω

4.28　**exciting** (adj) /ɪkˈsaɪtɪŋ/
making sb very interested or making sb want to do sth ● *James has got an exciting job – he's a firefighter.* ➣ excite (v), excitement (n), excited (adj) ❖ συναρπαστικός

4.29　**kiss** (v) /kɪs/
touch sb/sth with your lips to show you like them ● *Grandma always kisses us when we arrive at her house.* ➣ kiss (v) ❖ φιλάω

4.30　**next** (adj) /nekst/
sth that comes after sth else ● *Gina wants to go to the zoo next week.* ➣ next (n, adv) ❖ επόμενος

4.31　**tropical** (adj) /ˈtrɒpɪkl/
from the hottest areas of the world ● *I love pineapple and other tropical fruit.* ❖ τροπικός

4.32　**Chinese** (adj) /ˌtʃaɪˈniːz/
➣ China, Chinese (n) ❖ κινέζικος

4.33　**lucky** (adj) /ˈlʌki/
bringing sb good luck; having sth good or bad happen by chance ● *Mandy always writes with her lucky pen in the exams.* ➣ luck (n)
❖ τυχερός

4.34　**money** (n) /ˈmʌni/
sth you use to buy or pay for things ● *My grandparents give me money for my birthday and I usually buy clothes or books with it.*
❖ χρήμα, χρήματα, λεφτά

4.35　**packet** (n) /ˈpækɪt/
a paper bag or box ● *We need a packet of balloons for the party.* ❖ πακέτο

4.36　**mandarin orange** (n) /ˈmændərɪn ˈɒrɪndʒ/
a small kind of orange ● *These mandarin oranges are juicy and sweet.* ❖ μανταρίνι

4.37　**luck** (n) /lʌk/
sth good or bad that happens by chance
● *Good luck in your maths test!* ➣ lucky (adj)
❖ τύχη

4.38　**everywhere** (adv) /ˈevriweə(r)/
in all places ● *On New Year's Eve, there are parties everywhere.* ➣ everywhere (pron), everywhere (conj) ❖ παντού

4.39　**tart** (n) /tɑːt/
a sweet pie with fruit inside ● *Apple tarts are delicious with ice cream.* ❖ τάρτα, πίτα με γέμιση φρούτων

4.40　**coconut** (n) /ˈkəʊkənʌt/
a hard brown tropical nut with a soft white food and milky liquid inside; the soft white food from inside a coconut shell ● *Do you like drinking coconut milk?* ❖ καρύδα

4.41　**cookie** (n) /ˈkʊki/
a biscuit or small cake ● *Once a week, Alexia makes cookies for all the family. Her favourite kind is with fruit and nuts.* ❖ μπισκότο

4.42　**definitely** (adv) /ˈdefɪnətli/
for sure ● *Ian definitely wants to visit New York again. It's his favourite city.* ➣ definite (adj)
❖ σαφώς, σίγουρα

4.43　**dessert** (n) /dɪˈzɜːt/
a plate of sweet food or fruit as the last part of a meal ● *We're having chicken for our main meal and strawberries and ice cream for dessert.* ❖ επιδόρπιο

4.44　**present** (n) /ˈpreznt/
sth you give to sb, often for a special reason, e.g. birthday, wedding ● *What present do you want for your birthday? Do you like books or games?* ❖ δώρο

4.45　**market** (n) /ˈmɑːkɪt/
a place where sb can buy sth, often outside, and sometimes directly from the maker/farmer
● *On Tuesdays, we buy lots of fruit from the street market near our home.* ❖ (λαϊκή) αγορά

4.46　**prefer** (v) /prɪˈfɜː(r)/
like sth/sb more than sth/sb else ● *I don't like very sweet food for dessert. I prefer fruit.*
➣ preference (n) ❖ προτιμώ

4.47　**costume** (n) /ˈkɒstjuːm/
clothes sb wears to look like sb/sth else; clothes from a historic time or special place
● *The actors are wearing funny animal costumes for the play.* ❖ στολή

Seasons

spring	autumn
summer	winter

Vocabulary　　　Pages 46–47

4.48　**winter** (n) /ˈwɪntə(r)/
the coldest time of year between autumn and spring ● *Do you like winter sports like skiing?*
❖ χειμώνας

4.49　**spring** (n) /sprɪŋ/
the time of year between winter and summer
● *Spring is my favourite season because there are lots of flowers growing.* ❖ άνοιξη

4.50 **summer** (n) /'sʌmə(r)/
the hottest time of the year between spring and autumn • *In December, it's winter in Sweden, but it's summer in Australia!*
❖ καλοκαίρι

4.51 **autumn** (n) /'ɔːtəm/
the time of year between summer and winter • *In Britain, a lot of trees change their colours from green to brown and yellow in autumn.*
❖ φθινόπωρο

4.52 **warm** (adj) /wɔːm/
hot, but not a very high temperature • *Take some warm clothes for the camp. It gets cold at night.* ➣ warmth (n) ❖ ζεστός, θερμός

4.53 **Australia** (n) /ɒs'treɪljə/
➣ Australian (adj) ❖ Αυστραλία

4.54 **Halloween** (n) /ˌhæləʊ'iːn/
a celebration on 31st October, especially in the UK, USA and Canada • *We're having a Halloween party at school and this year we're all witches and cats!* ❖ Χαλοουίν, παραμονή των Αγίων Πάντων

4.55 **leaf** (n) /liːf/
a small flat green part of a tree • *In winter, there are no leaves on the trees in our garden.* ➣ leafy (adj) ❖ φύλλο
✎ Plural: leaves

4.56 **change** (v) /tʃeɪndʒ/
stop being in one state and become sth different • *Nancy usually changes her clothes after work and puts on jeans and a T-shirt.* ➣ change (n) ❖ αλλάζω

4.57 **October** (n) /ɒk'təʊbə(r)/
❖ Οκτώβριος, Οκτώβρης

4.58 **prepare** (v) /prɪ'peə(r)/
make sth ready for sth • *I'm tidying the house to prepare for the party.* ➣ preparation (n) ❖ προετοιμάζω

4.59 **pumpkin** (n) /'pʌmpkɪn/
a very big round orange vegetable with a hard skin • *The restaurant has good pumpkin soup in winter. It's delicious.* ❖ κολοκύθα

4.60 **dress up** (phr v) /dres 'ʌp/
wear special clothes, usually to look like sth/sb else • *What are you dressing up as for the party? I'm making a clown costume.*
❖ ντύνομαι, μεταμφιέζομαι

4.61 **trick or treating** (expr) /trɪk ɔː 'triːtɪŋ/
an activity that sb does at Halloween, especially in the USA or UK, where children dress up and go to other houses to ask for sweets or money • *We're going to our friends' houses to do trick or treating for Halloween.*
❖ έθιμο του Χαλοουίν με φάρσα ή κέρασμα

4.62 **neighbour** (n) /'neɪbə(r)
sb who lives next to or near your home • *Our neighbour's cat likes playing in our garden.*
❖ γείτονας

4.63 **excited** (adj) /ɪk'saɪtɪd/
feeling very happy about doing and really wanting to do sth • *It's Emmeline's birthday and she's excited about her party.* ➣ excite (v), excitement (n) ❖ ενθουσιασμένος

4.64 **best** (adv) /best/
the most; more than anything else • *From all the seasons, I like spring best.* ➣ best (n), best (adj) ❖ καλύτερα, περισσότερο

4.65 **invite** (v) /ɪn'vaɪt/
ask sb to come to sth or do sth with you • *My aunt sometimes invites us to her house at weekends.* ➣ invitation (n) ❖ προσκαλώ

4.66 **June** (n) /dʒuːn/
❖ Ιούνιος, Ιούνης

4.67 **month** (n) /mʌnθ/
one of twelve parts of the year • *I'm looking forward to August because that's the month we go on holiday.* ❖ μήνας

4.68 **be born** (v) /biː bɔːn/
begin your life • *Pierre was born in a town in France.* ❖ γεννιέμαι

4.69 **decoration** (n) /ˌdekə'reɪʃn/
sth to make a place look special or colourful • *In the USA, people cut pumpkins to make Halloween decorations.* ➣ decorate (v), decorative (adj) ❖ στολίδι

4.70 **barbecue** (n) /'baːbɪkjuː/
a meal outdoors with food cooked on an open fire • *Linda is making burgers for the barbecue in her garden.* ➣ barbecue (v) ❖ μπάρμπεκιου

4.71 **fancy dress** (n) /ˌfænsi 'dres/
special clothes that sb wears to look like sb/sth else for parties, etc. • *We're having a fancy dress party and everyone is dressed up as flowers or trees.* ❖ στολή (πχ για Απόκριες)

4.72 **bonfire** (n) /'bɒnfaɪə(r)/
a large fire outside to burn rubbish or for a celebration • *In Britain, people have bonfires as part of a traditional celebration on 5th November.* ❖ πυρά, μεγάλη εορταστική φωτιά

4.73 **Scotland** (n) /'skɒtlənd/
➣ Scot (n), Scottish (adj) ❖ Σκωτία

4.74 **January** (n) /'dʒænjuəri/
❖ Ιανουάριος, Γενάρης

4.75 **bride** (n) /braɪd/
a woman who is getting married, on her wedding day • *In the photo, the bride is wearing a simple wedding dress and holding some beautiful flowers.* ➣ bridal (adj) ❖ νύφη

4.76 **fizzy drink** (n) /'fɪzi drɪŋk/
a sweet drink that has bubbles in it • *I don't like fizzy drinks like cola. I prefer fruit juice.*
❖ αναψυκτικό

4.77   **sandal** (n) /ˈsændl/
an open shoe, usually worn in warm weather
● *You can't walk in the mountains with your beach sandals. Wear your walking boots.*
❖ πέδιλο, σανδάλι

4.78   **sandwich** (n) /ˈsænwɪtʃ/
a snack made with food between two pieces of bread ● *Ted's making cheese and tomato sandwiches for the picnic.* ❖ τοστ, σάντουιτς

4.79   **sausage** (n) /ˈsɒsɪdʒ/
very small pieces of meat or other food inside a long thin tube ● *The women in this mountain village make sausages with meat and vegetables from their farms.* ❖ λουκάνικο

4.80   **suit** (n) /suːt/
a jacket and trousers or skirt that go together
● *Brian is wearing his suit because he's going to an important meeting.* ❖ κοστούμι

4.81   **jumper** (n) /ˈdʒʌmpə(r)/
a piece of clothing with long sleeves, often made of wool, for the top part of the body
● *Wear your jumper. It's cold outside.*
❖ πουλόβερ

Grammar   Pages 48–49

4.82   **Diwali** (n) /diːˈwaːli/
an Indian celebration in autumn ● *In India, people decorate their homes with special lights for Diwali in autumn.* ❖ Diwali, η γιορτή των φώτων στην Ινδία

4.83   **November** (n) /nəʊˈvembə(r)/
❖ Νοέμβριος, Νοέμβρης

4.84   **noise** (n) /nɔɪz/
sth loud that you can hear ● *The neighbours are making a lot of noise, so I can't hear our TV.* ➣ noisy (adj) ❖ θόρυβος

4.85   **sari** (n) /ˈsaːri/
a traditional women's dress from India ● *Aisha usually wears jeans, but she is wearing a traditional sari for her sister's wedding.* ❖ σάρι

4.86   **fridge** (n) /frɪdʒ/
a device that you put food in to keep it cold or frozen ● *Is there any cheese in the fridge?*
❖ ψυγείο

4.87   **hope** (v) /həʊp/
want sth to happen very much ● *I hope you like this music. It's my favourite singer.*
➣ hope (n), hopeful (adj) ❖ ελπίζω

4.88   **invitation** (n) /ˌɪnvɪˈteɪʃn/
a card or paper that shows sb invites you to come to an event ● *Helena is having a party and she's giving invitations to all her friends.*
➣ invite (v) ❖ πρόσκληση

4.89   **festival** (n) /ˈfestɪvl/
an event or time where people do special activities to celebrate sth; a group of special events on one theme ● *Many tourists come to Edinburgh in August to enjoy music and street theatre at the festival.* ❖ φεστιβάλ, γιορτή

4.90   **Karaoke** (n) /ˌkæriˈəʊki/
a way that people have fun by using a machine to play music from famous songs so that sb can sing the words ● *Oh no! Dad wants to have a Karaoke night to sing those old songs again!* ❖ καραόκι

4.91   **candle** (n) /ˈkændl/
a small thin stick of coloured wax with a string inside that burns when you light it ● *Dan is blowing out the candles on his birthday cake.*
❖ κεράκι

4.92   **holiday** (n) /ˈhɒlədeɪ/
a day when schools, etc. are closed and people can relax ● *I'm looking forward to the school holidays. I'm going camping with my friends.* ❖ αργία, διακοπές, γιορτή

4.93   **traffic** (n) /ˈtræfɪk/
all the cars, buses, etc. travelling on a road
● *Sometimes the school bus is late because there's a lot of traffic in the morning.* ❖ κίνηση

4.94   **skiing** (n) /ˈskiːɪŋ/
the activity of moving across snow on skis
● *Pantelis goes skiing with his parents in Austria in winter.* ➣ ski (v) ❖ σκι

4.95   **news** (n) /njuːz/
information about interesting or important events that happened ● *There's some news on TV about the forest fire.* ❖ ειδήσεις

4.96   **during** (prep) /ˈdjʊərɪŋ/
from the start to the end of a certain time/event
● *I haven't got any free time during the week, so I go out at the weekend.* ❖ κατά τη διάρκεια

4.97   **slice** (n) /slaɪs/
a thin flat piece of sth ● *Zoe is eating a slice of bread with her soup.* ➣ slice (v) ❖ φέτα, λεπτό κομμάτι (πχ ψωμιού)

4.98   **whole** (adj) /həʊl/
all of sth ● *I can't eat the whole pizza. Two slices are enough.* ➣ whole (n) ❖ ολόκληρος

4.99   **offer** (v) /ˈɒfə(r)/
say that you will give sth to sb or do sth for them ● *The shop is offering two pizzas for the same price as one.* ➣ offer (n) ❖ προσφέρω

4.100   **dancer** (n) /ˈdaːnsə(r)/
sb who dances ● *Traditional Spanish music is playing and the dancers are performing on stage.* ➣ dance (v), dance, dancing (n)
❖ χορευτής, χορεύτρια

4.101   **get dressed** (expr) /get drest/
put on clothes ● *Wake up and get dressed. It's breakfast time.* ❖ ντύνομαι

4.102 **concert** (n) /ˈkɒnsət/
a performance with music and sometimes dancers ● *There's a famous singer in a concert at the stadium. Have you got a ticket?* ❖ συναυλία

4.103 **relative** (n) /ˈrelətɪv/
a family member ● *Tony's friends and relatives are all coming to see him in the play.* ➢ relate (v), related (adj) ❖ συγγενής

4.104 **language** (n) /ˈlæŋgwɪdʒ/
the system of how people talk or write that comes from one country or area ● *Chinese is a difficult language to learn.* ❖ γλώσσα

Months

January	July
February	August
March	September
April	October
May	November
June	December

Listening
Page 50

4.105 **international** (adj) /ˌɪntəˈnæʃnəl/
connected with more than one country ● *Roberto goes to an international school to learn English in summer. His classmates are from many different countries.* ❖ διεθνής

4.106 **March** (n) /mɑːtʃ/
❖ Μάρτιος, Μάρτης

4.107 **April** (n) /ˈeɪprəl/
❖ Απρίλιος, Απρίλης

4.108 **May** (n) /meɪ/
❖ Μάιος, Μάης

4.109 **Austria** (n) /ˈɒstriə/
➢ Austrian (n), Austrian (adj) ❖ Αυστρία

4.110 **last** (adj) /lɑːst/
the one that comes after all the other similar things ● *The concert finishes late, so we can take the last train home.* ➢ last (n), last (adv) ❖ τελευταίος

4.111 **British** (adj) /ˈbrɪtɪʃ/
➢ British, Britain (n) ❖ βρετανικός

4.112 **Bolivian** (adj) /bəˈlɪviən/
➢ Bolivia, Bolivian (n) ❖ βολιβιανός

4.113 **playground** (n) /ˈpleɪgraʊnd/
an area where children can play in front of a school building; an outdoor area where children can play ● *I like chatting to my friends in the playground during the break.* ❖ προαύλιο, αυλή του σχολείου

4.114 **gymnasium** (n) /dʒɪmˈneɪziəm/
a room or building for doing indoor sports ● *The students play volleyball in the school gymnasium.* ❖ κλειστό γήπεδο, γυμναστήριο 🖉 Abbrev: gym

4.115 **specific** (adj) /spəˈsɪfɪk/
connected with one thing; exact ● *I can understand the meaning of the song, but I don't know some specific words.* ➢ specify (v), specifically (adv) ❖ συγκεκριμένος, ακριβής

4.116 **preparation** (n) /ˌprepəˈreɪʃn/
all the things you do to get ready for sth ● *We're making pumpkin faces in preparation for our Halloween party.* ➢ prepare (v) ❖ προετοιμασία

4.117 **flag** (n) /flæg/
a piece of cloth with a pattern that is the symbol of a country ● *The Italian flag is green, white and red.* ❖ σημαία

4.118 **presentation** (n) /ˌpreznˈteɪʃn/
an event when sb performs sth or shows a piece of work to a group; an event where sb gets a prize/present from a group ● *The children are doing their presentations of international dances in the concert.* ➢ present (v) ❖ παρουσίαση

Speaking
Page 51

4.119 **Thanksgiving** (n) /ˌθæŋksˈgɪvɪŋ/
an important holiday at the end of autumn in the USA and Canada ● *Americans have a big family dinner for Thanksgiving at the end of November, but Canadians celebrate this in October.* ❖ Ημέρα ή Γιορτή των Ευχαριστιών

4.120 **February** (n) /ˈfebruəri/
❖ Φεβρουάριος, Φλεβάρης

4.121 **San Juan** (n) /sæn ˈhuæn/
the festival of San Juan (Saint John) in Spain on 23rd June ● *Spanish people celebrate San Juan with bonfires and beach parties.* ❖ Ισπανική γιορτή του Αγίου Ιωάννη (Σαν Χουάν)

4.122 **fourth** (number) /fɔːθ/
4th ❖ τέταρτος

4.123 **Carnival** (n) /ˈkɑːnɪvl/
❖ Απόκριες

4.124 **Valentine's Day** (n) /ˈvæləntaɪnz deɪ/
❖ ημέρα του Αγίου Βαλεντίνου

4.125 **tricky** (adj) /ˈtrɪki/
difficult ● *Some costumes are tricky to make, but they look good in the end.* ➢ trick (v), trick (n) ❖ ζόρικος, δύσκολος

4.126 **pronounce** (v) /prəˈnaʊns/
say a word using the correct sounds ● *Can you pronounce the word 'autumn'?* ➢ pronunciation (n) ❖ προφέρω

4.127 especially (adv) /ɪ'speʃəli/
very much; more than other things • *I love dressing up in costumes, especially at Carnival time.* ❖ ιδιαιτέρως

Celebrations

Nouns
Carnival
Diwali
Halloween
New Year
New Year's Eve
San Juan
Thanksgiving
Valentine's Day

barbecue
bonfire
bride
candle
concert
confetti
dancer
decoration
display
festival
fireworks
flag
fizzy drink
garland
holiday
hope
invitation
Karaoke
lantern

lotus flower
luck
news
preparation
present
presentation
procession
trick or treating
welcome

Clothes
costume
fancy dress
jumper
sari
suit

Verbs
count
decorate
dress up
explode
get dressed
hold hands
kiss
perform
prepare
take place

Writing
Pages 52–53

4.128 recipe (n) /'resəpi/
instructions on how to cook sth and what things you need for this • *This is a recipe for pumpkin pie. It's easy to make.* ❖ συνταγή

4.129 then (adv) /ðen/
at that moment in the past • *Betsy comes home from work at six o'clock, then she cooks dinner.* ❖ τότε, έπειτα

4.130 next (adv) /nekst/
coming after sth else • *First, clean the tomatoes. Next, cut them into pieces and put them in a bowl.* ➢ next (adj) ❖ μετά, έπειτα

4.131 finally (adv) /'faɪnəli/
after everything else • *Finally, put the food on the plates and it's ready to eat.* ➢ final (n) ❖ στο τέλος, τελικά

4.132 instruction (n) /ɪn'strʌkʃn/
sth that tells you what to do or how to do sth • *I can't find the instructions for this camera. Can you show me what to do?* ➢ instruct (v), instructor (n) ❖ οδηγίες, εντολή

4.133 for example (expr) /fɔː ɪg'zaːmpl/
used before you give an example of sth • *Some things are not good for us to eat or drink. For example, fizzy drinks and sweets are bad for our teeth.* ❖ για παράδειγμα ✎ Abbrev: e.g.

4.134 fry (v) /fraɪ/
cook sth in hot oil • *Fry the onions and then put in the tomatoes.* ➢ fried (adj) ❖ τηγανίζω

4.135 nationality (n) /ˌnæʃə'næləti/
the fact of belonging to a particular country; a group of people with the same history, language and traditions, etc. from one country • *Dawn was born in San Francisco, so her nationality is American.* ➢ nation (n), national (adj) ❖ εθνικότητα, υπηκοότητα

4.136 sushi (n) /'suːʃi/
a kind of Japanese food with rice put in small shapes with uncooked fish, etc. • *Mark doesn't like fish, so he isn't coming to the sushi bar with us.* ❖ σούσι

4.137 paella (n) /paɪ'elə/
traditional Spanish food with rice, fish, chicken and vegetables cooked together • *When we go to Barcelona, I want to eat some real Spanish paella.* ❖ παέγια, ισπανικό πιλάφι με θαλασσινά, κοτόπουλο και λαχανικά

4.138 curry (n) /'kʌri/
traditional Asian food with vegetables or meat cooked in a hot spicy sauce • *For dinner, we're having chicken curry with rice and Indian bread.* ➢ curried (adj) ❖ κάρι

4.139 guacamole (n) /ˌgwækə'məʊleɪ/
traditional Mexican food made with avocado mixed with tomatoes, onions, etc. • *For starters, they serve guacamole with thin pieces of carrot and other vegetables.* ❖ γκουακαμόλε

4.140 nachos (n) /'nætʃəʊz/
small pieces of Mexican bread with cheese, vegetables, sauces on top • *Do you like crispy nachos with beans and hot chili sauce?* ❖ νάτσο

4.141 Spanish (adj) /'spænɪʃ/
➢ Spain, Spanish (n) ❖ ισπανικός

4.142 Japanese (adj) /ˌdʒæpə'niːz/
➢ Japan, Japanese (n) ❖ ιαπωνικός

4.143 Russian (adj) /'rʌʃn/
➢ Russia, Russian (n) ❖ ρώσικος

4.144 cube (n) /kjuːb/
sth that is shaped like a box with six square sides • *Cut the carrots and potatoes into cubes and put them into the soup.* ➢ cube (v) ❖ κύβος

4.145 boil (v) /bɔɪl/
cook sth in very hot water • *The water is boiling. You can make a cup of tea now.* ➢ boiling, boiled (adj) ❖ βράζω

4.146 **pea** (n) /piː/
a small round green vegetable • *Grandma grows tomatoes and green peas in her garden.* ❖ αρακάς, μπιζέλι

4.147 **take off** (phr v) /teɪk ɒf/
remove sth • *Take the skin off the onions, then cut them into small pieces.* ❖ βγάζω

4.148 **chop** (v) /tʃɒp/
cut sth quickly into pieces, e.g. with a sharp knife • *The cook chopped the leaves off the carrots before cutting them into slices.* ❖ τεμαχίζω, ψιλοκόβω

4.149 **mix** (v) /mɪks/
put two or more things together to make sth • *Put the eggs into a bowl and mix them for a minute. Then mix in the sugar and flour.* ➤ mixture (n), mixed (adj) ❖ ανακατεύω

4.150 **vegetable** (n) /ˈvedʒtəbl/
a food that is part of a plant • *Carrots, beans and peas are all vegetables.* ❖ λαχανικό

4.151 **salt** (n) /sɔːlt/
a white substance that you can put on some food to change the taste • *This fish doesn't need any salt. Just put a little pepper on it.* ➤ salty (adj) ❖ αλάτι

4.152 **mayonnaise** (n) /ˌmeɪəˈneɪz/
a thick sauce made with eggs, vinegar and oil, used on salads, etc. • *Peter sometimes has egg and mayonnaise sandwiches for lunch.* ❖ μαγιονέζα

4.153 **pepper** (n) /ˈpepə(r)/
a large green, red or yellow fruit that you use as a vegetable in salads, etc.; a black or white powder made from seeds with a hot taste that you put on food • *Chop the red peppers and mix them with the tomatoes and onion to make a salad.* ❖ πιπεριά, πιπέρι

4.154 **pasta** (n) /ˈpæstə/
spaghetti, noodles, etc. • *Put the pasta into boiling water and cook it for ten minutes.* ❖ ζυμαρικά

4.155 **jar** (n) /dʒɑː(r)/
a glass container to keep food in • *There's a jar of honey in the cupboard.* ❖ βάζο για τρόφιμα

4.156 **refer** (v) /rɪˈfɜː(r)/
talk about a particular thing • *Jane refers to Sylvia as her best friend.* ➤ reference (n) ❖ αναφέρω

4.157 **forget** (v) /fəˈget/
not remember sth; stop thinking about sth • *Don't forget to buy some doughnuts at the bakery.* ❖ ξεχνάω

4.158 **onion** (n) /ˈʌnjən/
a round vegetable with a strong taste and smell • *Carol isn't really crying – she's chopping onions!* ❖ κρεμμύδι

4.159 **tomorrow** (adv) /təˈmɒrəʊ/
the day after today • *We're having a barbecue tomorrow. Do you want to come?* ❖ αύριο

Food

Nouns	pepper
coconut	pumpkin
cookie	recipe
cube	salt
curry	sandwich
dessert	sausage
guacamole	sushi
jar	tart
mandarin orange	vegetable
mayonnaise	
nachos	**Verbs**
onion	boil
paella	chop
pasta	fry
pea	mix

Video 4
The Magic of Diwali
Page 54

4.160 **sand** (n) /sænd/
very small pieces of rock, e.g. on a beach • *I love going to the beach, but I don't like getting sand in my shoes.* ➤ sandy (adj) ❖ άμμος, αμμουδιά

4.161 **garland** (n) /ˈgɑːlənd/
a circle of flowers made as a decoration • *The bride is wearing a garland of white flowers in her hair.* ❖ στεφάνι

4.162 **temple** (n) /ˈtempl/
a building like a church • *The Parthenon is the most famous Greek temple.* ❖ ναός

4.163 **darkness** (n) /ˈdɑːknəs/
a state which has very little or no light • *The road outside the farm is in darkness because there aren't any lights on. So take a flashlight with you.* ➤ dark (adj) ❖ σκοτάδι

4.164 **decorate** (v) /ˈdekəreɪt/
put things on sth to make it look better or more colourful • *We're decorating the room with balloons for the party.* ➤ decoration (n) ❖ στολίζω

4.165 **ground** (n) /graʊnd/
the surface of the earth • *There are lots of oranges on the ground under the orange tree.* ❖ έδαφος

4.166 **take place** (expr) /teɪk pleɪs/
happen • *The carnival takes place every year in early spring.* ❖ συμβαίνω, γίνομαι

4.167 **shape** (n) /ʃeɪp/
the outside form of sth • *We cut the paper into star shapes to make Christmas decorations.*
➢ shape (v) ❖ σχήμα

4.168 **lotus flower** (n) /ˈləʊtəs ˈflaʊə(r)/
a kind of flower that grows on a lake • *That frog is sitting on a lotus flower.* ❖ νούφαρο

4.169 **symbol** (n) /ˈsɪmbl/
an object or action that shows a particular feeling/idea • *People often give presents as a symbol of their love.* ❖ σύμβολο

4.170 **welcome** (n) /ˈwelkəm/
sth you do to make sb feel happy when they arrive • *The hotel offers visitors a traditional fruit drink as a welcome.* ➢ welcome (v), welcome (adj) ❖ καλωσόρισμα

Vocabulary Exercises

A Circle the odd one out.

1	festival	recipe	celebration
2	tart	guacamole	cookie
3	procession	concert	present
4	pasta	costume	curry
5	suit	sari	sushi
6	pea	sausage	onion

B Complete the seasons.

1 Trees change their colours from green to brown and yellow in _ _ _ _ _ _.
2 It's very cold and people go skiing in _ _ _ _ _ _.
3 There are lots of flowers starting to grow because it's _ _ _ _ _ _.
4 The warmest season of the year is _ _ _ _ _ _.

C Circle the correct words.

1 For dessert, they served us pineapple, coconut and other **tropical / typical** fruits.
2 Cut the carrots into **cubes / jars** and add them to the salad.
3 The festival takes **part / place** every year on the first Saturday of June.
4 I've got some **excited / exciting** news. We're having a party next week.
5 Paul has got an interesting new **job / work** in an office.
6 Have you got an **invitation / instruction** to Maggie and Rob's wedding?
7 They're making the costumes for the **fizzy / fancy** dress party.
8 Everybody is helping to **prepare / prefer** for the Carnival celebrations.
9 I'm cutting the **paella / pumpkin** to make a Halloween lantern.
10 People throw confetti at the bride and her husband as a **flag / symbol** of good luck.

D Complete the sentences with these words.

neighbour barbecue definitely everywhere weather midnight noise salt

1 Do you want to come to our _____ on Friday?
2 Are you inviting your _____ to the party?
3 Please stop making that _____! I can't sleep.
4 We switch off all the lights at _____ to celebrate the New Year.
5 This is _____ the best celebration of the year.
6 There are Christmas trees _____ in the city streets.
7 The _____ is often cold here in February.
8 Add some _____ and pepper to the salad and it's ready to eat.

E Complete the months and find the hidden celebration.

1. _ _ O _ _ _ _ _
2. _ _ _ _ _ H _
3. J _ _ _ _ _ _
4. _ _ _ B _ _ _ R _
5. _ _ N _
6. _ C _ _ _ _
7. _ _ _ _ L
8. _ _ _ _ _ Y
9. _ _ S _ _ _ _ _ R
10. _ _ G _ _ _
11. _ _ _ C _ _ _ E _
12. _ _ _ _ _

The hidden celebration is _ _ _ _ _ _ _ _ _ _ _ _ _ _.

4 Grammar

4.1 Countable Nouns

Τα περισσότερα ουσιαστικά (nouns) είναι αριθμήσιμα (countable) και έχουν ενικό και πληθυντικό αριθμό.
→ *banana* → *bananas*
Συνήθως χρησιμοποιούμε *a* με countable nouns στον ενικό.
→ ***a*** *cake*
ή *an* με countable nouns στον ενικό που αρχίζουν με ένα φωνήεν *a, e, i, o, u*.
→ ***an*** *egg*
→ ***an*** *apple*

Μπορούμε να χρησιμοποιήσουμε *some* ή έναν αριθμό (π.χ. *three*) με countable nouns στον πληθυντικό.
→ *There are **some** biscuits in the box.*
→ *I've got **two** dogs.*

Χρησιμοποιούμε *any* στις ερωτήσεις και αρνήσεις.
→ *Are there **any** flowers?*
→ *There aren't **any** trees.*

Χρησιμοποιούμε τα ρήματα στον ενικό με countable nouns στον ενικό.
→ *This **party is** fun.*
Χρησιμοποιούμε τα ρήματα στον πληθυντικό με countable nouns στον πληθυντικό.
→ *They have **parties** every month.*

Σημείωση: Μερικά countable nouns είναι ανώμαλα και δεν τελειώνουν σε *-s*. Χρησιμοποιούμε το ρήμα στον πληθυντικό με αυτά.
→ *The **children** are happy.*
→ *The **people** are dancing in the street.*

4.2 Uncountable Nouns

Μερικά ουσιαστικά είναι μη αριθμήσιμα (uncountable). Δεν έχουν πληθυντικό.

bread	fruit	time
cake	rubbish	traffic
food	snow	water

Πάντα χρησιμοποιούμε τα ρήματα στον ενικό με uncountable nouns.

→ *Snow **is** cold.*
→ *The food **is** on your plate.*
→ *The cake **is** very nice.*
Σημείωση: Όταν μιλάμε για ολόκληρα κομμάτια του φαγητού, χρησιμοποιούμε *a / an:*
→ *Who wants **a** cake/pizza?*
Όταν μιλάμε για μια φέτα ή ένα κομμάτι, χρησιμοποιούμε *some:*
→ *I want **some** cake/pizza.*

Μπορούμε να χρησιμοποιήσουμε *some* σε ερώτηση όταν προσφέρουμε φαγητό.
→ *Would you like **some** bread?*

4 Grammar

4.3 Quantifiers

Χρησιμοποιούμε *a lot of* ή *lots of* και με uncountable και με countable nouns στον πληθυντικό.

→ *Harry has got **lots of friends**.*

→ *There is **a lot of food** on the table.*

Χρησιμοποιούμε *a little* με uncountable nouns και *a few* με uncountable nouns στον πληθυντικό σε καταφατικές προτάσεις.

→ *There was **a little** milk left in the fridge.*

→ *There were **a few** women in the post office.*

Χρησιμοποιούμε *much* σε αρνητικές προτάσεις με uncountable nouns.

→ *We haven't got **much** water.*

Χρησιμοποιούμε *many* με countable nouns στον πληθυντικό.

→ *There are **many** decorations on the tree.*

Χρησιμοποιούμε *much* σε ερωτήσεις για uncountable nouns και *many* σε ερωτήσεις για countable nouns.

→ *How **much** cheese have you got?*

→ *How **many** apples are on the tree?*

Grammar Exercises

A Write the plural forms of the words.

1 pear   _____

2 party   _____

3 child   _____

4 cinema   _____

5 woman   _____

6 person   _____

7 piece   _____

8 man   _____

B Complete the dialogues with *a, an, some, any* or *–*.

1 **A:** What are you doing?
   B: I'm making _____ Christmas decorations.
2 **A:** What clothes are traditional at Carnival time?
   B: People usually wear funny costumes and _____ mask.
3 **A:** Where are the children?
   B: They're dancing at _____ festival.
4 **A:** What does your grandma do at Easter?
   B: She invites _____ of her friends for a barbecue.
5 **A:** Why are the boys at the bus stop?
   B: They're waiting, but there aren't _____ buses for another hour.
6 **A:** Where is Sarah going?
   B: She's going to _____ Italian restaurant with her friends.
7 **A:** What is outside the house?
   B: There's _____ rubbish in the big bin.
8 **A:** Can I have a sandwich?
   B: No. There isn't _____ bread.

C Complete the sentences with these words. Use each word only once.

a   an   any   lot   lots   many   much   some

1 There are _____ of people at the party.
2 Do you want _____ slice of pizza?
3 We've got a _____ of food to eat.
4 How _____ children are dancing?
5 Would you like _____ fruit juice?
6 There aren't _____ decorations in the street.
7 How _____ cheese is there in the fridge?
8 Diwali is _____ Indian festival.

5 A Perfect Day

Page 57

5.1 **perfect** (adj) /ˈpɜːfɪkt/
the best for a certain thing ● *It's a perfect day to go swimming.* ➣ perfection (n) ❖ τέλειος

5.2 **iguana** (n) /ɪˈgwɑːnə/
a large tropical lizard ● *Iguanas amazing lizards and they've got a third eye on top of their heads!* ❖ ιγκουάνα

5.3 **fish** (v) /fɪʃ/
catch a fish with a net or hook ● *The sign says you can't fish in this river. We have to protect the fish.* ➣ fishing (n) ❖ ψαρεύω

Reading Page 58

5.4 **journey** (n) /ˈdʒɜːni/
a trip from one place to another ● *We're going on a long journey by train from Paris to Istanbul.* ❖ ταξίδι

5.5 **build** (v) /bɪld/
make sth by putting things together ● *They're building a new hotel near my favourite beach.* ➣ building, builder (n) ❖ κτίζω

5.6 **snowman** (n) /ˈsnəʊmæn/
a shape like a person that sb makes from snow ● *There was a lot of snow last Saturday and the children had fun making a snowman in the park.* ❖ χιονάνθρωπος

5.7 **toboggan** (n) /təˈbɒgən/
sth made to carry sb/sth over snow and ice ● *Dad made a toboggan for us to ride down the hill in the snow.* ➣ toboggan (v) ❖ έλκηθρο ✎ Syn: sledge

5.8 **seaweed** (n) /ˈsiːwiːd/
a plant that grows in the sea ● *I don't like walking into the sea where there's lots of seaweed near the beach.* ❖ φύκια

5.9 **whale** (n) /weɪl/
a very large sea animal that looks like a fish ● *Sarah watched the whales swimming in the ocean and one was blowing water from the top of its head.* ❖ φάλαινα

5.10 **Dubai** (n) /duːˈbaɪ/
❖ Ντουμπάι

Word Focus Page 58

5.11 **slide** (v) /slaɪd/
move easily across sth wet or icy, etc.
● *I wanted to learn to ice skate, but my feet began to slide and I fell down.* ➣ slide (n) ❖ γλιστράω

5.12 **bridesmaid** (n) /ˈbraɪdzmeɪd/
a girl or woman who walks together with the bride during a wedding ● *Louise's three best friends were her bridesmaids at her wedding.* ❖ παράνυμφος

5.13 **turquoise** (n) /ˈtɜːkwɔɪz/
a green-blue colour ● *Under the sun and the blue sky, the sea looked turquoise.* ➣ turquoise (adj) ❖ τυρκουάζ

5.14 **lighthouse** (n) /ˈlaɪthaʊs/
a tall building near the sea with a bright light on top to show sailors where the coast is or where rocks are ● *At the end of the harbour wall, there's an old lighthouse so that ships can find the way in.* ❖ φάρος

5.15 **waterslide** (n) /ˈwɔːtəˌslaɪd/
a slide with water going down for sb to slide down into a pool ● *Luke's mum looked worried when he went on a really high waterslide at the swimming pool.* ❖ νερό-τσουλήθρα

5.16 **slide** (n) /slaɪd/
a structure that is high at one side and reaches the ground at the other so that sb can sit on the top and slide down ● *The children laughed as they slid down the slide in the playground.* ➣ slide (v) ❖ τσουλήθρα

5.17 **waterpark** (n) /ˈwɔːtəˌpaːk/
a park with swimming pools, slides and other things for children to play on ● *We're going on a day trip to the waterpark. I love playing on the waterslides there.* ❖ υδάτινο πάρκο

Reading Pages 58–59

5.18 **such** (det, pron) /sʌtʃ/
used before a noun to stress the meaning ● *This is such a beautiful place.* ❖ τόσο

5.19 **wake up** (phr v) /weɪk ʌp/
stop sleeping ● *What time do you usually wake up in the morning?* ❖ ξυπνάω

5.20 **snowball** (n) /ˈsnəʊbɔːl/
a ball sb makes from snow ● *Hey! Don't throw snowballs at the window!* ❖ χιονόμπαλα

5.21 **fight** (n) /faɪt/
a competition between two people or groups; an argument where people use physical strength to compete with sb ● *George had a fight with his brother because they both wanted to use the computer.* ➣ fight (v), fighter (n) ❖ αγώνας, μάχη

5.22 **soup** (n) /suːp/
a kind of food made with vegetables and/or meat boiled in water so they are soft ● *I had a big bowl of hot tomato soup for lunch.* ❖ σούπα

5.23 **roast** (adj) /rəʊst/
cooked inside an oven ● *Jill is cooking chicken and roast potatoes for her family.* ➣ roast (v), roast (n) ❖ ψητός, ψημένος

5.24 **take turns (in/at sth)** (expr) /teɪk tɜːnz ɪn ət sʌmθɪŋ/
do sth, e.g. play a game, one player after the other ● *The children are waiting to take turns at going down the waterslide.* ❖ παίζω κάτι με τη σειρά

5.25 **great-grandmother** (n) /ˈɡreɪt ˈɡrænmʌðə(r)/
your grandmother's or grandfather's mother ● *Mathew's great-grandmother is ninety years old.* ❖ πρόγιαγια

5.26 **hairdresser's** (n) /ˈheədresəz/
a place sb goes to have their hair cut or styled ● *Kelly is going to the hairdresser's so that she can look good on her holiday.* ➣ hairdresser (n) ❖ κομμωτήριο

5.27 **earring** (n) /ˈɪərɪŋ/
an item of jewellery that sb wears on their ear ● *Gloria is wearing a pair of gold earrings.* ❖ σκουλαρίκι

5.28 **reception** (n) /rɪˈsepʃn/
a party to celebrate a wedding ● *Have you got an invitation to Laila and Tom's wedding reception?* ❖ δεξίωση, γλέντι

Look!

Η λέξη **reception** έχει δύο διαφορετικές έννοιες. Σημαίνει η δεξίωση του γάμου.
We're having fun at the wedding reception.
Επίσης χρησιμοποιείται για τη ρεσεψιόν σε ξενοδοχείο.
We collected our room key from the hotel reception.

5.29 **fishing** (n) /ˈfɪʃɪŋ/
the activity of catching fish ● *In the evening, we often see people fishing from the harbour.* ➣ fish (v), fish (n) ❖ ψάρεμα

5.30 **sunrise** (n) /ˈsʌnraɪz/
the time that you can begin to see the sun in the sky in the morning ● *It was a long journey, so we got up very early and left home at sunrise.* ❖ ανατολή του ήλιου

5.31 **suddenly** (adv) /ˈsʌdənli/
very quickly and not expected ● *Suddenly, Bob saw a dog in the middle of the road, so he stopped the car.* ➣ sudden (n) ❖ ξαφνικά

5.32 **humpback whale** (n) /ˌhʌmpbæk ˈweɪl/
a kind of whale with a large round shape on its back ● *Humpback whales are so big! They can be up to 16 metres long.* ❖ μεγάπτερη φάλαινα

5.33 **in the distance** (expr) /ɪn ðə ˈdɪstəns/
far away ● *From the top of the hill, you can see the sea in the distance.* ❖ μακριά, στο βάθος

5.34 **distance** (n) /ˈdɪstəns/
the amount of space between two places ● *Thessaloniki is a very long distance from Kalamata.* ➣ distant (adj) ❖ απόσταση

5.35 **believe** (v) /bɪˈliːv/
think that sth is true ● *I don't believe you can catch a fish with your hands.* ➣ belief (n) ❖ πιστεύω

5.36 **pass** (v) /pæs/
move past sth/sb; succeed in an exam ● *We passed the playground and saw the students. They looked happy because they passed their exams.* ➣ pass (n) ❖ περνάω από, περνάω εξετάσεις

5.37 **lighthouse keeper** (n) /ˈlaɪthaʊs ˈkiːpə(r)/
sb who works in a lighthouse ● *Susan and Mike live in a lighthouse because their father is the lighthouse keeper.* ❖ φύλακας του φάρου

People

bridesmaid	lighthouse keeper
great-grandmother	organiser

5.38 **let** (v) /let/
allow sb to do sth ● *Our parents sometimes let us stay up late to watch a film together.* ❖ επιτρέπω

5.39 **science fiction** (n) /ˌsaɪəns ˈfɪkʃn/
a kind of book or film that has a story about characters in the future or from other planets, etc. ● *Ronald writes science fiction stories about a family from another planet.* ❖ επιστημονική φαντασία

5.40 **afterwards** (adv) /ˈɑːftəwədz/
after sth else happened; later ● *Stanley went swimming and afterwards, he had a hot bath.* ❖ μετά, έπειτα

5.41 **hire** (v) /ˈhaɪə(r)/
pay to use sth for a short time ● *They hired a car to drive around the island.* ➣ hire (v) ❖ ενοικιάζω

5.42 **quad bike** (n) /kwɒd/
a motorbike with four wheels ● *Remember to wear a helmet when you ride a quad bike on the farm road.* ❖ τετράτροχη μοτοσικλέτα

5.43 possible (adj) /ˈpɒsəbl/
that can happen • *It isn't possible to walk in the desert without water.* ➣ possibility (n), possibly (adv) ❖ δυνατός, πιθανός

5.44 brilliant (adj) /ˈbrɪliənt/
really good • *I've got a brilliant idea! Let's go to the waterpark.* ❖ υπέροχος

5.45 sure (adj) /ʃʊə(r)/
certain • *I'm sure I passed the English test.* ➣ sure (adv) ❖ σίγουρος

5.46 pity (n) /ˈpɪti/
a feeling that you are sorry or sad about sth • *It's a pity you can't come with us.* ➣ pity (v) ❖ κρίμα

5.47 helmet (n) /ˈhelmɪt/
a hard hat that you wear on your head to protect it • *Wear a helmet when you ride your skateboard.* ❖ κράνος

5.48 hurt (v) /hɜːt/
make sb/sth feel pain; feel pain • *Harry doesn't go fishing because he doesn't want to hurt any fish.* ➣ hurt (n, adv) ❖ πονάω

5.49 hit (v) /hɪt/
put your hand or an object against sb/sth quickly • *Daisy hit the ball hard and won the tennis match.* ➣ hit (n) ❖ χτυπάω

Vocabulary　　Pages 60–61

5.50 amusement park (n) /əˈmjuːzmənt pɑːk/
a place where people can pay to go on rides to have fun • *Let's go on some rides at the amusement park. It's fun!* ❖ λούνα παρκ
✎ Syn: funfair

5.51 wild (adj) /waɪld/
living in a natural place, not kept in a house, etc. • *You can't drive cars in the national park to protect the wild animals and plants.* ➣ wild (n) ❖ άγριος

5.52 snowboarding (n) /ˈsnəʊbɔːdɪŋ/
the sport/activity of riding a board on snow down a hill • *I like riding a toboggan, but I want to try snowboarding this winter.* ➣ snowboard (v, n), snowboarder (n) ❖ σνόουμπορντ (άθλημα, δραστηριότητα)

5.53 surfing (n) /ˈsɜːfɪŋ/
the sport/activity of standing on a board and riding on the sea • *My favourite water sport is surfing.* ➣ surf (v, n), surfer (n) ❖ σερφ (άθλημα, δραστηριότητα)

5.54 Ferris wheel (n) /ˈferɪs wiːl/
a large wheel that has seats for people to ride in at an amusement park • *The London Eye is a giant Ferris wheel in the centre of London.* ❖ μεγάλος τροχός στο λούνα παρκ

5.55 llama (n) /ˈlɑːmə/
a South American animal with a long neck and thick hair • *The old farmer uses his llamas to carry his vegetables to the market.* ❖ λάμα

5.56 rollercoaster (n) /ˈrəʊlə kəʊstə(r)/
a kind of small train that rides up and down at an amusement park • *My little brothers love going on the rollercoaster. It's so exciting for them!* ❖ τρενάκι σε λούνα παρκ

5.57 ride (n) /raɪd/
a short trip • *Do you want to go for a ride on the lake in our boat?* ➣ ride (v), rider (n) ❖ βόλτα

5.58 path (n) /pɑːθ/
a track made by people or animals walking or built for walking on • *Maria is making a new garden path around her house.* ❖ μονοπάτι

5.59 attend (v) /əˈtend/
go to sth; be present at sth • *We haven't got school today because our teachers are attending a meeting.* ➣ attendance (n) ❖ πηγαίνω, παρίσταμαι

5.60 hilltop (n) /ˈhɪltɒp/
the highest part of a hill • *You can see the whole town from the hilltop.* ❖ κορυφή του λόφου

5.61 fun run (n) /ˈfʌn rʌn/
a long distance run that people do to collect money for sth • *We're doing a three-mile fun run to collect money for our school trip.* ❖ αγώνας δρόμου για φιλανθρωπικό σκοπό

5.62 footpath (n) /ˈfʊtpɑːθ/
a path for people to walk on • *Cars or motorbikes are not allowed on the footpaths through the park.* ❖ μονοπάτι

5.63 scary (adj) /ˈskeəri/
sb/sth that makes sb feel afraid • *It was dark and scary inside the castle.* ➣ scare (v, n), scared (adj) ❖ τρομακτικός

5.64 have a go (expr) /hæv ə gəʊ/
try doing sth; take a turn • *Andrew's a good swimmer and now he wants to have a go at surfing.* ❖ κάνω μια προσπάθεια, δοκιμάζω

5.65 knowledge (n) /ˈnɒlɪdʒ/
the things sb knows about from learning or doing • *Marios has no knowledge of French, so he's trying to learn before he goes to study in France.* ➣ know (v), knowledgeable (adj) ❖ γνώση

5.66 skating rink (n) /ˈskeɪtɪŋ rɪŋk/
a place made for people to do ice skating or roller skating • *You can hire skates to wear at the skating rink.* ❖ πίστα πατινάζ, παγοδρόμιο

5.67 nervous (adj) /ˈnɜːvəs/
worried about or scared of sth • *Fiona was very nervous about learning to ride a horse.* ❖ αγχωμένος

5.68 **waste** (v) /weɪst/
use more of sth than you need • *The film starts at seven o'clock, so get ready now and don't waste time.* ➢ waste (n) ❖ σπαταλάω, χαλάω

5.69 **outdoor** (adj) /ˈaʊtdɔː(r)/
sth that is or happens outside • *Paul enjoys cycling, camping and other outdoor activities.* ➢ outdoors (adv) ❖ εξωτερικός, ανοιχτός

5.70 **indoor** (adj) /ˈɪndɔː(r)/
sth that is or happens inside • *The hotel has an indoor swimming pool where you can swim in any season.* ➢ indoors (adv) ❖ εσωτερικός, κλειστός

Compound Nouns

amusement park	hilltop
backpack	humpback whale
blood vessel	lighthouse keeper
bridesmaid	quad bike
day out	science fiction
earring	seaweed
footpath	snowball
fun run	snowman
great-grandmother	waterpark
hairdresser's	waterslide

Grammar **Pages 62–63**

5.71 **puddle** (n) /ˈpʌdl/
a small pool of water on the ground • *My dog got wet because it ran into the puddle on the path.* ❖ λακούβα με νερό

5.72 **pizzeria** (n) /ˌpiːtsəˈriːə/
a pizza restaurant • *Ursula and Derek are having a meal at a pizzeria near the museum.* ❖ πιτσαρία

5.73 **study** (v) /ˈstʌdi/
go to school, etc. to learn sth; spend time reading sth to learn; • *Did you study for the history test?* ➢ study, student (n) ❖ σπουδάζω, μελετάω

5.74 **popcorn** (n) /ˈpɒpkɔːn/
a kind of snack made from cooking grains of corn • *Sonia made popcorn and sandwiches for the party.* ❖ ποπ κορν

5.75 **university** (n) /ˌjuːnɪˈvɜːsəti/
a school where sb can study sth at a very high level • *Anne's sister is studying at university to become a doctor.* ❖ πανεπιστήμιο

Places

amusement park	path
footpath	pizzeria
hairdresser's	puddle
hilltop	skating rink
in the country	university
lighthouse	waterpark
middle	

5.76 **sunglasses** (n) /ˈsʌnɡlɑːsɪz/
a pair of glasses to protect your eyes from the light of the sun • *Lynn always wears her big hat and a pair of sunglasses when she goes to the beach.* ❖ γυαλιά ηλίου

5.77 **bedtime** (n) /ˈbedtaɪm/
the time when sb usually goes to sleep • *Max enjoys reading a book at bedtime.* ❖ ώρα που πάει κάποιος για ύπνο

5.78 **middle** (n) /ˈmɪdl/
the centre point of sth • *There was a lovely bowl of flowers in the middle of the table.* ❖ στη μέση

5.79 **ago** (adv) /əˈɡəʊ/
in the past (used after a time expression) • *It was my birthday three days ago.* ❖ πριν

5.80 **as** (conj) /əz/
in the way that; because • *As the teacher said, the trip was very interesting.* ➢ as (adv, prep) ❖ όπως

5.81 **exotic** (adj) /ɪɡˈzɒtɪk/
from a tropical country; exciting and different • *To finish the meal, the restaurant offered us some pineapple and other exotic fruit.* ❖ εξωτικός

5.82 **so** (conj) /səʊ/
used to show the reason, or purpose for sth; used to show the result of sth • *Simon got up early today, so he's really tired now.* ➢ so (adv, n) ❖ έτσι, οπότε

5.83 **lunchtime** (n) /ˈlʌntʃtaɪm/
the time that sb usually eats lunch • *Mabel often takes a walk in the park and eats a sandwich there at lunchtime.* ❖ ώρα του μεσημεριανού

5.84 **attach** (v) /əˈtætʃ/
join sth onto sth else • *Harris attached a photo of his bike to the advert.* ➢ attachment (n) ❖ βάζω, επισυνάπτω

Adjectives

brilliant	perfect
exotic	possible
indoor	roast
nervous	scary
outdoor	sure

Listening Page 64

5.85 **in common** (expr) /ɪn ˈkɒmən/
with the same kind of interests or
characteristics ● *Ilona and Olga have a lot
in common. For example, they are both from
Poland and they love science fiction books
and exploring.* ➤ common (adj) ❖ κοινό

5.86 **day out** (n) /ˌdeɪ ˈaʊt/
a one-day trip ● *We're having a day out on our
bikes tomorrow.* ❖ μονοήμερη εκδρομή

5.87 **cruise** (n) /kruːz/
a journey by ship to visit different places
● *Vassilis went on a six-day cruise around the
islands.* ➤ cruise (v), cruiser (n) ❖ κρουαζιέρα

5.88 **Caribbean** (n) /ˌkærɪˈbiːən/
➤ Caribbean (adj) ❖ η Καραϊβική

5.89 **romantic** (adj) /rəʊˈmæntɪk/
connected with love ● *We listened to romantic
songs on the radio.* ➤ romance (n)
❖ ρομαντικός

Speaking Page 65

5.90 **in the country** (expr) /ɪn ðə ˈkʌntri/
in an area with fields and farms far away
from town or cities ● *The club meets every
Saturday morning to go for a long walk over
the hills in the country.* ❖ στην εξοχή

5.91 **sightseeing** (n) /ˈsaɪtsiːɪŋ/
the activity of visiting places to look at
famous buildings, etc.● *The Wilsons are on a
sightseeing tour of Rome.* ➤ sightseer (n)
❖ περιήγηση σε αξιοθέατα

5.92 **backpack** (n) /ˈbækpæk/
a bag that you carry on your back ● *Jim put
his camera in his backpack to go sightseeing.*
➤ backpack (v) ❖ σακίδιο πλάτης

5.93 **souvenir** (n) /ˌsuːvəˈnɪə(r)/
sth you buy to remember a place you visit,
sometimes to give as a present ● *I bought
some souvenirs at the museum to remember
my trip to New York.* ❖ σουβενίρ

5.94 **feeling** (n) /ˈfiːlɪŋ/
sth that you feel, e.g. happiness, love, hate,
thirst ● *I can understand my dog's feelings.
He jumps around moving his tail when he's
happy and excited.* ➤ feel (v)
❖ αίσθηση, συναίσθημα

5.95 **opinion** (n) /əˈpɪnjən/
what sb thinks or believes about sth ● *What's
your opinion of the waterpark? Is it a good
place to visit?* ❖ γνώμη

Writing Pages 66–67

5.96 **feel** (v) /fiːl/
have a certain feeling ● *Everybody felt tired
and hungry after the long walk.* ➤ feeling (n)
❖ αισθάνομαι

5.97 **experience** (n) /ɪkˈspɪəriəns/
sth you did or sth that happened to you
● *Irene's grandmother is writing a book about
her travel experiences.* ➤ experience (v)
❖ πείρα, εμπειρία

5.98 **organiser** (n) /ˈɔːgənaɪzə(r)/
sth like a notebook to keep information of
plans and other things to remember; sb who
plans events ● *Agnes uses her tablet as
an organiser for her homework and other
activities.* ➤ organise (v), organised (adj)
❖ ατζέντα

5.99 **appointment** (n) /əˈpɔɪntmənt/
a time and date that sb plans to meet sb or be
somewhere ● *What time is your appointment
at the hairdresser's?* ❖ ραντεβού

5.100 **meeting** (n) /ˈmiːtɪŋ/
an event when people meet together to talk
about sth important ● *We're having a parents'
meeting to talk about what we need for our
camping trip.* ➤ meet (v) ❖ συνάντηση

5.101 **hot air balloon** (n) /ˌhɒt ˈeə bəluːn/
a very large balloon that is filled with hot air to
move high above the ground, usually with a
large basket below that carries people
● *I flew over Central Park in New York in a
hot air balloon. It was amazing!* ❖ αερόστατο

5.102 **competition** (n) /ˌkɒmpəˈtɪʃn/
an event that people take part in to see who is
the best at sth ● *John felt nervous before the
surfing competition.* ➤ compete (v), competitor
(n), competitive (adj) ❖ διαγωνισμός, αγώνας

5.103 **view** (n) /vjuː/
what sb can see from somewhere ● *There's
a great view of the city from the restaurant on
top of the hotel.* ➤ view (v) ❖ θέα

5.104 **moment** (n) /ˈməʊmənt/
a particular short period of time● *Starting his first job was a special moment for Frank.*
❖ στιγμή

5.105 **memory** (n) /ˈmeməri/
the part of the brain that makes sb remember sth; sth that sb remembers ● *Janet is good at history because she has a great memory. She never forgets anything!* ❖ μνήμη, ανάμνηση

5.106 **draft** (n) /drɑːft/
sth that sb writes quickly before checking this to do the final writing ● *Alice made three drafts of her story before she wrote the book.* ➢ draft (v) ❖ πρόχειρο

Activities

appointment	lunchtime
bedtime	meeting
build a snowman	reception
competition	ride
cruise	rollercoaster
day out	sightseeing
experience	skating rink
Ferris wheel	slide
fishing	snowboarding
fun run	sunglasses
hot air balloon	surfing
journey	toboggan
laughter	waterslide
laughter yoga	

Video 5
Laughter Yoga!   Page 68

5.107 **laughter** (n) /ˈlɑːftə(r)
the action of laughing; the sound made by laughing ● *The film was very funny and the cinema was filled with laughter.* ➢ laugh (v)
❖ γέλιο

5.108 **yoga** (n) /ˈjəʊɡə/
an activity to exercise the body and focus the mind with different movements and controlled breathing ● *Andrea does yoga twice a week at the gym.* ❖ γιόγκα
✎ laughter yoga ❖ γιόγκα γέλιου

5.109 **communicate** (v) /kəˈmjuːnɪkeɪt/
give information by talking or writing, etc. ● *We can send emails to communicate with people all round the world.* ➢ communication (n)
❖ επικοινωνώ

5.110 **energy** (n) /ˈenədʒi/
the strong feeling made by a group of people or from a place or thing; power ● *Nicky believes that we can get good energy from plants in the house.* ➢ energise (v), energetic (adj) ❖ ενέργεια

5.111 **healthy** (adj) /ˈhelθi/
good for you because it helps stop you getting ill; being well; not being ill ● *I prefer to drink something healthy like fruit juice and not fizzy drinks.* ➢ health (n) ❖ υγιής, υγιεινός

5.112 **heart** (n) /hɑːt/
the part of the body that makes the blood go around ● *Grandad had a problem with his heart, so he went to hospital and the doctors helped it work better.* ❖ καρδιά

5.113 **blood vessel** (n) /ˈblʌd vesl/
a tube that blood goes through in the body ● *Doing sports can help to keep our blood vessels healthy.* ❖ αιμοφόρο αγγείο

5.114 **condition** (n) /kənˈdɪʃn/
the state of how sth/sb is ● *Liam cycles to work to keep himself in good condition.*
❖ (φυσική) κατάσταση

5.115 **positive** (adj) /ˈpɒzətɪv/
good or helpful ● *Joe's visit to the yoga club was a positive experience for him.*
➢ positive (n) ❖ θετικός

5.116 **social** (adj) /ˈsəʊʃl/
connected with activities people do to spend time together ● *I enjoy going to different social events like barbecues and parties.*
➢ social, society (n) ❖ κοινωνικός

Vocabulary Exercises

A Match to make compound nouns.

1	humpback	☐	a	park
2	laughter	☐	b	balloon
3	lighthouse	☐	c	keeper
4	amusement	☐	d	whale
5	quad	☐	e	fiction
6	skating	☐	f	bike
7	hot air	☐	g	rink
8	science	☐	h	yoga

B Complete the sentences with the compound nouns from A.

1 You can hire a(n) _____ _____ to travel around the island.
2 We saw the _____ _____ swimming far away in the sea.
3 I watched a(n) _____ _____ film about a journey in the 23rd century.
4 Let's take our skates and go to the _____ _____.
5 Tom felt really happy and relaxed when he joined the _____ _____ club.
6 We're going to fly in a(n) _____ _____ and look down at the view.
7 The children had a lot of fun at the _____ _____.
8 The _____ _____ works in that tall building on top of the cliffs.

C Circle the correct words.

1 My friends and I took **rides / turns** to play on the waterslide.
2 Janet and Steve are on a two-week **meeting / cruise** in the Caribbean.
3 I'm **sure / possible** that animal is a whale.
4 We got up early and watched the **memory / sunrise**.
5 Bill feels **nervous / scary** about travelling by ship.
6 Did you **build / hire** a car to drive around the island?
7 The quad bike **hit / hurt** a tree and we fell off.
8 Don't forget to wear your **earring / helmet** on your bike.
9 My parents didn't **let / leave** me go snowboarding.
10 We saw lots of **roast / wild** animals like iguanas and llamas at the zoo.

D Complete the paragraph with these words.

> country   day out   pity   puddle   snowball   soup   toboggan   view

My great-grandmother lives in the [1] _____ and I like visiting her. There's a lovely [2] _____ of the mountains from her house. In February, I went there for a [3] _____ with my parents. I took my [4] _____ to slide down the hill. My cousins were there and I had a [5] _____ fight with them. Suddenly, our two dogs jumped in a [6] _____ and we all got wet. Then my great-grandmother brought us some hot [7] _____ and bread. It was a perfect day and it was a [8] _____ that we didn't stay for a week.

E Do the crossword.

Across

3 a party to celebrate a wedding
4 a bag that you carry on your back
8 a kind of small train that rides up and down at an amusement park
9 the time that you can begin to see the sun in the sky in the morning
10 a girl or woman who walks together with the bride during a wedding

Down

1 a hard hat that you wear on your head to protect it
2 a path for people to walk on
5 a journey by ship to visit different places
6 something you buy to remember a place you visit
7 a plant that grows in the sea

5 Grammar

5.1 Past Simple *To Be*

Κατάφαση
I **was**. We/you/they **were**. He/she/it **was**.

Άρνηση
I **was not (wasn't)**. We/you/they **were not (weren't)**. He/she/it **was not (wasn't)**.

Ερώτηση
Was I? **Were** we/you/they? **Was** he/she/it?

Σύντομες απαντήσεις	
Yes, I was. **Yes**, we/you/they were. **Yes**, he/she/it was.	**No**, I wasn't. **No**, we/you/they weren't. **No**, he/she/it wasn't.

Χρησιμοποιούμε το ρήμα *to be* στον Past Simple:
με επίθετα ή ουσιαστικά.
→ I **was** happy.
→ You **were** a good skater.
→ The fish **was** small.
για τοποθεσίες ή χρόνους.
→ They **were** in the park at six o'clock.
ως βοηθητικό ρήμα για να σχηματίσουμε άλλους χρόνους.
→ I **was** swimming.
→ We **were** playing football.
→ His boots **were** made in China.

5.2 Past Simple

Κατάφαση
I/he/she/it/we/you/they play**ed**.

Άρνηση
I/he/she/it/we/you/they **didn't** play.

Ερώτηση
Did I/he/she/it/we/you/they play?

Σύντομες απαντήσεις	
Yes, I/he/she/it/we/you/they **did**.	**No**, I/he/she/it/we/you/they **didn't**.

Ορθογραφία:
dance → danc**ed**   stop → sto**pped**   study → stud**ied**   stay → sta**yed**

Σημείωση: Κάποια ρήματα είναι ανώμαλα και δεν ακολουθούν αυτούς τους ορθογραφικούς κανόνες. Δες τη λίστα ανωμάλων ρημάτων στις σελίδες 185–186 του Student's Book. Είναι καλή ιδέα να μάθεις μαζί τα ανώμαλα ρήματα που μοιάζουν στον τρόπο σχηματισμού. Για παράδειγμα, τα ρήματα *cut, hit, put* και *read* δεν αλλάζουν στον Past Simple. Ή, τα ρήματα *draw, fly, grow* και *throw* καταλήγουν όλα σε -ew στον Past Simple (*drew, flew, grew, threw*).

Χρησιμοποιούμε Past Simple για:
κάτι που ξεκίνησε και τελείωσε στο παρελθόν.
→ *She **visited** the lighthouse a week ago.*
γεγονότα που έγιναν στο παρελθόν το ένα μετά το άλλο.
→ *Sam **arrived** at the beach, **picked** up his board and **started** surfing.*

Σημείωση: Κάποιες συνηθισμένες χρονικές εκφράσεις που χρησιμοποιούνται συχνά με τον Past Simple είναι:
yesterday, last night/week/month/summer, a week/month/year ago, twice a week, once a month, at the weekend.

Grammar Exercises

A Circle the correct words.

1 My uncle **go** / **went** fishing last week.
2 The wedding reception **was** / **did** in a big hotel.
3 We **move** / **moved** to Paris two years ago.
4 Those cakes **was** / **were** really delicious.
5 Nicky **studied** / **studying** French at university.
6 **Did** / **Were** you build a snowman?
7 I **didn't** / **wasn't** see any llamas at the zoo.
8 Did your friends **have** / **had** a good time last night?

B Write the words in the correct order to make questions. Then complete the short answers.

1 ? / Mike / school / did / on / go / the / trip

_____

No, he _____.

2 ? / your / were / sunglasses / the / table / on

_____

No, they _____.

3 ? / were / yesterday / at / party / the / you

_____

Yes, we _____.

4 ? / hot / you / chocolate / did / drink

_____

Yes, I _____.

5 ? / in / the / race / the / I / was / first

_____

No, you _____.

6 ? / your / bike / mum / was / the / ride / on

_____

Yes, she _____.

C **Complete the sentences with the Past Simple form of the verbs in brackets.**

1 We _____ (stop) under the trees for our picnic.

2 My friend and I _____ (run) for ten kilometres last Sunday.

3 _____ (be) your parents in the hot air balloon?

4 The weather _____ (not be) very warm yesterday.

5 Hundreds of people _____ (take part) in the fun run.

6 Wendy _____ (buy) lots of souvenirs in the market.

7 Kevin _____ (not like) that ride at the amusement park.

8 _____ (you / enjoy) yourself at the skating rink last week?

6 Welcome To The Jungle

Page 69

6.1 **welcome** (excl) /'welkəm/
used to tell sb that you are happy they arrived in a place • *Welcome to our island! I hope you like it here.* ➣ welcome (v, n) ❖ καλωσόρισες, καλωσορίσατε

6.2 **jungle** (n) /'dʒʌŋgl/
a thick tropical forest • *Maureen is exloring the Amazon jungle to find strange tropical plants.* ❖ ζούγκλα

6.3 **imperial moth** (n) /ɪm'pɪəriəl mɒθ/
a large American moth (butterfly) that is yellow and purple • *Imperial moths fly in the forests of North and South America.* ❖ είδος μεγάλης, Αμερικάνικης πεταλούδας με κίτρινες και μοβ αποχρώσεις

6.4 **hide** (v) /haɪd/
go into a place where nobody can see you; put sth/sb in a place where nobody can find them • *The students hid under their desks to play a trick on their teacher on 1st April.* ➣ hide (n), hidden (adj) ❖ κρύβω, κρύβομαι

6.5 **Ecuador** (n) /'ekwədɔː(r)/
➣ Ecuadorian (adj) ❖ Εκουαδόρ

Reading
Page 70

66.6 **unusual** (adj) /ʌn'juːʒuəl/
not usual or common • *It's unusual to see snow in summer here.* ❖ σπάνιος, ασυνήθιστος

6.7 **look like sb/sth** (phr v) /lʊk laɪk 'sʌmbədi sʌmθɪŋ/
be similar to sb/sth • *Some insects can hide easily because they look like leaves or grass.* ❖ μοιάζω

6.8 **butterfly** (n) /'bʌtəflaɪ/
an insect with large colourful wings • *I enjoy watching the butterfies flying around the flowers in the park in spring.* ❖ πεταλούδα

6.9 **armadillo** (n) /ˌɑːmə'dɪləʊ/
a small animal with a shell like very hard skin on its back • *Armadillos look strange because they've got hard backs, but underneath they're soft and furry.* ❖ αρμαδίλλος

6.10 **turtle** (n) /'tɜːtl/
a large reptile like a tortoise that lives in the sea • *Hara helps protect the eggs of sea turtles on the beach before the baby turtles come out and run into the sea.* ❖ θαλάσσια χελώνα

6.11 **sunbittern** (n) /'sʌnˌbɪtən/
a kind of large South American bird that lives near rivers in the jungle • *The explorer saw a sunbittern that flew down and caught a fish in the Amazon.* ❖ ήταυρος/τρανομουγκάνα της Νότιας Αμερικής (είδος πουλιού)

6.12 **gecko** (n) /'gekəʊ/
a small lizard • *I didn't see the gecko at first because it was the same colour as the kitchen wall.* ❖ γκέκο, σαμιαμίδι (είδος σαύρας)

6.13 **sloth** (n) /sləʊθ/
a slow-moving animal that lives in the trees in South and Central America • *Sloths are usually slow, but they can move fast to save themselves.* ❖ βραδύπους

6.14 **tarantula** (n) /tə'ræntʃələ/
a kind of large hairy spider from hot countries • *It's not a good idea to have a pet tarantula. They can bite you!* ❖ ταραντούλα

Word Focus
Page 70

6.15 **endangered** (adj) /ɪn'deɪndʒəd/
used to describe an animal or plant that there are not many of and that might disappear completely • *Don't pick these flowers – they are endangered plants.* ➣ endanger (v) ❖ υπό εξαφάνιση

6.16 **species** (n) /'spiːʃiːz/
type of living thing (e.g. animals, plants) • *We saw different species of lizards at the zoo.* ❖ είδος

6.17 **disappear** (v) /ˌdɪsə'pɪə(r)/
stop existing; be lost • *Many forests are disappearing because they are cut down to build more houses.* ➣ disappearance (n), disappearing (adj) ❖ εξαφανίζω

6.18 **planet** (n) /'plænɪt/
a large round object that moves around a star (sun) in space • *Do you believe we can live on another planet?* ❖ πλανήτης

6.19 **camouflage** (n) /'kæməflɑːʒ/
sth that covers sth/sb so they look like part of the place where they are and can't be seen • *The snake's colour was a perfect camouflage and it looked like another part of the tree.* ➣ camouflage (v) ❖ καμουφλάζ

6.20 **disguise** (n) /dɪs'gaɪz/
sth that hides how sth/sb looks by making them look different • *The actor wore a big hat and sunglasses as a disguise when she went shopping.* ➣ disguise (v) ❖ μεταμφίεση

65

6.21 **predator** (n) /ˈpredətə(r)/
an animal that kills and eats other animals
• *Birds and other predators often kill baby
turtles when they come out of their eggs.*
➢ predatory (adj) ❖ αρπακτικό

6.22 **claw** (n) /klɔː/
a sharp nail on an animal's foot • *The cat
caught the bird with its sharp claws.* ➢ claw (v)
❖ νύχι ζώου, δαγκάνα

6.23 **sharp** (adj) /ʃɑːp/
sth with a point or edge that cuts sth easily
• *Be careful with that knife – it's very sharp!*
❖ κοφτερός, μυτερός

6.24 **nail** (n) /neɪl/
the hard sharp part on the end of a finger or
toe • *My sister has nice long nails and she
likes painting them different colours.* ❖ νύχι

6.25 **prey** (n) /preɪ/
an animal that other animals kill to eat
• *We watched a video of a lion hunting its
prey.* ➢ prey (v) ❖ λεία, θήραμα

6.26 **attack** (v) /əˈtæk/
suddenly try to hurt or kill sth/sb • *A cat
attacked Tom's dog to protect her kittens.*
➢ attack (n) ❖ επιτίθεμαι

6.27 **poison** (n) /ˈpɔɪzn/
sth that makes sb/sth ill or can kill if you eat
or drink it • *Socrates drank the poison and it
killed him.* ➢ poison (v), poisonous (adj)
❖ δηλητήριο

6.28 **substance** (n) /ˈsʌbstəns/
any kind of material • *The plant is covered
with a sticky substance.* ❖ ουσία

6.29 **harm** (v) /hɑːm/
hurt or damage • *Don't harm the bees! We
need to protect them.* ➢ harm (n), harmful
(adj) ❖ βλάπτω, τραυματίζω

Reading
Pages 70–71

6.30 **photographer** (n) /fəˈtɒɡrəfə(r)/
sb who takes photos as a job • *Alan hired a
photographer to take the wedding photos.*
➢ photograph (v), photograph,
photography (n) ❖ φωτογράφος

6.31 **photograph** (v) /ˈfəʊtəɡrɑːf/
take a photo of sth/sb • *Sharon climbed to the
top of the hill to photograph the view.*
➢ photograph, photographer, photography (n)
❖ φωτογραφίζω

6.32 **attention** (n) /əˈtenʃn/
the act of listening to or watching sth/sb
carefully • *The kittens cried to get their
mother's attention.* ❖ προσοχή

6.33 **Madagascar** (n) /ˌmædəˈɡæskə(r)/
❖ Μαδαγασκάρη

6.34 **danger** (n) /ˈdeɪndʒə(r)/
the chance that sth will happen to hurt or kill
sb/sth • *I don't want to go cycling because
of the dangers on the road.* ➢ endanger (v),
dangerous (adj) ❖ κίνδυνος

6.35 **lose** (v) /luːz/
not have sth that you had before because
sb/sth takes it; be unable to find sth/sb
• *My dog lost a bit of his ear in a fight with the
neighbour's dog!* ➢ loss (n), lost (adj) ❖ χάνω

6.36 **trick** (v) /trɪk/
make sb believe that sth is true • *Samantha
tricked the police by wearing a large hat.*
➢ trick (n) ❖ ξεγελώ, εξαπατώ

6.37 **get away** (phr v) /get əˈweɪ/
escape • *The rabbit ran into its burrow to get
away from the fox.* ➢ getaway (n, adj)
❖ δραπετεύω

6.38 **mammal** (n) /ˈmæml/
an animal that has babies (not eggs) and
feeds them with its milk • *Whales are the
biggest mammals on the planet.* ❖ θηλαστικό

6.39 **herbivore** (n) /ˈhɜːbɪvɔː(r)/
an animal that only eats plants • *Cows are
herbivores. That's why they eat grass and
leaves.* ➢ herbivorous (adj) ❖ φυτοφάγος

6.40 **nocturnal** (adj) /nɒkˈtɜːnl/
active at night and asleep during the day
• *Bats are nocturnal animals, so they fly
around at night.* ❖ νυχτόβιος

6.41 **hang** (v) /hæŋ/
hold onto sth from the top so that the bottom
part is free; attach sth on a surface so it hangs
down • *The monkey hung onto the tree with
only one arm and watched us.* ❖ κρεμώ,
κρεμιέμαι

6.42 **upside down** (adv) /ˌʌpsaɪd ˈdaʊn/
in a position with the top part at the bottom
and the bottom part at the top • *That picture
looks strange. Did you hang it upside down?*
➢ upside-down (adj) ❖ ανάποδα

6.43 **Brazil** (n) /brəˈzɪl/
➢ Brazilian (n, adv) ❖ Βραζιλία

6.44 **Bolivia** (n) /bəˈlɪviə/
➢ Bolivian (n, adj) ❖ Βολιβία

6.45 **bend** (v) /bend/
move or make sth move from a straight
position in one direction • *The tree bent over
in the strong wind.* ➢ bend (n), bent (adj)
❖ λυγίζω

6.46 **roll up** (phr v) /ˌrəʊl ˈʌp/
make sth into a smaller round shape
• *Hetty rolled up her socks and put them into
her backpack.* ❖ τυλίγω

6.47 **touch** (v) /tʌtʃ/
put your hand or part of your body on sth; be right beside sth with no space in between
• *It was scary when the tarantula touched my arm.* ➤ touch (n), touching (adj) ❖ αγγίζω

6.48 **Venezuela** (n) /ˌvenəˈzweɪlə/
➤ Venezuelan (n, adj) ❖ Βενεζουέλα

6.49 **average** (adj) /ˈævərɪdʒ/
ordinary; normal • *The weather is colder than average for this month.* ➤ average (n) ❖ μέσος όρος, κοινός

6.50 **carnivore** (n) /ˈkɑːnɪvɔː(r)/
an animal that eats meat • *Cats and dogs are carnivores, but they eat vegetables, too.* ➤ carnivorous (adj) ❖ σαρκοφάγος

6.51 **waterway** (n) /ˈwɔːtəweɪ/
a river or canal that boats can travel on • *You can hire a boat for a holiday on the waterways of central England.* ❖ κανάλι

6.52 **webbed** (adj) /webd/
used to describe the feet of a bird or animal that has flat pieces of skin between its toes
• *Ducks have webbed feet so that they can move fast in water.* ➤ web (n) ❖ ενωμένος με νηκτική μεμβράνη

6.53 **wing** (n) /wɪŋ/
a part of the side of a bird's body that makes it fly • *Penguins can't fly because they've got such short wings.* ❖ φτερό, φτερούγα

6.54 **amphibian** (n) /æmˈfɪbiən/
an animal that can live on land or water
• *A lot of reptiles like frogs and lizards are amphibians.* ➤ amphibious (adj) ❖ αμφίβιο

6.55 **newspaper** (n) /ˈnjuːzpeɪpə(r)/
a set of pages with news, adverts, articles, etc. that is made every day or week • *Grandma buys a newpaper every day to read about what's happening in the world.* ❖ εφημερίδα

6.56 **natural** (adj) /ˈnætʃrəl/
made by nature; not made by people; normal
• *The sea is the only natural home for dolphins.* ➤ nature (n), naturally (adv) ❖ φυσικός
✎ Opp: unnatural ❖ αφύσικος, μη φυσικός

6.57 **habitat** (n) /ˈhæbɪtæt/
a place where a living thing usualy lives
• *A river is a natural habitat for frogs and fish.* ❖ περιβάλλον, οικότοπος

Places

aquarium	jungle
cage	planet
habitat	waterway

Vocabulary

6.58 **beak** (n) /biːk/
the hard outside part of a bird's mouth • *The parrot broke the nut open with its beak.* ❖ ράμφος

6.59 **leather** (n) /ˈleðə(r)/
material made from the skin of animals
• *Jane is wearing a pair of black leather boots.* ❖ δέρμα

6.60 **fin** (n) /fɪn/
a thin part like a wing on a fish that it uses for swimming • *Fish move their fins all the time to keep swimming.* ❖ πτερύγιο

6.61 **fur** (n) /fɜː(r)/
the thick hair on an animal's body • *The mother cat cleaned the fur of her kittens.* ➤ furry (adj) ❖ τρίχωμα, γούνα

6.62 **scale** (n) /skeɪl/
one of many thin plates on the skin of a fish or reptile • *The fisherman cleaned the scales off the fish before selling them at the market.* ➤ scaly (adj) ❖ λέπια

6.63 **skin** (n) /skɪn/
the natural outside cover of the body • *The hot sun made Wendy's white skin go red.* ❖ επιδερμίδα, δέρμα

6.64 **dolphin** (n) /ˈdɒlfɪn/
a sea animal like a large fish • *Did you see any dolphins swimming near your boat?* ❖ δελφίνι

6.65 **goose** (n) /guːs/
a large bird like a big duck with a longer neck
• *We saw lots of wild geese and ducks on the lake.* ❖ χήνα
✎ Plural: geese

6.66 **ostrich** (n) /ˈɒstrɪtʃ/
a very large bird with long legs, a long neck and short wings • *Ostriches are bigger than any other birds, but they can't fly.* ❖ στρουθοκάμηλος

6.67 **calf** (n) /kɑːf/
a young cow • *Cows produce milk to feed their calves.* ❖ μοσχάρι
✎ Plural: calves

6.68 **lay (eggs)** (v) /leɪ eggz/
When a bird, insect or reptile lays eggs, it pushes them out of its body. • *Tortoises lay their eggs in the ground.* ❖ γεννάω (αυγά)

6.69 **tadpole** (n) /ˈtædpəʊl/
a baby frog when it comes out of its egg
• *Frogs lay their eggs in this river, so it's full of tadpoles now.* ❖ γυρίνος

6.70   **develop** (v) /dɪ'veləp/
grow; grow bigger • *Angela and Len's daughter is developing into a teenager.*
➤ development (n) ❖ αναπτύσσω, αναπτύσσομαι

6.71   **lung** (n) /lʌŋ/
one of the two parts of the body that you use to breathe air • *It's good to walk in the forest to fill your lungs with clean air.* ❖ πνεύμονας

Parts of the Body

beak	nail
blood	neck
claw	scale
fin	skin
fur	tongue
lung	wing

6.72   **breathe** (v) /briːð/
move air into and out of your lungs through your nose or mouth • *People can't breathe underwater.* ➤ breath (n) ❖ αναπνέω

6.73   **poisonous** (adj) /'pɔɪzənəs/
sth with poison inside; that can kill or make you ill if you touch or eat it • *You can't eat that plant because it's poisonous.* ➤ poison (v, n) ❖ δηλητηριώδης

6.74   **rhinoceros** (n) /raɪ'nɒsərəs/
a large animal that has one or two horns on its nose and thick skin • *Some species of rhinoceros are endangered because of people hunting them.* ❖ ρινόκερος
✎ Abbrev: rhino

6.75   **leopard** (n) /'lepəd/
a large cat from Africa or Asia with a spotty pattern on its fur • *A leopard's yellow and brown fur is good camouflage in the long grass and trees.* ❖ λεοπάρδαλη

6.76   **furry** (adj) /'fɜːri/
covered with soft fur • *Tracy saw a furry animal catching a bird. I'm sure it was a cat.* ➤ fur (n) ❖ τριχωτός, μαλλιαρός

6.77   **dangerous** (adj) /'deɪndʒərəs/
able or possible to harm sth/sb • *Grass snakes aren't dangerous to humans.* ➤ danger (n) ❖ επικίνδυνος

6.78   **ugly** (adj) /'ʌgli/
not nice loooking • *The hotel was an ugly old building in the centre of the city.* ❖ άσχημος

6.79   **tiny** (adj) /'taɪni/
very small • *Look at that tiny yellow spider on the rock.* ❖ μικροσκοπικός

6.80   **heavy** (adj) /'hevi/
sb/sth that weighs a lot; difficult to lift up or carry • *This box is really heavy. Can you help me to carry it?* ❖ βαρύς

6.81   **snail** (n) /sneɪl/
a small animal with a very soft body that moves slowly with a shell on its back • *After the rain, the garden was full of snails.* ❖ σαλιγκάρι

Grammar   Pages 74–75

6.82   **noisy** (adj) /'nɔɪzi/
sb/sth that makes a lot of noise; full of noises • *The village church bell is very noisy and it wakes us up in the morning.* ➤ noise (n) ❖ θορυβώδης

6.83   **rat** (n) /ræt/
a small animal like a large mouse • *The old castle had rats looking for food in the kitchen.* ❖ αρουραίος

6.84   **polar bear** (n) /'pəʊlə beə(r)/
a large white bear that lives near the North Pole • *Polar bears are an endangered species.* ❖ πολική αρκούδα

6.85   **tiger** (n) /'taɪgə(r)/
a large cat that has black stripes on orange-yellow fur • *Tigers live alone and not in big groups like lions.* ❖ τίγρης

6.86   **giraffe** (n) /dʒə'rɑːf/
a tall African animal with a very long neck and long legs • *I took a photo of the giraffe that was eating leaves from the top of a tree.* ❖ καμηλοπάρδαλη

6.87   **neck** (n) /nek/
the part of the body that joins the head to the shoulders • *His neck hurt from working on the computer for hours.* ❖ λαιμός, αυχένας

6.88   **parrot** (n) /'pærət/
a colourful tropical bird that can make sounds like sb talking • *In their natural habitat, parrots make their homes in holes in trees.* ❖ παπαγάλος

6.89   **zebra** (n) /'zebrə/
a wild animal like a horse with black and white stripes • *Zebras are social animals that like to live in large groups.* ❖ ζέβρα

6.90   **brown bear** (n) /ˌbraʊn beə(r)/
a large brown coloured bear that lives in forests in Europe, Asia and North America • *Brown bears look cute in pictures, but they can be dangerous animals.* ❖ καφέ αρκούδα

6.91 **swimmer** (n) /ˈswɪmə(r)/
sb who swims ● *Tassia is a very good swimmer and she enjoys swimming in the sea every day.* ➢ swim (v), swimming (n)
❖ κολυμβητής

6.92 **hippopotamus** (n) /ˌhɪpəˈpɒtəməs/
a large animal with thick skin and short legs that lives in rivers or lakes in Africa
● *Hippopotamuses like to spend the day in a river to keep cool, then they come out to eat grass in the evening.* ❖ ιπποπόταμος
✎ Abbrev: hippo

6.93 **crocodile** (n) /ˈkrɒkədaɪl/
a large reptile with a long mouth and a long tail
● *Don't go in the river. It's full of crocodiles.*
❖ κροκόδειλος

6.94 **sound** (v) /saʊnd/
seem to be from what sb says; have a particular sound; give a particular idea
● *That sounds like a good idea!* ➢ sound (n)
❖ ακούγομαι, φαίνεται

6.95 **cheetah** (n) /ˈtʃiːtə/
a large cat with yellow fur and black spots, which runs very fast ● *A cheetah can run faster than any other animal.* ❖ τσίτα

6.96 **eagle** (n) /ˈiːgl/
a very large bird that kills small animals for food ● *The eagle flew down and caught the rabbit in its beak.* ❖ αετός

6.97 **toucan** (n) /ˈtuːkæn/
a tropical bird that is mainly black with a very large beak ● *Toucans are wild birds, native to the jungles of Central and South America.*
❖ τουκάν

6.98 **siren** (n) /ˈsaɪrən/
a machine that makes a very loud noise as a signal ● *The drivers moved their cars off the road quickly when they heard the fire sirens.*
❖ σειρήνα

6.99 **flap** (v) /flæp/
move up and down quickly; move or make sth move from side to side ● *The eagle flapped its wings and flew high above the trees.* ➢ flap (n)
❖ φτερουγίζω, κουνάω

6.100 **strong** (adj) /strɒŋ/
with a lot of power ● *Elephants are stronger than giraffes.* ➢ strength (n) ❖ δυνατός

Animals

armadillo	polar bear
brown bear	rat
bug	rhinoceros
butterfly	scorpion
calf	sloth
camel	snail
cheetah	sunbittern
cricket	tadpole
crocodile	tarantula
dolphin	tiger
eagle	toucan
gecko	turtle
giraffe	worm
goose	zebra
hippopotamus	
horned lizard	**Types of Animal**
imperial moth	amphibian
Komodo dragon	carnivore
leopard	herbivore
ostrich	mammal
panther chameleon	predator
parrot	prey

Listening Page 76

6.101 **lovely** (adj) /ˈlʌvli/
beautiful; enjoyable ● *We had a lovely walk in the park.* ❖ ωραίος, χαριτωμένος

6.102 **sound** (n) /saʊnd/
a noise; sth that you can hear ● *Dolphins make some strange sounds to send messages to each other.* ➢ sound (v) ❖ ήχος

6.103 **camel** (n) /ˈkæml/
an animal with a long neck and two humps on its back that you can ride in the desert
● *In hot deserts, people often use camels to carry things.* ❖ καμήλα

6.104 **scarf** (n) /skɑːf/
an item of clothing that sb wears around their neck ● *Wear a scarf to keep your neck warm. It's very cold tonight.* ❖ κασκόλ, φουλάρι
✎ Plural: scarves

6.105 **gift** (n) /gɪft/
a present ● *Frances gave her parents some flowers as a present.* ➢ give (v) ❖ δώρο

Speaking Page 77

6.106 **company** (n) /ˈkʌmpəni/
sb/sth you like being with or spend time with; being with other people ● *Pets are good company for children.* ❖ παρέα

6.107 **busy** (adj) /ˈbɪzi/
having a lot of things to do • *Betty is very busy doing her homework, so she can't go out tonight.* ❖ απασχολημένος

6.108 **exercise** (n) /ˈeksəsaɪz/
physical activities sb does to stay healthy • *Going for walks with my dog is good exercise.* ➤ exercise (v) ❖ άσκηση, γυμναστική

6.109 **relaxing** (adj) /rɪˈlæksɪŋ/
helping you to rest and not feel worried • *Eleanor listens to relaxing music while she's cooking.* ➤ relax (v), relaxation (n), relaxed (adj) ❖ χαλαρωτικός

6.110 **seed** (n) /siːd/
a small part of a plant that a new plant can grow from • *John put seeds in the ground last month and some lovely plants are growing.* ❖ σπόρος

Adjectives

average	poisonous
busy	relaxing
dangerous	sharp
endangered	sticky
furry	strong
heavy	timid
lovely	tiny
natural	ugly
nocturnal	unusual
noisy	webbed

Writing
Pages 78–79

6.111 **fact** (n) /fækt/
a piece of information that is true for sure • *Don't believe everything you read on the Internet. Check the facts first.* ➤ factual (adj) ❖ γεγονός

6.112 **file** (n) /faɪl/
a collection of information about sth/sb kept together in one place • *Don't forget to give each file a different name so you can find it.* ➤ file (v) ❖ φάκελος

6.113 **contraction** (n) /kənˈtrækʃn/
the short form of a verb • *'We're' is a contraction of 'we are'.* ❖ σύντομη μορφή (των λέξεων)

6.114 **paper clip** (n) /ˈpeɪpə klɪp/
a small piece of metal or plastic bent to hold papers together • *The police officer attached the photo to the file with a paper clip.* ❖ συνδετήρας

6.115 **panther chameleon** (n) /ˈpænθə kəˈmiːliən/
a large type of lizard that can change colour to match the place it is in • *Panther chameleons can hide in the jungles of Madagascar by changing colour.* ❖ πάνθηρας χαμαιλέοντας

6.116 **cricket** (n) /ˈkrɪkɪt/
a small brown insect that makes a lound sound with its wings, especially when the weather is hot • *It was a very hot day and we heard the sound of crickets in the trees outside our hotel.* ❖ γρύλος, τριζόνι

6.117 **worm** (n) /wɜːm/
a long thin animal with a soft body and no bones that lives in the ground • *Bill put a worm in his fishing net to catch a fish.* ❖ σκουλίκι

6.118 **male** (adj) /meɪl/
referring to a male animal; a boy or man • *Male tigers are larger than the females.* ➤ male (n) ❖ αρσενικός

6.119 **female** (adj) /ˈfiːmeɪl/
referring to a female animal; a girl or woman • *A female dog looks after her puppies.* ➤ female (n) ❖ θηλυκός

6.120 **gram** (n) /græm/
a very small measure of weight • *A kitten is about 100 grams when it's born.* ❖ γραμμάριο

6.121 **tongue** (n) /tʌŋ/
the long soft part of the mouth that you use to talk or taste, etc. • *Snakes look scary when they put out their tongues, but that's how they smell things.* ❖ γλώσσα (στο στόμα)

6.122 **diet** (n) /ˈdaɪət/
the food sb eats; a pattern of eating • *Like cows and sheep, kangaroos live on a diet of grass and leaves.* ➤ diet (v), dietary (adj) ❖ διατροφή

6.123 **size** (n) /saɪz/
how large sth/sb is • *How big is a baby elephant? Is it the same size as an adult human?* ➤ size (v) ❖ μέγεθος

6.124 **weight** (n) /weɪt/
how heavy sb/sth is • *The blue whale can be up to 136 tonnes in weight. That's heavy!* ➤ weigh (v) ❖ βάρος

6.125 **weigh** (v) /weɪ/
be a particular weght; measure sth/sb to find out their weight • *Human babies weigh an average of 3.4 kilograms when they are born.* ➤ weight (n) ❖ ζυγίζω, ζυγίζομαι

6.126 **transfer** (v) /trænsˈfɜː(r)/
move sth from one place to another; copy • *Remember to transfer your notes from your draft into paragraphs.* ➤ transfer (n) ❖ μεταφέρω

6.127 **hurry** (n) /ˈhʌri/
the need to do sth very quickly • *I'm not in a hurry to find a new home. I have lots of time.* ➤ hurry (v) ❖ βιασύνη

6.128 **cage** (n) /keɪdʒ/
a box shape made with metal bars to keep birds or other animals inside • *Animals are not happy to live in cages where they can't move around.* ➣ cage (v), caged (adj) ❖ κλουβί

6.129 **aquarium** (n) /əˈkweəriəm/
a container for fish or other animals to live in; a building where sb can go to see fish and other sea animals • *We visited the aquarium at the zoo and saw some small sharks.* ❖ ενυδρείο

6.130 **timid** (adj) /ˈtɪmɪd/
shy and easily scared • *Most birds are timid and they fly away when people go near them.* ❖ ντροπαλός, δειλός

Verbs

attack	lay (eggs)
bend	look like sb/sth
breathe	lose
capture	photograph
develop	roll up
disappear	smell
flap	sound
get away	spray
hang	touch
harm	trick
hide	weigh
hunt	

Video 6
Tip of my Tongue!

Page 80

6.131 **tip** (n) /tɪp/
the thin end part of an object • *Our black cat has got a tiny white part on the tip of her tail.* ❖ άκρη

6.132 **Komodo dragon** (n) /kəˌməʊdəʊ ˈdrægən/
a species of large lizard from Indonesia • *A Komodo dragon can weigh up to 70 kilograms!* ❖ δράκος του Κομόντο (είδος σαύρας)

6.133 **smell** (v) /smel/
use your nose to see how sth smells; have a particular smell • *Snakes don't have noses, so they use their tongues to smell things.* ➣ smell (n), smelly (adj) ❖ μυρίζω

6.134 **horned lizard** (n) /hɔːnd ˈlɪzəd/
a species of small desert lizard with horns on its head • *Horned lizards are an endangered species and they eat ants in the desert.* ❖ είδος σαύρας με κέρατα

6.135 **scorpion** (n) /ˈskɔːpiən/
a small animal that has eight legs and a long tail • *Jeremy went to hospital after the scorpion stung him with its poisonous tail.* ❖ σκορπιός

6.136 **spray** (v) /spreɪ/
put lots of small drops of liquid onto sth/sb • *Faisal sprayed the garden plants to protect them from insects.* ➣ spray (n) ❖ ψεκάζω

6.137 **blood** (n) /blʌd/
the red liquid that flows in your body • *Maya cut her finger on the knife and got blood on her clothes.* ➣ bleed (v) ❖ αίμα

6.138 **hunt** (v) /hʌnt/
chase sth/sb to catch or kill them • *People aren't allowed to hunt animals in the national park.* ➣ hunt, hunting, hunter (n) ❖ κυνηγάω

6.139 **bug** (n) /bʌg/
an insect • *Katie put cream on her skin to stop bugs from biting her in the forest.* ❖ έντομο, ζουζούνι

6.140 **sticky** (adj) /ˈstɪki/
having a surface that sth sticks to • *Roberto's hands are sticky with flour because he's making bread.* ➣ stick (v) ❖ κολλώδης, που κολλάει

6.141 **capture** (v) /ˈkæptʃə(r)/
catch sb/sth and take them prisoner • *The lion captured the calf and ate it.* ➣ capture (n) ❖ πιάνω, αιχμαλωτίζω

6.142 **Indonesia** (n) /ˌɪndəˈniːʒə/
➣ Indonesian (adj) ❖ Ινδονησία

Vocabulary Exercises

A Complete the word groups with these words.

armadillo butterfly cricket dolphin eagle gecko giraffe goose ostrich scorpion tadpole turtle

Land Animal	Sea/River Animal	Bird	Bug
_____	_____	_____	_____
_____	_____	_____	_____
_____	_____	_____	_____

B Choose the correct words (A, B or C).

1 The Indian elephant is a(n) ____ species, but it's a friendly animal.
  A dangerous   **B** poisonous   **C** endangered

2 Animals like bats are ____ and they hunt for food at night.
  A nocturnal   **B** relaxing   **C** natural

3 The eagle killed a small rabbit with its sharp ____.
  A beak   **B** fin   **C** wing

4 Most ____ brown bears live for about 25 years and the oldest are up to 50 years old.
  A ugly   **B** unusual   **C** average

5 That plant is poisonous. Don't ____ it!
  A attack   **B** touch   **C** trick

6 The chameleon's skin is a good ____ for hiding because it changes colour.
  A camouflage   **B** substance   **C** species

7 Don't ____ the grass snake. It isn't dangerous.
  A flap   **B** bend   **C** harm

8 This parrot's natural ____ is the jungle.
  A aquarium   **B** habitat   **C** disguise

C Unjumble the words to find the kinds of animals.

1 malmam   _____
2 hibaanmpi   _____
3 rype   _____
4 vocairern   _____
5 rebivhero   _____
6 torredap   _____

D Match the meanings a–f to the words 1–6 from C.

☐ **a** an animal that can live on land or water
☐ **b** an animal that eats meat
☐ **c** an animal that has babies (not eggs) and feeds them with its milk
☐ **d** an animal that only eats plants
☐ **e** an animal that kills and eats other animals
☐ **f** an animal that other animals kill to eat

E Find ten animals and write them on the lines.

C	H	O	R	M	E	C	L	E	O	N	T
R	A	L	U	S	E	R	T	I	G	E	B
O	P	E	Y	T	W	O	R	M	L	E	H
C	R	O	D	R	H	C	O	C	D	I	L
H	I	P	P	O	P	O	T	A	M	U	S
E	R	A	T	U	N	D	B	M	O	N	L
E	N	R	O	C	Z	I	R	E	K	E	O
T	Y	D	U	A	E	L	L	L	H	R	T
A	V	D	C	M	B	E	R	D	T	U	H
H	C	H	A	M	E	L	E	O	N	E	L
W	O	R	N	L	O	N	B	O	T	L	E

1 _____   6 _____
2 _____   7 _____
3 _____   8 _____
4 _____   9 _____
5 _____   10 _____

6 Grammar

6.1 Comparative Adjectives

Adjective	Comparative
small	small**er**
cute	cut**er**
big	big**ger**
noisy	nois**ier**
dangerous	**more** dangerous
good	**better**
bad	**worse**

Συνήθως σχηματίζουμε τον comparative (συγκριτικό βαθμό) προσθέτοντας την κατάληξη *-er* στο επίθετο ή το επίρρημα. Αν το επίθετο ή το επίρρημα έχει περισσότερες από δύο συλλαβές, τότε χρησιμοποιούμε τη λέξη *more*. Χρησιμοποιούμε τη λέξη *than* μετά από τον comparative σε μια πρόταση.
→ *An elephant is **bigger than** a tiger.*
→ *Snakes are **more dangerous than** frogs.*

Μερικά επίθετα είναι ανώμαλα και σχηματίζουν τον comparative με διαφορετικούς τρόπους.
→ *George is a **worse** swimmer **than** his sister.*

Χρησιμοποιούμε τον comparative για να συγκρίνουμε δύο πρόσωπα ή πράγματα.

6.2 Other Comparative Structures

Χρησιμοποιούμε *as* + επίθετο + *as* για να δείξουμε ότι δύο πρόσωπα, ζώα ή πράγματα είναι παρόμοια.
→ *Tigers are **as dangerous** as lions.*

Χρησιμοποιούμε *not as/so ... as* για να δείξουμε ότι δύο πρόσωπα, ζώα ή πράγματα είναι διαφορετικά.
→ *A lion is**n't as tall as** a giraffe.*

6.3 *How* + Adjective

Χρησιμοποιούμε *How* + επίθετο σε μια ερώτηση όταν θέλουμε πιο συγκεκριμένες πληροφορίες.
→ ***How heavy** is that brown bear?*
→ ***How tall** is this building?*
→ ***How old** is your cat?*

6.4 Adjective and Sense Verbs

Χρησιμοποιούμε επίθετα μετά από sense verbs (ρήματα αισθήσεων) για να πούμε πως κάτι *looks, sounds, smells, tastes* και *feels*.
→ *This cake **tastes good**.*
→ *The snake's skin **feels soft**.*
→ *The plants **look dangerous**.*

Χρησιμοποιούμε sense verbs + *like* + ουσιαστικό για να συγκρίνουμε αυτό που βλέπουμε, ακούμε, μυρίζουμε, γευόμαστε ή αγγίζουμε.
→ *It **feels like** water.*
→ *It **looks like** an insect.*
→ *It **sounds like** a bell.*

Grammar Exercises

A Complete the sentences with the comparative form of the adjectives in brackets. Remember to use *than* where necessary.

1 Looking after a cat is _____ (easy) looking after a dog.
2 A tarantula is _____ (dangerous) a tortoise.
3 Poisonous snakes are _____ (bad) mosquitoes.
4 A giraffe is _____ (big) a rabbit.
5 My sister is a _____ (good) swimmer than me.
6 A dog is _____ (friendly) a goldfish.

B Complete the sentences with *as ... as* or *not as ... as*.

1 A feather is _____ heavy _____ butterfly.
2 A rhinoceros is _____ fast _____ a horse.
3 Snakes are _____ cute _____ kittens.
4 A butterfly looks _____ beautiful _____ a flower.
5 A lion is _____ timid _____ a mouse.
6 The blue whale is _____ heavy _____ a lorry!

C Match the questions and answers.

1 How long is a British grass snake? ☐
2 How heavy is a penguin? ☐
3 How old is your cat? ☐
4 How does a snake's skin feel? ☐
5 What does a puffin sound like? ☐
6 What does a leopard look like? ☐

a It sounds like a police siren.
b It looks like a very big yellow cat with brown spots.
c It's heavier than a puffin.
d It can be up to 80 centimetres long.
e It's seven years old.
f It feels soft.

D Complete the sentences with one word in each space.

1 What's that noise? It sounds _____ a frog.
2 _____ fast can a chicken run?
3 A whale's heart is _____ big as a car.
4 A kangaroo's back legs are longer _____ its front legs.
5 You _____ sad. Is something wrong?
6 Chameleons are _____ interesting than other reptiles because they can change colour.

7 Invent It!

7.1 **invent** (v) /ɪnˈvent/
make or design sth that has not been made
before ● *Who invented the phone? Was it
Alexander Graham Bell?* ➢ inventor (n),
invention (n), inventive (adj) ❖ εφευρίσκω

7.2 **device** (n) /dɪˈvaɪs/
an object that is used for a particular purpose
● *A torch is a useful device that helps us see
at night outside.* ❖ συσκευή

7.3 **robotic** (adj) /rəʊˈbɒtɪk/
made as a robot; controlled by a computer
● *The company uses machines with robotic
arms to make cars.* ➢ robot, robotics (n)
❖ ρομποτικός

7.4 **jockey** (n) /ˈdʒɒki/
sb who rides a horse in a race ● *The jockey
nearly fell off his horse in the middle of the
race.* ➢ jockey (v) ❖ τζόκεϊ

7.5 **Oman** (n) /əʊˈmɑːn/
➢ Omani (n, adj) ❖ Ομάν

Reading

7.6 **invention** (n) /ɪnˈvenʃn/
sth new that sb has created that has never
been made before ● *The telephone was an
important invention. It changed the way people
communicate.* ➢ invent (v), inventor (n),
inventive (adj) ❖ εφεύρεση

7.7 **dark** (n) /dɑːk/
the state of being without light ● *Cats and bats
can see in the dark.* ➢ darken (v), darkness
(n), dark (adj) ❖ σκοτάδι

7.8 **usefulness** (n) /ˈjuːsfəlnəs/
the fact of being helpful to do sth ● *I'm not
sure about the usefulness of remote controlled
lights in the house.* ➢ use (v, n), useful (adj)
❖ χρησιμότητα

7.9 **useful** (adj) /ˈjuːsfəl/
helping to do sth ● *Smartphones are useful
for sending photos and information.* ➢ use (v),
use, usefulness (n) ❖ χρήσιμος

Word Focus

7.10 **eco-friendly** (adj) /ˌiːkəʊ ˈfrendli/
not dangerous to the environment ● *Electric
cars are eco-friendly because they don't need
petrol.* ❖ φιλικός στο περιβάλλον

7.11 **environment** (n) /ɪnˈvaɪrənmənt/
the air, water, land around us ● *We must
protect the environment and not throw
litter everywhere.* ➢ environmental (adj),
environmentally (adv) ❖ περιβάλλον

7.12 **preserve** (v) /prɪˈzɜːv/
prevent food from going bad by treating it
in a particular way ● *You can preserve fruit
by cooking it with sugar.* ➢ preservative (n),
preservation (n) ❖ διατηρώ

7.13 **fresh** (adj) /freʃ/
produced or picked not long ago ● *I love
eating fresh bread from the bakery.* ➢ freshen
(v), freshness (n), freshly (adv) ❖ φρέσκος

7.14 **resist** (v) /rɪˈzɪst/
not be harmed by sth; try not to do sth that you
want to do ● *My tent is made of material that
can resist the rain.* ➢ resistance (n)
❖ αντιστέκομαι

7.15 **biodegradable** (adj) /ˌbaɪəʊdɪˈɡreɪdəbl/
able to be broken down naturally into small
parts as part of nature ● *This box is made of
biodegradable paper.* ❖ βιοδιασπώμενος
✎ Opp: non-biodegradable
❖ μη-βιοδιασπώμενος

7.16 **organism** (n) /ˈɔːɡənɪzəm/
a living thing ● *Hundreds of tiny organisms live
in a piece of cheese.* ❖ οργανισμός

7.17 **hiccups** (n) /ˈhɪkʌps/
sounds that come from your throat when you
eat sth too quickly ● *Tricia got hiccups after
drinking a big glass of fruit juice.* ➢ hiccup (v)
❖ λόξιγκας

7.18 **throat** (n) /θrəʊt/
the part of the body inside the neck that food
and drink goes through ● *Nadia didn't feel well
because her throat hurt.* ❖ λάρυγγας, λαιμός

7.19 **lollipop** (n) /ˈlɒlipɒp/
a sweet on a stick ● *Do you want an ice cream
or an ice lollipop?* ❖ γλειφιτζούρι

7.20 **earthquake** (n) /ˈɜːθˌkweɪk/
shaking of the ground ● *Rescue workers
saved the family from the building that fell
down in the earthquake.* ❖ σεισμός

7.21 **sudden** (adj) /ˈsʌdn/
happening very quickly when you don't expect
it ● *The sudden change of weather stopped us
having a barbecue.* ➢ suddenly (adv)
❖ ξαφνικός

7.22 **violent** (adj) /ˈvaɪələnt/
acting in a way that can hurt sb/sth ● *Don't
annoy the cat because it might get violent.*
➢ violence (n) ❖ βίαιος

7.23 **movement** (n) /ˈmuːvmənt/
going from one place to another • *We saw a movement in the sea near the boat and then the dolphins appeared.* ➣ move (v, n), movable (adj) ❖ κίνηση

Reading   Pages 84–85

7.24 **inventor** (n) /ɪnˈventə(r)/
sb who has an idea to make sth that nobody made before • *Tim Berners-Lee was the inventor of the Internet.* ➣ invent (v), invention (n), inventive (adj) ❖ εφευρέτης

7.25 **win** (v) /wɪn/
be the best in a race, competition, etc. • *Uncle Fred won a car in a TV phone-in quiz.* ➣ win, winner (n) ❖ κερδίζω, νικάω

7.26 **normally** (adv) /ˈnɔːməli/
usually • *I normally get up early, but today I woke up at 10 o'clock.* ➣ normal (adj) ❖ συνήθως, κανονικά

7.27 **technology** (n) /tekˈnɒlədʒi/
the science used to discover and design new things • *Modern technology helps us to do jobs at home more easily and quickly.* ➣ technological (adj) ❖ τεχνολογία

7.28 **UV** (n) /ˌjuː ˈviː/
ultraviolet; a type of light from the sun or a special lamp • *A UV light can read hidden information from bank cards.* ❖ υπεριώδης ακτινοβολία

7.29 **technique** (n) /tekˈniːk/
a particular way of doing sth, especially sth that needs a special skill • *Firefighters learn special techniques to save people from fires.* ➣ technical (adj), technically (adv), technician (n) ❖ τεχνική

7.30 **chemical** (n) /ˈkemɪkl/
a substance made through a chemical process • *Fish can't live in this lake because it's full of chemicals.* ➣ chemical (adj) ❖ χημική ουσία

7.31 **instead of** (prep) /ɪnˈsted əv/
in the place of sth/sb else • *Theo cycles to work instead of driving his car.* ➣ instead (adv) ❖ αντί για

7.32 **plastic** (n) /ˈplæstɪk/
a strong material made from oil that is processed • *It's better to take your own shopping bag instead of using bags made of plastic.* ➣ plastic (adj) ❖ πλαστικό

7.33 **plate** (n) /pleɪt/
a flat dish to put food on • *I ate some pizza and a plate of salad.* ❖ πιάτο

7.34 **unlike** (prep) /ˌʌnˈlaɪk/
different from; not like • *Unlike other birds, penguins can't fly.* ❖ διαφορετικός από, αντίθετα, ανόμοιος

7.35 **cure** (n) /kjʊə(r)/
sth that makes an illness stop so sb feels healthy again • *Sleep is the best cure for feeling tired!* ➣ cure (v), curable (adj) ❖ θεραπεία

7.36 **cider** (n) /ˈsaɪdə(r)/
a drink made from apple juice • *Cider is a common drink, especially in the south of England.* ❖ μηλίτης, ποτό από μήλο

7.37 **vinegar** (n) /ˈvɪnɪgə(r)/
a liquid made from wine, grain or cider that is used to flavour food • *Put some oil and vinegar on the salad before you serve it.* ❖ ξίδι

7.38 **earthworm** (n) /ˈɜːθwɜːm/
a worm that lives in the ground • *Grandpa says that earthworms are good for the garden, so we don't harm them.* ❖ σκουλήκι, γαιοσκώληκας

7.39 **teenage** (adj) /ˈtiːneɪdʒ/
aged between 13 and 19 years old • *Stephen lived in Manchester during his teenage years before he started working.* ➣ teen, teenager (n) ❖ εφηβικός

7.40 **prototype** (n) /ˈprəʊtətaɪp/
the first design of sth new that is a model for similar things made later • *The company made the prototype for the first electric car.* ❖ πρότυπο, πρωτότυπο

7.41 **destroy** (v) /dɪsˈtrɔɪ/
damage sth so badly that it can't be used; ruin • *We are destroying the environment by throwing away so much plastic.* ➣ destruction (n), destructive (adj) ❖ καταστρέφω

7.42 **dentist** (n) /ˈdentɪst/
sb who takes care of people's teeth as a job • *The dentist checks my teeth every six months.* ➣ dental (adj) ❖ οδοντίατρος

7.43 **machine** (n) /məˈʃiːn/
sth that has moving parts and works with power from electricity, etc. to do a job • *Our washing machine is 15 years old, but it still washes clothes well.* ❖ μηχανή

Vocabulary   Pages 86–87

7.44 **computer screen** (n) /kəmˌpjuːtə skriːn/
a flat surface that you can see pictures and information on from a computer • *The photos from her camera looked great on the computer screen.* ❖ οθόνη υπολογιστή

7.45 **handle** (n) /ˈhændl/
a part of a door, window, etc., that you move to open it; a part of an object that you use to hold it • *She turned the handle to open the door, but it was locked.* ➣ handle (v) ❖ πόμολο, λαβή, χερούλι

7.46 **earphones** (n) /ˈɪəfəʊnz/
a device you wear in your ears to listen to a phone, radio, etc., without other people hearing ● *Rick is listening to music from his tablet through his earphones.*
❖ ακουστικά (ψείρες)

7.47 **remote control** (n) /rɪˌməʊt kənˈtrəʊl/
a device that sb can use to control a machine from a distance ● *The cameras outside the building work by remote control.* ➤ remote-controlled (adj) ❖ τηλεχειριστήριο

7.48 **charger** (n) /ˈtʃɑːrʒə/
a device for putting electricity into a battery ● *Can I use your phone charger? I need to charge my smartphone.* ➤ charge (v), charge (n) ❖ φορτιστής

7.49 **plug in** (phr v) /plʌg ɪn/
connect a machine to an electric source ● *You can plug in your phone charger on the wall next to the computer.* ➤ plug (v, n) ❖ βάζω στην μπρίζα
✎ Opp: unplug ❖ βγάζω απ'την μπρίζα

7.50 **turn on** (phr v) /tɜːn ɒn/
switch on ● *It's time for the news. Can you turn on the car radio?* ❖ ανοίγω (για συσκευή)

7.51 **television** (n) /ˈtelɪvɪʒn/
a machine with a screen that you can watch programmes on; a TV ● *This old television works very well. I don't need a new one with a giant screen.* ❖ τηλεόραση

7.52 **turn off** (phr v) /tɜːn ɒf/
switch off ● *Please turn off all the lights and close the doors before you go out.*
❖ κλείνω (για συσκευή)

7.53 **metal** (n) /ˈmetl/
a very hard shiny material (e.g. steel, iron, gold) used to make tools, machines, etc. ● *This bike is made of light metal so it can move quickly.* ➤ metallic (adj) ❖ μέταλλο

7.54 **wood** (n) /wʊd/
the material that comes from trees ● *The famous Trojan Horse was made of wood.* ➤ wooden (adj) ❖ ξύλο

7.55 **glass** (n) /glæs/
a clear material made from sand, used to make windows, etc. ● *These windows are made of a special kind of glass that doesn't break.* ➤ glass, glaze (v) ❖ γυαλί

> ## Look!
> Να θυμάσαι πως η λέξη **glass** έχει δυο διαφορετικές έννοιες.
> Σημαίνει γυαλί.
> *The computer screen is made of glass.*
> Επίσης σημαίνει ποτήρι.
> *She's drinking a glass of water.*
> Στον πληθυντικό **glasses** είναι γυαλιά (μυωπίας ή ηλίου).
> *Dad wears glasses for reading.*
> *Have you got your hat and sunglasses for the beach?*

> ## Materials
> chemical   plastic
> glass   wood
> metal

7.56 **rectangular** (adj) /rekˈtæŋgjələ(r)/
in a shape with two long parallel sides and two shorter sides ● *Florence's phone has rectangular screen that is 12 cm long and 7 cm wide.* ➤ rectangle (n) ❖ ορθογώνιος

7.57 **square** (adj) /skweə(r)/
shaped with four sides of the same size ● *There's a square table in the kitchen.* ➤ square (n) ❖ τετράγωνος

7.58 **silver** (adj) /ˈsɪlvə(r)/
a white or grey metal, used to make money, jewellery, etc. ● *Dad gave Mum a lovely silver necklace as a present.* ➤ silver (n) ❖ ασημένιος

7.59 **round** (adj) /raʊnd/
shaped like a circle ● *There's a round clock at the top of the tower.* ➤ round (v, n) ❖ στρογγυλός

7.60 **oval** (adj) /ˈəʊvl/
shaped like an egg ● *The salad was on an oval dish in the middle of the table.* ➤ oval (n) ❖ οβάλ, ωοείδης

7.61 **enormous** (adj) /ɪˈnɔːməs/
very large ● *They live in an enormous house that has twelve rooms and a swimming pool.* ❖ τεράστιος

7.62 **compass** (n) /ˈkʌmpəs/
a small, round device that points to north to help find directions ● *Ursula's phone was off, so she found the path by using a map and her old compass.* ❖ πυξίδα

Adjectives

biodegradable	round
eco-friendly	shiny
enormous	silver
fresh	square
full	sudden
oval	useful
rectangular	violent
robotic	

Grammar

Pages 88–89

7.63 pencil sharpener (n) /ˈpensl ʃɑːpnə(r)/
sth used to make pencils sharp ● *Take your pencil sharpener to school. Your pencil might break during the lesson.* ❖ ξύστρα

7.64 solar system (n) /ˈsəʊlə sɪstəm/
a group of planets that moves around the same star, which is their sun ● *Do you know how many planets are in our solar system?* ❖ ηλιακό σύστημα

7.65 wheel (n) /wiːl/
a round object that helps a vehicle move along the road ● *Alan's bike hit a rock and one of the wheels fell off.* ➤ wheel (v) ❖ τροχός, ρόδα

7.66 rocket (n) /ˈrɒkɪt/
a long, thin spacecraft; a kind of bomb that moves very fast through the air ● *What year did the first rocket travel in space around Earth?* ➤ rocket (v) ❖ πύραυλος

7.67 dishwasher (n) /ˈdɪʃwɒʃə(r)/
a machine for washing cups, plates, etc. ● *The dishwasher wasn't working, so Nigel washed all the dishes by hand.* ❖ πλυντήριο πιάτων

7.68 drone (n) /drəʊn/
a device like a small helicopter with a camera that flies by remote control; a small plane with no pilot moved by a remote control from a computer ● *We used a drone to take some amazing photos and videos of the castle from the air.* ➤ drone (v) ❖ ρομποτάκι, ιπτάμενη κάμερα, drone

7.69 scientist (n) /ˈsaɪəntɪst/
sb who studies science and works to find out more about sth scientific ● *Scientists say that the ice in the Arctic and Antarctic is melting.* ➤ science (n), scientific (adj) ❖ επιστήμονας

7.70 GPS (n) /dʒiː piː es/
a device that shows the position of sb/sth on a map; global positioning system ● *We found the road easily because our GPS showed us where we were.* ❖ σύστημα δορυφορικής πλοήγησης

7.71 pilot (n) /ˈpaɪlət/
sb who flies a plane ● *The pilot flew the plane up through the clouds.* ➤ pilot (v) ❖ πιλότος, κυβερνήτης

People

dentist	jockey
engineer	pilot
inventor	scientist

7.72 predict (v) /prɪˈdɪkt/
say that sth will happen in the future ● *Can you predict where you will be in twenty years from now?* ➤ prediction (n) ❖ προβλέπω

7.73 upstairs (adv) /ˌʌpˈsteəz/
on/to the floor of a building above the one where sb is ● *The house has three bedrooms upstairs.* ➤ upstairs (adv) ❖ στον επάνω όροφο
✎ Opp: downstairs ❖ στον κάτω όροφο

7.74 telescope (n) /ˈtelɪskəʊp/
a device that makes faraway things look close so sb can look through it and see them clearly ● *Sheila looked through the telescope and saw the moon up close.* ➤ telescopic (adj) ❖ τηλεσκόπιο

7.75 toothbrush (n) /ˈtuːθbrʌʃ/
a small brush for cleaning teeth ● *Don't forget to take your toothbrush on the camping trip.* ❖ οδοντόβουρτσα

7.76 suitcase (n) /ˈsuːtkeɪs/
a large bag with flat sides that you can pack clothes in to take for travelling ● *Salman packed his clothes into his suitcase and took a taxi to the airport.* ❖ βαλίτσα

Listening

Page 90

7.77 floor (n) /flɔː(r)/
the part of a room that sb walks on ● *The glass fell on the stone floor and broke.* ❖ πάτωμα, δάπεδο

7.78 anywhere (adv) /ˈeniweə(r)/
in any place (usually used in questions and negative sentences) ● *I can't find my sunglasses anywhere.* ❖ οπουδήποτε

7.79 movie (n) /ˈmuːvi/
a film ● *Let's watch a movie on TV tonight.* ❖ ταινία, έργο

7.80 function (n) /ˈfʌŋkʃn/
the use or purpose of sth ● *What is the function of an MP3 player? Does it play music?* ➤ function (v), functional (adj) ❖ χρήση

Speaking

7.81 **exhibition** (n) /ˌeksɪˈbɪʃən/
a show of paintings, interesting objects, etc.
that people can go to see ● *Keira is having an
exhibition of her photographs next week.*
➢ exhibit (v, n) ❖ έκθεση

7.82 **floor** (n) /flɔː(r)/
the rooms on one level of a building ● *Our
company office is on the second floor.*
❖ όροφος

7.83 **space** (n) /speɪs/
the place beyond the Earth's atmosphere
● *You can look into space and see stars
clearly with a telescope.* ❖ διάστημα

7.84 **lift** (n) /lɪft/
a machine that moves people and things to a
higher level in a building ● *Let's use the lift to
go up to the sixth floor.* ➢ lift (v) ❖ ασανσέρ,
ανελκυστήρας

7.85 **flight** (n) /flaɪt/
travel in the air; a journey by plane, helicopter,
etc. ● *The documentary showed the flight of
an eagle above the mountains.* ➢ fly (v)
❖ πτήση

7.86 **ground floor** (n) /ˌɡraʊnd flɔː(r)/
the part of a building that is on the same level
as the ground where you enter it ● *We live on
the ground floor and we've got a small garden
outside.* ❖ ισόγειο

7.87 **entrance** (n) /ˈentrəns/
the place that leads to a building or room
● *Wait for me outside the entrance to the
exhibition centre.* ➢ enter (v), entry (n)
❖ είσοδος

7.88 **science** (n) /ˈsaɪəns/
the study of how things work in nature and
how to create things in the world ● *Irene wants
to study science to become an inventor one
day.* ➢ scientist (n), scientific (adj) ❖ επιστήμη

Writing

7.89 **illustration** (n) /ˌɪləˈstreɪʃn/
a picture ● *This book about flowers is full
of colourful illustrations.* ➢ illustrate (v),
illustrator (n) ❖ εικονογράφηση, ζωγραφιά

7.90 **sundial** (n) /ˈsʌndaɪəl/
a kind of clock that shows the time by the
position of a shadow made when the sun
shines ● *The group agreed to meet beside the
old sundial in the town square.* ❖ ηλιακό ρολόι

7.91 **typewriter** (n) /ˈtaɪpraɪtə(r)/
a machine used to write on paper by pressing
metal keys ● *My grandmother didn't have
a laptop at university, so she wrote her
homework with a typewriter.* ❖ γραφομηχανή

7.92 **gramophone** (n) /ˈɡræməfəʊn/
an old machine that played music from records
● *Years ago, my grandparents listened to
music on their gramophone.* ❖ γραμόφωνο

7.93 **electricity** (n) /ɪˌlekˈtrɪsəti/
energy that moves through wires to give power
to machines, lights, etc. ● *I can't switch on the
computer because the electricity is off.*
➢ electric (adj) ❖ (ηλεκτρικό) ρεύμα

7.94 **sharpen** (v) /ˈʃɑːpən/
make sth sharp at the point or edge ● *This
pencil doesn't write. I need to sharpen it.*
➢ sharpener (n), sharp (adj) ❖ ξύνω, ακονίζω

7.95 **pencil case** (n) /ˈpensl keɪs/
a small bag or box for pencils, pens, etc.
● *Make sure your sharpener is in your pencil
case for school.* ❖ κασετίνα

7.96 **MP3 player** (n) /ˌem piː ˈθriː pleɪə(r)/
a small, portable device that you can transfer
information or music into from a computer
● *Andy puts music on his MP3 player to listen
to on the bus.* ❖ συσκευή αναπαραγωγής MP3

7.97 **finger** (n) /ˈfɪŋɡə(r)/
one of the five long thin parts of a hand ● *You
can write on your smartphone by using your
finger on the screen.* ❖ δάχτυλο (χεριού)

7.98 **wrist** (n) /rɪst/
a part of the body between the arm and the
hand ● *Shirley usually uses her computer for
ten hours a day, so now her wrist hurts a lot.*
❖ καρπός (χεριού)

7.99 **fit** (v) /fɪt/
be the correct size for sb/sth ● *My feet hurt
because these new boots don't fit me very
well.* ➢ fit (n) ❖ εφαρμόζω καλά, χωράω

Verbs

destroy	preserve
fit	resist
invent	sharpen
plug in	turn on/off
predict	win

7.100 **solar** (adj) /ˈsəʊlə(r)/
using power from the sun's heat or light
● *In our house, we use solar energy to get
hot water.* ❖ ηλιακός

7.101 **cooker** (n) /ˈkʊkə/
a piece of equipment for cooking food on or in
● *The cooker isn't working so we can't make
roast chicken for dinner.* ➢ cook (v, n)
❖ ηλεκτρική κουζίνα

7.102 **shiny** (adj) /'ʃaɪni/
bright and smooth ● *Tony's dirty old car was shiny and clean again after he washed it.* ➢ shine (v) ❖ γυαλιστερός

7.103 **nutribullet®** (n) /ˌnjuːtriˈbʊlɪt/
a make of blender (a machine to mix food or drinks) ● *I put all the fruit into the nutribullet® to mix a healthy drink for breakfast.*
❖ μάρκα μπλέντερ nutribullet®

7.104 **Fitbit** (n) /'fɪtbɪt/
a make of watch that can also measure heartbeat, etc. ● *Runners can wear a Fitbit to check their speed and how fast their heart beats during training.* ❖ μάρκα ρολογιού που μετράει και τους παλμούς, κτλ.

7.105 **walking stick** (n) /'wɔːkɪŋ stɪk/
a long piece of wood or metal that sb uses to help them walk ● *Grant uses two walking sticks to help him go up hills when he walks in the country.* ❖ μπαστούνι

Technology: Nouns

brake	pencil sharpener
charger	prototype
compass	remote control
computer screen	rocket
cooker	science
device	solar system
dishwasher	space
drone	speed
earphones	sundial
electricity	technique
GPS	telescope
gramophone	television
handle	typewriter
invention	UV
lift	walking stick
machine	wheel
MP3 player	

7.106 **full** (adj) /fʊl/
whole; complete ● *I don't eat a full dinner at school. I usually have a sandwich.* ➢ full (adv) ❖ ολόκληρος, πλήρης, γεμάτος

7.107 **deadline** (n) /'dedlaɪn/
the latest time or date when sb must do sth ● *Did you send your form for the competition? The deadline for entries is next Monday.*
❖ προθεσμία

7.108 **prize** (n) /praɪz/
sth you win for being the best at sth ● *Who won the first prize in the science competition?* ❖ βραβείο

Video 7
An Exciting Invention
Page 94

7.109 **brake** (n) /breɪk/
a part of a bike, car, etc. that makes it stop or go slowly ● *Remember to check the brakes on your bike before you go cycling.* ➢ brake (v)
❖ φρένο

7.110 **engineer** (n) /ˌendʒɪˈnɪə(r)/
a person who designs and builds roads, bridges, etc. ● *The engineers discovered how to make electric cars.* ➢ engineering (n, adj)
❖ μηχανικός

7.111 **million** (num) /'mɪljən/
the number 1,000,000 ❖ εκατομμύριο

7.112 **attraction** (n) /əˈtrækʃn/
an interesting activity or place to see; sth that makes sth/sb interesting or fun ● *The biggest attraction at the amusement park is the roller coaster.* ➢ attract (v), attractive (adj)
❖ παιχνίδι στο λούνα παρκ, πόλος έλξης

7.113 **make sure** (expr) /meɪk ʃʊə(r)/
do sth so that you know sth will happen or sth is true ● *Make sure the electricity is off before you go away on holiday* ❖ σιγουρεύομαι

7.114 **sandbag** (n) /'sændbæg/
a large bag full of sand usually used to protect a place against bad weather, fire or an attack ● *In winter, some houses in the village had sandbags outside their windows and doors to protect them from the heavy rain.*
❖ αμμόσακος

7.115 **speed** (n) /spiːd/
how fast sth moves ● *This car can go at a speed of 150 kilometres per hour.* ➢ speed (v), speedy (adj) ❖ ταχύτητα

7.116 **high season** (n) /ˌhaɪ ˈsiːzn/
the time of year when most people want to travel, go to hotels, etc. especially for holidays ● *Hotel rooms cost a lot more during the high season.* ❖ υψηλή σεζόν/περίοδος
✎ Opp: low season ❖ χαμηλή σεζόν/περίοδος

Vocabulary Exercises

A Match to make compound nouns.

1 pencil ☐   a stick
2 ground ☐   b sharpener
3 walking ☐   c system
4 solar ☐   d player
5 remote ☐   e season
6 computer ☐   f control
7 high ☐   g floor
8 MP3 ☐   h screen

B Complete the sentences with the compound nouns from A.

1 We live on the _____ _____ of a high building.
2 Can you see all the planets in the _____ _____ with your telescope?
3 Jane listened to music on her _____ _____.
4 This pencil doesn't write well. I need my _____ _____.
5 Oh, no! Why is there no picture on my _____ _____?
6 The hotels near the beach are always busy in the _____ _____.
7 Grandpa's _____ _____ helps him to go upstairs more quickly.
8 Where's the _____ _____? I want to turn off the TV.

C Circle the correct words.

1 Can I plug in my phone **charger** / **handle** for a few minutes?
2 The **dentist** / **pilot** welcomed the passengers when they got on the plane.
3 Let's go to see the robots at the science **exhibition** / **illustration**.
4 What time is the **lift** / **flight** to Athens? I can drive you to the airport.
5 I haven't got a rubber in my **pencil case** / **suitcase**. Can I borrow yours?
6 Can scientists really **predict** / **invent** when an earthquake will happen?
7 Smartphones are usually **rectangular** / **round** in shape.
8 I thought I saw a snake in the garden, but it was just a big **earthworm** / **earthquake**.

D Complete the sentences with the words you did not circle in C.

1 Ted drew a funny _____ to put on his blog.
2 Ben always walks upstairs instead of taking the _____.
3 The wheels on this _____ make it easy to move when it's full of clothes.
4 The _____ destroyed the whole village.
5 Is the kitchen table _____ or square?
6 Push the _____ down to open the door.
7 Did Tim Berners-Lee _____ the Internet?
8 My tooth hurts, so I've got an appointment with the _____.

E Complete the sentences with words formed from the words in bold.

1 A washing machine is _____ because it cleans clothes quickly.   USE
2 The teenage _____ won a prize for her new idea.   INVENT
3 I heard a loud noise and felt a sudden _____ when the earthquake happened.   MOVE
4 Milk doesn't _____ go bad after a day in the fridge.   NORMAL
5 Which _____ invented the toothbrush?   SCIENCE
6 I need something to _____ my pencil.   SHARP
7 We've got a new electric _____ in the kitchen.   COOK
8 The robots were the main _____ at the science exhibition.   ATTRACT

7 Grammar

7.1 Superlative Adjectives

Adjective	Superlative
small	the small**est**
brave	the brav**est**
hot	the ho**ttest**
easy	the eas**iest**
interesting	the **most** interesting
far	the **farthest**
good	the **best**
bad	the **worst**

Χρησιμοποιούμε τον superlative (υπερθετικό βαθμό) για να συγκρίνουμε ένα πρόσωπο ή πράγμα με άλλα ομοειδή πρόσωπα ή πράγματα. Συνήθως σχηματίζουμε τον superlative προσθέτοντας την κατάληξη -*est* στο επίθετο. Αν το επίθετο έχει περισσότερες από δύο συλλαβές, τότε χρησιμοποιούμε τη λέξη *most*. Χρησιμοποιούμε τη λέξη *the* πριν από τον superlative.

→ *February is **the wettest** month of the year.*
→ *The fridge is **the most useful** device in the kitchen.*

7.2 Expressing Purpose

Μπορούμε να χρησιμοποιήσουμε τις ακόλουθες εκφράσεις για να εκφράσουμε σκοπό:
is/are used for ακολουθείται από ένα ρήμα + -*ing*.
is/are used to ακολουθείται από ένα απαρέμφατο.
I/you/we use something to ακολουθείται από ένα απαρέμφατο.

→ *An oven **is used for** baking cakes.*
→ *It's **used to** bake cakes.*
→ *We **use** an oven **to** bake cakes and roast meat or vegetables.*

Σημείωση: Μερικές φορές μπορούμε να παραλείψουμε *is/are used*. Για παράδειγμα:
*It's a machine **for** cooking food.*

7.3 *Will*

Κατάφαση
I/he/she/it/we/you/they **will** go.

Άρνηση
I/he/she/it/we/you/they **will not (won't)** go.

Ερώτηση
Will I/he/she/it/we/you/they go?

Σύντομες απαντήσεις	
Yes, I/he/she/it/we/you/they **will**.	**No**, I/he/she/it/we/you/they **won't**.

Μπορούμε να χρησιμοποιήσουμε *will* για:
προβλέψεις για το μέλλον και για να μιλήσουμε για το τι πιστεύουμε ότι θα συμβεί.

→ *We **will travel** to other planets for holidays.*
→ *I think buses **won't need** a driver.*
→ *It **won't rain** next week.*

Grammar Exercises

A Complete the sentences with the correct superlative form of the adjectives in brackets. Remember to use *the*.

1 Kathy is _____ (young) inventor in the competition.

2 I think the telephone was the _____ (important) invention of the 19th century.

3 This is _____ (good) smartphone in the shop.

4 Which television has got _____ (flat) screen?

5 The North Pole is _____ (far) part of the Earth from the Sun in December.

6 What is _____ (useful) website on the Internet?

7 This solar cooker is _____ (shiny) object in the garden.

8 Which is _____ (bad) ride in the amusement park?

B Circle the correct words.

1 A plane is for **travel / travelling** long distances.

2 You use a dishwasher to **clean / cleaning** the plates.

3 An oven is **use / used** to bake bread.

4 What machine do you use **for / to** washing clothes?

5 We **use / are used** our phones to talk and send messages.

6 This device is used **for / to** charge phones.

7 What is this device used **for / to**?

8 Those machines **use / are used** to transport astronauts into space.

C Complete the sentences with *will* or *won't* and the words in brackets.

1 I think it _____ (be) a good day tomorrow.

2 More people _____ (use) bicycles to travel in cities.

3 The scientist _____ (not attend) the next exhibition.

4 Dogs _____ (not learn) to speak English.

5 Robots _____ (build) better homes for people in the future.

6 _____ (you / be) famous when you're older?

7 In the future, trains _____ (not have) drivers.

8 _____ (we / live) on other planets in 2050?

8 Snap!

8.1   **snap** (excl) /snæp/
sth you say in a card game called 'Snap' when you put down a card the same as the card below or when two things are the same
• *Snap! We're wearing the same shoes.*
➢ snap (v), snap (n) ❖ «σναπ»

8.2   **Buddhist** (adj) /ˈbʊdɪst/
➢ Buddhism, Buddhist (n) ❖ βουδιστής

8.3   **monk** (n) /mʌŋk/
a man in a religious group who lives in a monastery • *When we went to Mystras, one of the monks was lighting candles in the church.*
❖ μοναχός, καλόγερος

8.4   **hide-and-seek** (n) /ˌhaɪd ən ˈsiːk/
a game in which children hide and then one child tries to find them • *Let's play hide-and-seek in the park.* ❖ κρυφτό

8.5   **Cambodia** (n) /kæmˈbəʊdiə/
➢ Cambodian (n, adj) ❖ Καμπότζη

Reading

8.6   **card game** (n) /ˈkaːd ɡeɪm/
a game played with cards • *Walter's favourite card game is Snap.* ❖ παιχνίδι με τράπουλα

8.7   **video game** (n) /ˈvɪdiəʊ ɡeɪm/
a game with pictures that move on a screen when sb presses buttons • *On wet days, I enjoy reading books or playing video games.*
❖ ηλεκτρονικό παιχνίδι

8.8   **rule** (n) /ruːl/
sth that says what sb must do to play or do sth in the correct way • *The rule says you can have an extra turn and move again when you throw a six.* ➢ rule (v) ❖ κανόνας

8.9   **dice** (n) /daɪs/
a small cube with different numbers or spots on each side to use in a game • *She threw the dice and got two sixes.* ➢ dice (v) ❖ ζάρι

8.10   **counter** (n) /ˈkaʊntə(r)/
a piece used for playing in a board game
• *Put all the counters on the first square to start the game.* ➢ count (v) ❖ μάρκα, πούλι (σε παιχνίδι)

8.11   **shuffle** (v) /ˈʃʌfl/
mix up playing cards • *Dan shuffled the cards and gave ten to each person.* ➢ shuffle (n)
❖ ανακατεύω τα χαρτιά

8.12   **playing cards** (n) /ˈpleɪɪŋ kaːdz/
numbered cards used for playing different card games • *I put down all my playing cards and won the game.* ❖ χαρτιά, τράπουλα

8.13   **deal** (v) /diːl/
hand out • *It's my turn to deal the cards.*
➢ deal, dealer (n) ❖ μοιράζω (τα χαρτιά)

8.14   **player** (n) /ˈpleɪə(r)/
sb who is playing a game • *This is a game for two to six players.* ➢ play (v), play (n)
❖ παίχτης

8.15   **ladder** (n) /ˈlædə(r)/
a device made from two long pieces of wood or metal joined together with steps for climbing up or down a wall, etc.• *Lisa climbed up the ladder to paint the wall.* ❖ σκάλα

8.16   **land** (v) /lænd/
arrive somewhere; come down onto the ground • *When you land on a snake, you have to go back to another square.* ➢ landing, land (n) ❖ πέφτω πάνω σε, προσγειώνομαι

8.17   **shout** (v) /ʃaʊt/
say sth very loudly • *James put down his last card and shouted 'Snap!'* ➢ shout (n)
❖ φωνάζω

8.18   **go** (n) /ɡəʊ/
a turn or move in a game • *It's my go now. Where's the dice?* ➢ go (v) ❖ σειρά

8.19   **winner** (n) /ˈwɪnə(r)/
a person, team or animal that wins sth • *Well done! Your team is the winner!* ➢ win (v, n)
❖ νικητής

Word Focus

8.20   **dot** (n) /dɒt/
a small round mark; a symbol like a full stop
• *You have to draw a line to join the dots to make the picture.* ➢ dot (v) ❖ τελεία, βούλα

8.21   **represent** (v) /ˌreprɪˈzent/
be a symbol that means sth • *This chess piece represents the king.* ➢ representative, representation (n) ❖ συμβολίζω

8.22   **vertical** (adj) /ˈvɜːtɪkl/
that is straight up and down • *Sam painted a vertical line up the wall from the bottom to the top.* ➢ vertical (n), vertically (adv) ❖ κάθετος, κατακόρυφος

8.23   **reach** (v) /riːtʃ/
put your hand out far enough to touch sth; arrive at a place • *I can't reach the books on the top shelf. I need a ladder.* ➢ reach (n)
❖ φτάνω

8.24   **pack** (n) /pæk/
a set of playing cards • *There are usually 52 playing cards in a pack.* ➢ pack (v)
❖ τράπουλα

8.25 **competitive** (adj) /kəm'petətɪv/
sb who tries hard to do sth better than others
• *Diane is really competitive and doesn't like losing games.* ➢ compete (v), competition (n)
❖ ανταγωνιστικός

Reading
Pages 96–97

8.26 **electronics** (n) /ɪˌlek'trɒnɪks/
the use of electronic technology, e.g. computers • *Playing outside with a ball is more fun than using electronics all the time.*
❖ ηλεκτρονικά

8.27 **better** (adj) /'betə(r)/
the comparative form of 'good' • *Olga is getting better at swimming.* ❖ καλύτερος

8.28 **remove** (v) /rɪ'muːv/
take sth away from or off sth • *Please remove the game from the table so I can serve dinner.*
➢ removal (n) ❖ αφαιρώ, βγάζω, παίρνω

8.29 **block** (n) /blɒk/
a small square or rectangular piece of wood or plastic used in a game for building, etc.; a piece of square or rectangular used as part of building • *Maggie joined the coloured blocks together to make a castle.* ➢ block (v)
❖ τούβλο, τουβλάκι, κύβος

8.30 **come over** (phr v) /kʌm 'əʊvə(r)/
come to sb's home for a visit • *Come over to my place tonight and we can play some games.* ❖ έρχομαι για επίσκεψη

8.31 **charades** (n) /ʃə'rɑːdz/
a game where players take turns to act out words for others to guess • *Last night we played charades to guess animals. It was very funny.* ❖ παντομίμα

8.32 **mime** (v) /maɪm/
act out words or a story by moving your body without talking • *Jeff flapped his arms and jumped around the room to mime a butterfly.*
➢ mime (n) ❖ μιμούμαι

8.33 **scissors** (n) /'sɪzəz/
sth that has two sharp sides joined together for cutting paper or cloth • *I can't find the scissors to cut my nails.* ❖ ψαλίδι

8.34 **electronic** (adj) /ɪˌlek'trɒnɪk/
with many small parts that use electricity
• *Please switch off all electronic devices in the theatre.* ➢ electronics (n) ❖ ηλεκτρονικός

8.35 **bored** (adj) /bɔːd/
tired and not interested • *This video game isn't very good. I got bored with it after ten minutes.*
➢ bore (v, n), boredom (n), boring (adj)
❖ βαριεστημένος

8.36 **non-** (prefix) /nɒn/
not (before nouns, adjectives, adverbs) • *My sisters prefer playing with non-electronic toys like Lego.* ❖ μη, που δεν έχει/είναι

Vocabulary
Pages 98–99

8.37 **spin** (v) /spɪn/
make sth move round quickly • *Spin the wheel on the board to see which colour to put your arm or leg on.* ➢ spin (n) ❖ περιστρέφω, γυρνάω

8.38 **score** (n) /skɔː(r)/
the total number of points or goals in a game or sport • *Nobody can beat Mum's top score in Scrabble.* ➢ score (v) ❖ σκορ, βαθμολογία

8.39 **roll** (v) /rəʊl/
make sth move or move in a circular movement on a surface • *Julie rolled the ball across the grass to hit the smaller balls.*
➢ roll (n) ❖ ρίχνω, κυλάω, τσουλάω

8.40 **cheat** (v) /tʃiːt/
do sth in a way that is dishonest or not fair to get sth you want • *Don't look at my cards! You're cheating.* ➢ cheat (n) ❖ κλέβω, κάνω ζαβολιά

8.41 **fair** (adj) /feə(r)/
done in a correct way • *That's not fair! It was my turn to play, not yours.* ➢ fairness (n), fairly (adv) ❖ δίκαιος
✏ Opp: unfair ❖ άδικος

8.42 **backwards** (adv) /'bækwədz/
in a direction that goes back to a position you were in before • *The card says you have to move two squares backwards.* ❖ πίσω, όπισθεν

8.43 **second** (det, num) /'sekənd/
the number 2nd ❖ δεύτερος

8.44 **third** (det, num) /θɜːd/
the number 3rd ❖ τρίτος

8.45 **fifth** (det, num) /fɪfθ/
the number 5th ❖ πέμπτος

8.46 **sixth** (det, num) /sɪksθ/
the number 6th ❖ έκτος

8.47 **twelfth** (det, num) /twelfθ/
the number 12th ❖ δωδέκατος

8.48 **twenty first** (det, num) /ˌtwenti 'fɜːst/
the number 21st ❖ εικοστός πρώτος

8.49 **thirty-second** (det, num) /'θɜːti 'sekənd/
the number 32nd ❖ τριακοστός δεύτερος

8.50 **twenty-fifth** (det, num) /ˌtwenti fɪfθ/
the number 25th ❖ εικοστός πέμπτος

8.51 **four hundredth** (det, num) /fɔː 'hʌndrədθ/
the number 400th ❖ τετρακοσιοστός

Numbers

1st	first	10th	tenth
2nd	second	11th	eleventh
3rd	third	12th	twelfth
4th	fourth	20th	twentieth
5th	fifth	21st	twenty-first
6th	sixth	25th	twenty-fifth
7th	seventh	32nd	thirty-second
8th	eighth	400th	four hundredth
9th	ninth		

8.52 **tournament** (n) /'tʊənəmənt/
a competition where sets of games are played until only one winner is left • *Marianna won the tennis tournament after winning all the matches.* ❖ τουρνουά

8.53 **anniversary** (n) /ˌænɪ'vɜːsəri/
the date that is the same as the date an important event happened in the past • *Hazel and Joe are celebrating their tenth wedding anniversary.* ❖ επέτειος

8.54 **wallet** (n) /'wɒlɪt/
a small flat case for carrying money in • *I've got twenty euros in my wallet.* ❖ πορτοφόλι

8.55 **create** (v) /kri'eɪt/
make sth new • *We tried to create two teams to play football, but there weren't enough players.* ➤ creation (n), creative (adj) ❖ δημιουργώ

8.56 **impossible** (adj) /ɪm'pɒsəbl/
not possible • *It's impossible to play this game with only one person.* ➤ (im)possibility (n) ❖ αδύνατος
✎ Opp: possible ❖ δυνατός, πιθανός

8.57 **educational** (adj) /ˌedʒu'keɪʃənl/
sth that sb can learn sth from • *Card games can be educational for children because they practise counting.* ➤ educate (v), education, educator (n) ❖ εκπαιδευτικός

8.58 **teach** (v) /tiːtʃ/
tell or show sb how to do sth • *My grandfather is good at chess and he taught me to play it.* ➤ teacher, teaching (n) ❖ διδάσκω

Grammar   Pages 100–101

8.60 **sequence** (n) /'siːkwəns/
the order that events happen in • *The police officer asked about the sequence of events before the necklace disappeared.* ➤ sequence (v), sequencing (n) ❖ σειρά, ακολουθία

8.61 **until** (conj, prep) /ən'tɪl/
up to a particular time • *They played the game until there were no more letters.* ❖ μέχρι (που)

8.62 **eventually** (adv) /ɪ'ventʃuəli/
after a long time or a sequence of events • *The bus was very late, but it arrived eventually.* ➤ eventual (adj) ❖ τελικά

8.63 **at first** (expr) /ət fɜːst/
at/in the beginning • *At first, nobody wanted to play, but then everybody joined in.* ❖ στην αρχή

8.64 **on my own** (expr) /ɒn maɪ əʊn/
by myself; alone; without help from anybody • *When my parents can't drive me home, I cycle back from school on my own.* ❖ μόνος μου

8.65 **hero** (n) /'hɪərəʊ/
sb who does sth very good or brave • *Mario wants to become a football hero like Ronaldo.* ➤ heroic (adj) ❖ ήρωας

8.66 **power** (n) /'paʊə(r)/
ability to do sth • *When you get a high score, you get more power to stay in the game longer.* ➤ powerful (adj) ❖ δύναμη

8.67 **tidy** (v) /'taɪdi/
clear up and put things in their correct place • *My friends are coming over, so I'm tidying the house.* ➤ tidy (adj), tidily (adv) ❖ τακτοποιώ, συμμαζεύω

8.68 **uniform** (n) /'juːnɪfɔːm/
clothes sb wears to show they belong to a particular job or group • *Nurses in this hospital have to wear a blue uniform.* ❖ στολή

8.69 **booklet** (n) /'bʊklət/
a small book with information about sth • *Read the instruction booklet to see how to put the cupboard together.* ❖ φυλλάδιο

8.70 **replace** (v) /rɪ'pleɪs/
put sth/sb in the place of sth/sb else • *She took the four houses off the Monopoly board and replaced them with a hotel.* ➤ replacement (n) ❖ αντικαθιστώ, αλλάζω

8.71 **option** (n) /'ɒpʃn/
sth you can choose to do • *Kostas lost the game when there were no other options for him to move on the chess board.* ➤ opt (v), optional (adj) ❖ επιλογή

8.72 **continue** (v) /kən'tɪnjuː/
keep on doing sth; go on • *Our game of Monopoly continued for two days until my brother won.* ➤ continuous, continual (adj), continuously, continually (adv) ❖ συνεχίζω

8.73 **point** (n) /pɔɪnt/
a mark or unit that sb scores or wins in a game • *Jackie got extra points for putting her letters on the pink squares in Scrabble.* ➤ point (v) ❖ πόντος

8.74 **diagonally** (adv) /daɪ'æɡənəli/
in a way that makes a sloping line • *The path goes diagonally across the field.* ➤ diagonal (n, adj) ❖ διαγώνια

8.75 **vertically** (adv) /ˈvɜːtɪkli/
straight up and down • *Alice put the word on the board vertically from the top line to the middle line.* ➤ vertical (n, adj) ❖ κάθετα, κατακόρυφα
✎ Opp: horizontally ❖ οριζόντια

8.76 **horizontally** (adv) /ˌhɒrɪˈzɒntəli/
flat and parallel to the ground and not up and down • *I dealt the cards horizontally in a line across the table.* ➤ horizon (n), horizontal (adj) ❖ οριζόντια
✎ Opp: vertically ❖ κάθετα, κατακόρυφα

Listening   Page 102

8.77 **Battleships™** (n) /ˈbætlʃɪps/
❖ το επιτραπέζιο παιχνίδι Ναυμαχία

8.78 **table tennis** (n) /ˈteɪbl tenɪs/
a game like tennis played on a table with a small net across the middle • *I often play table tennis in the sports club.* ❖ πινγκ πονγκ

8.79 **parcel** (n) /ˈpɑːsl/
sth in a packet to send by post or to give as a present • *It is Tina's birthday and she's opening a big parcel from her grandparents.* ➤ parcel (v) ❖ δέμα

8.80 **Sardines** (n) /ˌsɑːˈdiːnz/
a game like hide-and-seek where as many people as possible try to hide together in a small space • *The children played Sardines at the party and there were five people in the wardrobe in the end.* ❖ το παιχνίδι σαρδέλες
✎ sardine = a small fish ❖ σαρδέλα

8.81 **trumps** (n) /trʌmps/
the set of winning cards in a game • *Hearts are trumps for this game.* ➤ trump (v), trump (adj) ❖ ατού (τραπουλόχαρτο που συμβατικά νικάει τα άλλα)

8.82 **Trivial Pursuit™** (n) /ˈtrɪviəl pəˈsjuːt/
❖ το επιτραπέζιο παιχνίδι Trivial Pursuit™

8.83 **toy shop** (n) /ˈtɔɪ ʃɒp/
a shop that sells toys • *I'm going to the toy shop to buy a present for my little cousin.* ❖ παιχνιδοπωλείο

Speaking   Page 103

8.101 **zumba** (n) /ˈzʊmbə/
a type of aerobics mixed with Latin dancing steps • *Dancing to the music makes zumba classes more fun than basic aerobics.* ❖ ζούμπα

8.84 **geography** (n) /dʒiˈɒɡrəfi/
the study of the world's land, sea, countries, population, etc. • *Our geography teacher is teaching us about how rivers are made.* ➤ geographic (adj) ❖ γεωγραφία

8.85 **entertainment** (n) /ˌentəˈteɪnmənt/
activities or performances for people to have fun • *What do you do for entertainment? Do you go to the cinema?* ➤ entertain (v), entertainer (n), entertaining (adj) ❖ ψυχαγωγία

8.86 **history** (n) /ˈhɪstri/
the study of the events that happened in the past • *My favourite period of history is the Golden Century of ancient Greece.* ➤ historian (n), historic, historical (adj) ❖ ιστορία

8.87 **literature** (n) /ˈlɪtrətʃə(r)/
the study of books, poems and plays that are important pieces of writing • *John studies literature and he wants to write children's stories.* ➤ literate, literary (adj) ❖ φιλολογία

8.88 **nature** (n) /ˈneɪtʃə(r)/
all the things that are natural and not made by people • *We moved to the country to live closer to nature.* ➤ natural (adj), naturally (adv) ❖ φύση

8.89 **leisure** (n) /ˈleʒə(r)/
the time sb spends when they are not studying or working • *Stephanie works a lot and she hasn't got much leisure time.* ➤ leisurely (adj) ❖ αναψυχή
✎ Syn: free time

8.90 **runner** (n) /ˈrʌnə(r)/
sb who runs in a race or goes running as a hobby • *We saw the first runners arriving at the end of the race.* ➤ run (v, n), running (n) ❖ δρομέας

8.91 **general** (adj) /ˈdʒenrəl/
usual; not specific; about many different subjects • *This film is of general interest to teenagers.* ➤ generalise (v), generally (adv) ❖ γενικός

Writing   Pages 104–105

8.92 **experiment** (n) /ɪkˈsperɪmənt/
a scientific test to see what sth does • *Penny did an experiment with salt and water in the science class.* ➤ experiment (v), experimental (adj) ❖ πείραμα

8.93 **guess** (v) /ɡes/
say what you think sth is without knowing all the facts • *When it was my turn, I guessed the right answer.* ➤ guess (n) ❖ μαντεύω

8.94 **correctly** (adj) /kəˈrektli/
in the correct way • *Did you spell that word correctly?* ➤ correct (v, adj), correction (n) ❖ σωστά
✎ Opp: incorrectly ❖ λάθος, λανθασμένα

8.95 **divide** (v) /dɪˈvaɪd/
break sth into parts to share between people • *I divided the cake into pieces to give some to everybody.* ➤ division (n) ❖ χωρίζω

8.96 **musical chairs** (n) /ˌmjuːzɪkl ˈtʃeəz/
a party game in which children run round
to music and sit on a chair when the music
stops, but there are never enough chairs for all
players • *The children played musical chairs
until there was only one chair left to sit on.*
❖ το παχνίδι «μουσικές καρέκλες»

8.97 **artist** (n) /ˈɑːtɪst/
a person who does painting, drawing or other
kinds of art • *Picasso was a great artist.*
➢ art (n), artistic (adj) ❖ καλλιτέχνης

Video 8
Testing!   **Page 106**

8.98 **test** (v) /test/
do experiments on sth to see if it is safe or
works well • *They're testing the toys to make
sure the material is safe for babies.* ➢ test (n)
❖ ελέγχω, εξετάζω

8.99 **teddy bear** (n) /ˈtedi beə(r)/
a toy bear • *Mum has got her old teddy bear
from when she was a baby.* ❖ αρκουδάκι

8.100 **train set** (n) /ˈtreɪn ˌset/
a toy train that moves along small tracks • *The
children had fun playing with the train set on
the floor for hours.* ❖ σετ τρενάκι με ράγες

8.101 **marble** (n) /ˈmɑːbl/
a small coloured glass ball used for children's
games • *Vincent rolled the marble across the
floor and it went under the sofa.* ❖ μπίλια

8.102 **expert** (n) /ˈekspɜːt/
a person who knows a lot about sth or can do
sth very well • *You're an expert at literature.
So who wrote The BFG?* ➢ expert (adj)
❖ ειδικός

8.103 **drop** (v) /drɒp/
let/make sth fall down • *Be careful! Don't drop
that toy box.* ➢ drop (n) ❖ ρίχνω, αφήνω να
πέσει

8.104 **burn** (v) /bɜːn/
make sth go on fire • *We called the firefighters
when the building started to burn.* ➢ burn (n),
burnt (adj) ❖ καίω, καίγομαι

8.105 **stuffing** (n) /ˈstʌfɪŋ/
the material put inside to fill sth • *The stuffing
is starting to come out of my old toy dog.*
➢ stuff (v), stuffed (adj) ❖ γέμισμα

8.106 **break** (v) /breɪk/
lose a part or stop working; damage sth so it
stops working or parts come off it • *The toy
train broke when I dropped it.* ➢ break (n),
broken (adj) ❖ σπάω, χαλάω

8.107 **coordinate** (v) /kəʊˈɔːdɪneɪt/
make the parts of your body work together
• *The toy helps babies to coordinate their
hand movements with what they see.*
➢ coordination (n) ❖ συντονίζω

8.108 **fall** (v) /fɔːl/
drop down; drop off sth • *The robot's arms fell
off.* ➢ fall (n) ❖ πέφτω

8.109 **easily** (adv) /ˈiːzəli/
without any problem • *We won the game
easily.* ➢ ease (n), easy (adj) ❖ εύκολα

8.110 **soft toy** (n) /ˌsɔːft ˈtɔɪ/
a toy often shaped like an animal with soft
stuffing • *Karen's room is full of soft toys and
board games.* ❖ χνουδωτό, μαλακό παιχνίδι

8.111 **run away** (phr v) /rʌn əˈweɪ/
escape; get away • *The rabbit ran away when
it saw us.* ➢ runaway (n, adj) ❖ το σκάω,
δραπατεύω

Vocabulary Exercises

A Match to make compound nouns.

1	teddy	☐	a	tennis
2	train	☐	b	game
3	table	☐	c	cards
4	musical	☐	d	set
5	playing	☐	e	bear
6	video	☐	f	chairs

B Complete the sentences with the words from A.

1 Bob built the track for his ＿＿＿＿＿ ＿＿＿＿＿ all around his bedroom floor.
2 Ten of the ＿＿＿＿＿ ＿＿＿＿＿ are missing. There are only 42 here, so we can't play the game.
3 Lee hit the ball over the net and won the last match in the ＿＿＿＿＿ ＿＿＿＿＿ tournament.
4 My baby brother takes his ＿＿＿＿＿ ＿＿＿＿＿ to bed at night.
5 We laughed a lot running round the room and playing ＿＿＿＿＿ ＿＿＿＿＿ at the party.
6 Don't sit in front of the screen playing that ＿＿＿＿＿ ＿＿＿＿＿ all day.

C Circle the correct words.

1 If you land on a **ladder** / **winner**, you can move forward on the board.
2 It isn't fair to **cheat** / **deal** in any game.
3 She **landed** / **rolled** the dice and got two sixes.
4 Make sure you **shuffle** / **tidy** the cards to mix them well before you begin the game.
5 Duncan mimed the word 'robot' when we played **electronics** / **charades** at the party.
6 Hilda is good at spelling and she always gets a high **score** / **block** at *Scrabble*.
7 I asked my friends to **come over** / **run away** to my house this evening to play cards.
8 Did you **spin** / **guess** all the answers on your own? Or did you find them on the Internet?

D Write the numbers in words.

1 2nd   ＿＿＿＿＿＿＿
2 5th   ＿＿＿＿＿＿＿
3 8th   ＿＿＿＿＿＿＿
4 21st   ＿＿＿＿＿＿＿
5 12th   ＿＿＿＿＿＿＿
6 500th ＿＿＿＿＿＿＿
7 3rd   ＿＿＿＿＿＿＿
8 32nd   ＿＿＿＿＿＿＿

E **Find the six quiz subjects. Then match them to the questions below.**

G	E	O	L	T	U	R	L	O	L	Y	T	L
E	N	T	E	N	L	G	O	L	A	N	A	I
I	P	O	I	I	E	E	R	E	P	A	I	T
T	H	R	S	T	I	O	Y	I	H	T	N	E
E	O	Y	U	E	S	G	E	N	T	U	M	R
R	G	E	R	R	O	R	Y	R	A	R	T	A
E	N	T	E	R	T	A	I	N	M	E	N	T
A	I	N	M	E	G	P	E	N	T	K	N	U
Y	P	H	I	S	T	H	A	I	N	M	A	R
H	I	S	T	O	R	Y	F	K	E	N	T	E

1   When was the battle of Marathon? _____
2   Where is the natural habitat of polar bears? _____
3   Is the museum far from here? _____
4   What's the capital city of France? _____
5   Who wrote *Treasure Island*? _____
6   Which actor played Spiderman? _____

8 Grammar

8.1 Zero Conditional

If clause	Main clause
Present Simple	Present Simple

Χρησιμοποιούμε Zero Conditional για να μιλήσουμε για πραγματικές ή αληθινές καταστάσεις στο παρόν.
➔ *If you run in the marathon, you **get** a special T-shirt.*
Μπορούμε να χρησιμοποιήσουμε το *when* αντί για το *if* για να μιλήσουμε για πράγματα ή καταστάσεις που είναι πιο βέβαιες.
➔ *When we **play** charades, we **have** lots of fun.*

Σημείωση: Όταν το *if* και το *when* μπαίνουν στην αρχή μιας πρότασης, ένα κόμμα διαχωρίζει τα δύο μέρη.
Μπορούμε όμως να βάλουμε την υπόθεση με το *if* ή το *when* δεύτερη, δηλαδή να πούμε:
*We have lots of fun **when** we play charades.*
Σε αυτήν την περίπτωση, το κόμμα δεν χρειάζεται.

8.2 Sequencing

Υπάρχουν πολλά επιρρήματα και εκφράσεις που μας βοηθούν για να ταξινομήσουμε και να δείξουμε την σειρά των γεγονότων. Επιρρήματα όπως *after, before* και *while* μπορούν να προηγηθούν του υποκειμένου + του ρήματος ή του ρήματος + *-ing*.
➔ ***Before I go** to school, I have breakfast.*
➔ ***After packing** my school bag, I go to school.*

Επίσης μπορούμε να χρησιμοποιήσουμε *as soon as, until, eventually, in the end.*
➔ *The students sit down **as soon as** the teacher arrives.*
➔ *You can't go out **until** you finish your homework.*
➔ ***Eventually**, the bus arrived after 45 minutes!*
➔ *I wanted to play video games, but **in the end** I went to the park.*

8.3 *Must*

Χρησιμοποιούμε *must* + bare infinitive (γυμνό απαρέμφατο) για να:
πούμε ότι κάτι είναι απαραίτητο.
➔ *You **must have** at least two people to play this game.*
μιλήσουμε για υποχρεώσεις.
➔ *I **must do** my homework before I go out.*

8.4 *Mustn't*

Χρησιμοποιούμε *mustn't* + bare infinitive (γυμνό απαρέμφατο) για να μιλήσουμε για κάτι που δεν επιτρέπεται.
➔ *You **mustn't look** at the other players' cards.*

8.5 *Have To*

Χρησιμοποιούμε *have to* για να:
πούμε ότι κάτι είναι απαραίτητο.
➔ *You **have to take** another card if you can't move.*
μιλήσουμε για υποχρέωση.
➔ *I **have to help** my little brother to play the game.*

8.6 *Mustn't & Don't Have To*

Υπάρχει μια σημαντική διαφορά ανάμεσα στο *mustn't* και στο *don't have to*.
Χρησιμοποιούμε *mustn't* για να δείξουμε ότι κάτι δεν επιτρέπεται και χρησιμοποιούμε *don't have to* για να δείξουμε ότι δεν υπάρχει υποχρέωση.
➔ *You **mustn't** make a noise in the library.*
➔ *We **don't have to** cook today. We can go to a restaurant.*

8 Grammar

8.7 Can & Can't

Χρησιμοποιούμε *can* και *can't* + infinitive (απαρέμφατο) για να:
μιλήσουμε για δυνατότητα.

→ She **can climb** the hill easily.

→ They **can't speak** French very well.

ζητήσουμε άδεια.

→ **Can** I **play** a game on your laptop?

→ Yes, you **can play** for half an hour.

→ No, you **can't play** with my laptop. I need it for work.

Grammar Exercises

A Match to make sentences.

1	If you throw a six, ☐	**a** but in the end we played *Monopoly*.
2	After losing all his money, ☐	**b** you get an extra go.
3	You lose a turn ☐	**c** if you read the instructions.
4	We wanted to go for a walk, ☐	**d** give each player seven cards.
5	Before starting the game, ☐	**e** until we got bored with it.
6	When you're on your own, ☐	**f** when you land on a red square.
7	The game is easy ☐	**g** he sold all his houses and hotels.
8	We played the board game for hours ☐	**h** you can play this video game.

B Choose the correct answers (A, B or C).

1 ___ we go to bed, let's play one more game of *Scrabble*.

   A Before   **B** When   **C** While

2 I ___ play this game on my own. It needs two players.

   A can   **B** can't   **C** don't have to

3 You ___ clean your bike. It's really dirty!

   A have to   **B** can't   **C** mustn't

4 Players ___ choose any colour they like to answer a question.

   A have to   **B** can   **C** must

5 ___, there were no more letters in the bag and we counted our scores.

   A After   **B** Until   **C** Eventually

6 As soon ___ the pizza comes, we can stop for a break.

   A as   **B** if   **C** when

7 Let's wait ___ our friends arrive and then start the game.

   A after   **B** until   **C** eventually

8 My aunt ___ wear a uniform at work. She's a police officer.

   A can   **B** must   **C** has

C Complete the sentences with *must, mustn't, don't have to* or *doesn't have to*.

1 You _____ leave litter in the park.
2 Jane _____ tidy the kitchen tonight. She can do it tomorrow.
3 We _____ play an electronic game – we can play cards instead.
4 I _____ leave now, or I'll miss my bus.
5 Players _____ pass 'Go' to collect more money.
6 The block _____ be yellow – you can use any colour.
7 My parents _____ go to work tomorrow, so we're going on a trip.
8 I _____ forget to order the food for the games night.

9 In The Extreme!

Page 109

9.1 **in the extreme** (expr) /ɪn ðə ɪkˈstriːm/
much more than normal • *Some outdoor sports are dangerous in the extreme.*
➢ extreme (adj), extremely (adv) ❖ ακραία
✎ Syn: extremely

9.2 **geologist** (n) /dʒiˈɒlədʒɪst/
a person who studies geology • *Geologists are trying to find better ways to measure earthquakes.* ➢ geology (n), geological (ad)
❖ γεωλόγος

9.3 **take care** (expr) /teɪk kɜː(r)/
be careful • *Take care so you don't fall off the banana boat.* ❖ προσέχω

9.4 **volcano** (n) /vɒlˈkeɪnəʊ/
a mountain that has (or had) hot gases and hot melted rocks coming out of a hole on its top
• *Greece has many live volcanoes, for example, Santorini and Methana.*
➢ volcanic (adj) ❖ ηφαίστειο

9.5 **edge** (n) /edʒ/
the top of the outside part of sth
• *Don't stand so close to the edge of the cliff.*
❖ άκρη, χείλος

9.6 **Hawaii** (n) /həˈwaɪˌiː/
➢ Hawaiian (n, adj) ❖ Χαβάη

Reading
Page 110

9.7 **kitesurfing** (n) /ˈkaɪtsɜːfɪŋ/
the sport of riding on a board on water and holding a large kite that gets pushed by the wind • *A large wave hit the kitesurfer and he fell into the sea.* ➢ kitesurf (v), kitesurfer (n)
❖ κάιτ σερφ

9.8 **banana boat** (n) /bəˈnɑːnə bəʊt/
a small rubber boat shaped like a large banana filled with air • *I fell off the banana boat into the sea.* ❖ φουσκωτή μπανάνα (παιχνίδι θαλάσσης)

9.9 **soapbox racing** (n) /ˈsəʊpbɒks/
the sport of racing in homemade racing carts
• *Ben goes soapbox racing at weekends. He loves racing down hills.* ❖ αγώνας με χειροποίητο κάρο

9.10 **paragliding** (n) /ˈpærəɡlaɪdɪŋ/
a sport in which you jump from a high place with a kind of parachute you can stear until you reach the ground • *We saw people paragliding from the top of the mountain down to a field below.* ➢ paraglide (v), paraglider (n)
❖ αλεξίπτωτο πλαγιάς

9.11 **extreme** (adj) /ɪkˈstriːm/
much more than normal • *Frank is scared to do extreme sports like kitesurfing.*
➢ extreme (n), extremely ❖ ακραίος

9.12 **frightening** (adj) /ˈfraɪtnɪŋ/
sb/sth that makes you afraid • *It was very frightening when we got lost in the snow.*
➢ frighten (v), fright (n), frightened (adj), frighteningly (adv) ❖ τρομακτικός

9.13 **careful** (adj) /ˈkeəfl/
taking care not to get hurt or damage sth
• *Be careful when you go climbing.* ➢ care (v), care (n), carefully (adv) ❖ προσεκτικός

9.14 **exhausting** (adj) /ɪɡˈzɔːstɪŋ/
very tiring; making you very tired • *Walking in thick snow is really exhausting.* ➢ exhaust (v), exhaustion (n), exhausted (adj)
❖ εξαντλητικός, κοπιαστικός, επίπονος

9.15 **blog** (n) /blɒɡ/
a piece of writing on a website about events, opinions, etc. • *Did you read Ed's blog about his trip to China?* ➢ blog (v), blogger (n)
❖ μπλογκ

9.16 **article** (n) /ˈɑːtɪkl/
a piece of writing about sth in a newspaper or magazine, etc. • *This website has an interesting article about scuba diving.* ❖ άρθρο

Word Focus
Page 110

9.17 **compete** (v) /kəmˈpiːt/
take part in a competition or sport • *Hundreds of runners compete in the marathon every year.* ➢ competitor (n), competition (n), competitive (adj), competitively (adv)
❖ διαγωνίζομαι, ανταγωνίζομαι

9.18 **glide** (v) /ɡlaɪd/
move easily through the air without moving wings; move easily and quietly • *The paragliders jumped off the cliff and glided down to the beach.* ➢ gliding, glider (n)
❖ πετάω ή κινούμαι με ευχέρεια

9.19 **slope** (n) /sləʊp/
an area of land on the side of a hill or mountain • *They skied down the slope of the mountain.* ➢ slope (v) ❖ πλαγιά

9.20 **gentle** (adj) /ˈdʒentl/
not extreme; quiet and kind • *There was a gentle wind blowing that kept us cool.*
➢ gentleness (n), gently (adv) ❖ απαλός

9.21 **give up** (phr v) /ɡɪv ʌp/
stop trying or doing sth; decide to stop • *The rescue team gave up and stopped looking for the lost climbers.* ❖ παρατώ, εγκαταλείπω

9.22   **decide** (v) /dɪˈsaɪd/
think about different options and choose one
● *Heather decided not to go sailing because of the weather.* ➣ decision (n), decisive (adj), decisively (adv) ❖ αποφασίζω

9.23   **paralysed** (adj) /ˈpærəlaɪzd/
not able to move your body or part of it ● *I was so scared that I felt paralysed before I jumped.* ➣ paralyse (v), paralysis (n) ❖ παράλυτος

Reading   Pages 110–111

9.24   **post** (v) /pəʊst/
put a piece of writing or a picture on a website ● *George posted photos of the racing team on the website.* ➣ post (n) ❖ ποστάρω, αναρτώ, δημοσιεύω

9.25   **snowboard** (n) /ˈsnəʊbɔːd/
the sport/activity of riding a board on snow down a hill; a board used for snowboarding ● *You can do snowboard lessons at the ski centre.* ➣ snowboard (v), snowboarding, snowboarder (n) ❖ σανίδα σνόουμπορντ

9.26   **wingsuit** (n) /ˈwɪŋsuːt/
a kind of skydiving suit with material between the arms to make it easier to fly slowly ● *Jill looked like a giant bird as she flew down the hill in her wingsuit.* ❖ στολή με φτερά, wingsuit

9.27   **take off** (phr v) /teɪk ɒf/
leave the ground (for planes, etc.) ● *The plane took off and flew up into the clouds.* ➣ take-off (n) ❖ απογειώνομαι

9.28   **quietly** (adv) /ˈkwaɪətli/
in a quiet way; without making any or much noise ● *Colin sat quietly taking photos of the birds.* ➣ quiet (n, adj) ❖ ήσυχα, αθόρυβα, σιγά

9.29   **landing** (n) /ˈlændɪŋ/
the act of bring a plane, etc., down onto the ground after flying ● *The helicopter made a perfect landing on top of the building.* ➣ land (v) ❖ προσγείωση

9.30   **be worth** (expr) /bi wɜːθ/
be useful enough to do; have a value ● *The trip cost a lot of money, but it was worth it.* ❖ αξίζω, αξίζει τον κόπο

9.31   **derby** (n) /ˈdɑːbi/
a competition between teams or players from the same place ● *They watched the derby match between Olympiakos and AEK.* ❖ αγώνας ντέρμπι

9.32   **come along** (phr v) /kʌm əˈlɒŋ/
go somewhere with sb ● *We're going to watch the soapbox race. Do you want to come along?* ❖ έρχομαι μαζί

9.33   **motor** (n) /ˈməʊtə(r)/
a machine that makes sth work ● *Mike turned on the motor and the boat started to move.* ➣ motor (v), motor (adj) ❖ κινητήρας

9.34   **bend** (n) /bend/
a turn on a road ● *Slow down when you drive round the bend.* ➣ bend (v) ❖ στροφή

9.35   **racer** (n) /ˈreɪsə(r)/
a person or animal taking part in a race ● *She is a famous ski racer.* ➣ race (v, n) ❖ οδηγός αγώνων ταχύτητας, δρομέας

9.36   **time** (v) /taɪm/
check/count how much time sb takes to do sth ● *I timed myself running home across the park and it took me sixteen minutes.* ➣ timer, timing, time (n) ❖ χρονομετρώ

9.37   **kit** (n) /kɪt/
a set of parts that you need to make sth; a set of equipment needed for sth ● *Linda followed the intructions to make the model ship from a kit.* ❖ κιτ, σετ, εξοπλισμός

9.38   **book** (v) /bʊk/
ask sb to keep sth for you to use later ● *Richard booked his ticket for the plane to Geneva.* ➣ booking (n) ❖ κλείνω (τραπέζι, δωμάτιο, κλπ.), κάνω κράτηση

9.39   **hand cycling** (n) /hænd ˈsaɪklɪŋ/
a sport in which you make a bike move with your hands instead of your legs ● *Hand cycling is a great sport for people who can't use their legs.* ❖ χειροκίνητη ποδηλασία

9.40   **dizzy** (adj) /ˈdɪzi/
feeling like everything is spinning around you as if you're going to fall ● *Going up a ladder makes me feel dizzy.* ➣ dizziness (n) ❖ ζαλισμένος

9.41   **carousel** (n) /ˌkærəˈsel/
a round platform with places for children to sit on that spins around, usually in a playground or amusement park ● *The children enjoyed their ride on the carousel at the fair.* ❖ καρουζέλ
✎ Syn: merry-go-round, roundabout

9.42   **Mozambique** (n) /ˌməʊzæmˈbiːk/
➣ Mozambican (n, adj) ❖ Μοζαμβίκη

9.43   **offer** (n) /ˈɒfə(r)/
sth sb says they will give or do ● *The hotel has a special offer of three nights for the price of two.* ➣ offer (v) ❖ προσφορά

9.44   **sportswoman** (n) /ˈspɔːtswʊmən/
a woman who plays a sport ● *Nadia was the youngest sportswoman representing her country in the Olympics.* ❖ αθλήτρια
✎ Also: sportsman, sportsperson

9.45   **determination** (n) /dɪˌtɜːmɪˈneɪʃn/
the power to continue doing sth very difficult without giving up ● *The survivors kept walking with determination until they found help.* ➣ determine (v), determined (adj) ❖ αποφασιστικότητα

9.46 **medal** (n) /ˈmedl/
a flat piece of metal that sb gets as a prize for winning sth or doing sth very brave • *David won a gold medal for swimming in the national competition.* ❖ μετάλλιο

9.47 **chest** (n) /tʃest/
the top of the front part of your body • *The marathon runners all wore numbers on their chests.* ❖ στήθος

9.48 **carry on** (phr v) /ˈkæri ɒn/
continue doing sth; continue moving • *Liz carried on driving until she found a good place for a picnic.* ❖ συνεχίζω

9.49 **take up** (phr v) /teɪk ʌp/
start doing sth new, e.g. a hobby or sport • *Millie is always out at weekends because she's taken up cycling.* ❖ ξεκινώ κάτι καινούργιο (π.χ. χόμπι ή άθλημα)

9.50 **sensation** (n) /senˈseɪʃn/
a feeling • *I had a sharp sensation in my wrist and I knew it was broken.* ➢ sense (v) ❖ αίσθηση

9.51 **dream** (n) /driːm/
sth you want to do, be or have in the future • *His dream is to climb Mount Everest one day.* ➢ dream (v), dreamer (n) ❖ όνειρο, όραμα

9.52 **come true** (exp) /kʌm truː/
really happen • *Her dream to take part in the Olympics came true in 2016.* ❖ πραγματοποιώ, γίνεται πραγματικότητα

Phrasal Verbs & Expressions

be worth	in the extreme
carry on	take care
come along	take off
dream come true	take up
give up	

Vocabulary   Pages 112–113

9.53 **equipment** (n) /ɪˈkwɪpmənt/
the things you need to do a job or an activity • *You don't need any special equipment on the trip. Just wear comfortable clothes and shoes.* ❖ εξοπλισμός

9.54 **skydiving** (n) /ˈskaɪdaɪvɪŋ/
a sport in which sb jumps out of a plane and falls without opening a parachute for as long as possible • *Jumping out of a plane to do skydiving is exciting, but it's very dangerous.* ➢ skydive (v), skydiver (n) ❖ ελεύθερη πτώση με αλεξίπτωτο

9.55 **scuba diving** (n) /ˈskuːbə ˈdaɪvɪŋ/
swimming underwater using a container of air that you have on your back and a tube that you use to breathe • *My dream is to go scuba diving in the Caribbean Sea.* ❖ αυτόνομη κατάδυση (με φιάλη οξυγόνου)

9.56 **wetsuit** (n) /ˈwetsuːt/
an item of waterproof clothing made of rubber that fits over the whole body • *Lazaros wears his wetsuit to swim in the sea when it's cold in winter.* ❖ στολή κατάδυσης, αδιάβροχη στολή

9.57 **flipper** (n) /ˈflɪpə(r)/
a kind of rubber shoe with a long flat part that helps sb swim quickly • *I can't swim fast today because I don't have my flippers.* ❖ βατραχοπέδιλο

9.58 **ski** (n) /skiː/
a long thin board that you wear on your boot to move across snow • *You can hire skis at the winter sports centre.* ➢ ski (v), skiing, skier (n) ❖ πέδιλο του σκι, χιονοπέδιλο

9.59 **goggles** (n) /ˈgɒglz/
special glasses to cover your eyes for sports in the snow or swimming • *I don't like swimming in the pool without my goggles because the water gets in my eyes.* ❖ γυαλιά κολύμβησης/σκι, προστατευτικά γυαλάκια

9.60 **board** (n) /bɔːd/
a long thin piece of hard material used in sports like surfing. • *This board is made of wood and I use it for surfing.* ❖ σανίδα

9.61 **swimwear** (n) /ˈswɪmweə(r)/
the clothes you wear to go swimming • *This website sells bikinis and other swimwear.* ❖ μαγιό

9.62 **knee** (n) /niː/
the joint between the top and bottom parts of the leg • *Vanessa hurt her knee when she fell and she can't walk easily.* ❖ γόνατο

9.63 **knee pad** (n) /niː pæd/
protective clothing for knees • *Skateboarders should wear knee pads to protect them when they fall.* ❖ επιγονατίδα

9.64 **elbow** (n) /ˈelbəʊ/
the middle joint of your arm that connects the top and lower part • *I hit my elbow on the door as I went out.* ❖ αγκώνας

9.65 **elbow pad** (n) /ˈelbəʊ pæd/
a piece of hard material (e.g. plastic or rubber) that you wear on your arm to protect your elbow • *The biker didn't break his arm because he was wearing elbow pads.* ❖ περιαγκωνίδα, προστατευτικό αγκώνα

9.66 **ice axe** (n) /ˈaɪs aks/
a tool for climbers to cut steps in ice • *The explorers used ice axes to make holes in the ice.* ❖ πιολέ, ορειβατική σκαπάνη

9.67 **crampon** (n) /ˈkræmpɒn/
a metal plate with sharp points that climbers can put on their boots to walk on ice • *The walkers slid and fell on the icy slope because they didn't have crampons on their shoes.*
❖ καρφί (για ορειβατικές μπότες)

9.68 **parachute** (n) /ˈpærəʃuːt/
a large piece of cloth that opens to form an umbrella shape held by sb when they jump out of a plane to make them fall to the ground slowly • *She jumped out of the plane and soon her parachute opened.* ➢ parachute (v), parachutist (n) ❖ αλεξίπτωτο

Equipment

board	kit	snowboard
crampon	knee pad	swimwear
elbow pad	map	trapeze
flipper	motor	wetsuit
glove	parachute	wingsuit
goggles	rope	
ice axe	ski	

9.69 **earth** (n) /ɜːθ/
the planet Earth; the ground • *The earth goes round the sun.* ❖ Γη
✎ Also: Earth

9.70 **joint** (n) /dʒɔɪnt/
a part of the body that connects two bones • *My joints hurt the day after I ran in the race.* ➢ join (v) ❖ άρθρωση

9.71 **wave** (n) /weɪv/
a large mass of water flowing, e.g. in the sea • *Suddenly, a big wave hit the side of the boat.* ➢ wave (v) ❖ κύμα

9.72 **skydiver** (n) /ˈskaɪdaɪvə(r)/
sb who does skydiving • *No, it isn't a giant bird. It's a skydiver!* ➢ skydive (v), skydiving (n) ❖ αλεξιπτωτιστής

9.73 **frightened** (adj) /ˈfraɪtnd/
feeling scared • *Are you frightened of walking in the dark?* ➢ frighten (v), fright (n), frightening (adj) ❖ φοβισμένος, τρομαγμένος

9.74 **disappointed** (adj) /ˌdɪsəˈpɔɪntɪd/
unhappy when sth doesn't go as well as you wanted it to • *Sally felt disappointed that there were no tickets left for the show.* ➢ disappoint (v), disappointing (adj), disappointment (n) ❖ απογοητευμένος

9.75 **disappointing** (adj) /ˌdɪsəˈpɔɪntɪŋ/
not as good as you thought sth would be • *The skiing course was disappointing. I didn't learn very much.* ➢ disappoint (v), disappointed (adj), disappointment (n) ❖ απογοητευτικός

9.76 **brave** (adj) /breɪv/
not afraid to do sth • *I'm not brave enough to jump out of a plane.* ➢ bravely (adv) ❖ θαρραλέος, γενναίος

9.77 **bravely** (adv) /ˈbreɪvli/
in a brave way • *Ahmed bravely dived into the sea and saved the child.* ➢ brave (adj) ❖ θαρραλέα, γενναία

9.78 **noisily** (adv) /ˈnɔɪzɪli/
in a noisy way • *The cars raced noisily round the track.* ➢ noise (n), noisy (adj) ❖ με θόρυβο

9.79 **dangerously** (adv) /ˈdeɪndʒərəsli/
in a dangerous way • *They surfed dangerously close to the rocks.* ➢ endanger (v), danger (n), dangerous (adj) ❖ επικίνδυνα

9.80 **diver** (n) /ˈdaɪvə(r)/
sb who works underwater, usually with special equipment; sb who dives for fun or sport • *The diver took photos of strange fish at the bottom of the sea.* ➢ dive (v, n) ❖ δύτης

9.81 **slowly** (adj) /ˈsləʊli/
not quickly; at a slow speed • *Luke skated slowly on the ice at first.* ➢ slow (v), slow (adj) ❖ σιγά, αργά

9.82 **coral** (n) /ˈkɒrəl/
a hard red, pink or white substance that forms on the bottom of the sea from the bones of very small animals • *The pink rocks we saw in the sea were actually coral.* ➢ coral (adj) ❖ κοράλλι

9.83 **skier** (n) /ˈskiːə(r)/
a person who skis • *In winter, the mountain village is full of skiers going to the slopes.* ➢ ski (v, n), skiing (n) ❖ σκιέρ

9.84 **bungee jumping** (n) /ˈbʌndʒi dʒʌmpɪŋ/
a sport in which you jump off a high place, like a bridge or a cliff, with an elastic rope tied to your feet • *People sometimes do bungee jumping from the bridge at Corinth.* ❖ μπάντζι τζάμπινγκ, σπορ με σάλτο από γέφυρα ή άλλο ψηλό σημείο

9.85 **amaze** (v) /əˈmeɪz/
surprise sb very much • *Ian amazed us with his skateboarding moves.* ➢ amazement (n), amazed, amazing (adj) ❖ καταπλήσσω, προκαλώ κατάπληξη

9.86 **amazed** (adj) /əˈmeɪzd/
very surprised • *We were amazed at Grandpa's bungee jumping experience.* ➢ amaze (v), amazement (n), amazing (adj) ❖ κατάπληκτος, μαγεμένος

9.87 **elastic** (adj) /ɪˈlæstɪk/
made of rubber material that stretches easily • *This jacket has got elastic around the wrists.* ➢ elastic (n) ❖ ελαστικός, εύκαμπτος

9.88 **rope** (n) /rəʊp/
very strong thick string used to tie things
• *The climbers used strong ropes to help them climb the mountain.* ❖ σκοινί

9.89 **ankle** (n) /ˈæŋkl/
the part of the body that connects the foot to the leg • *Eva fell and broke her ankle during the race.* ❖ αστράγαλος

Body Parts

ankle	joint
chest	knee
elbow	

Grammar Pages 114–115

9.90 **marathon** (n) /ˈmærəθən/
a long distance race, usually about 42 kilometres • *The road was closed because hundreds of people were running in the marathon.* ➢ marathon (adj) ❖ μαραθώνιος

9.91 **host** (v) /həʊst/
organise an event and invite people to take part • *Which country is hosting the next Olympic Games?* ➢ host (n) ❖ διοργανώνω

9.92 **dive** (v) /daɪv/
jump into water with your arms and head going in first • *We dived off the rocks into the sea.* ➢ dive, diver, diving (n) ❖ βουτώ, κάνω κατάδυση

9.93 **vitamin** (n) /ˈvɪtəmɪn/
sth that you get from food that you need to grow and be healthy • *Fresh fruit has more vitamins than sweets or crisps.* ❖ βιταμίνη

9.94 **biking** (n) /ˈbaɪkɪŋ/
the sport of riding a bicycle or motorbike
• *I like biking in the country, but I haven't tried fat biking.* ➢ bike (v), bike, biker (n) ❖ ποδηλασία

9.95 **biker** (n) /ˈbaɪkə(r)/
sb who rides a bicycle or motorbike • *There are special paths in the city for bikers to cycle on.* ➢ bike (v), bike, biking (n) ❖ ποδηλάτης

9.96 **sandy** (adj) /ˈsændi/
covered with sand • *Walking on a sandy beach is good exercise.* ➢ sand (n) ❖ αμμώδης

9.97 **excite** (v) /ɪkˈsaɪt/
make sb feel excited • *The idea of travelling around the world excited him.* ➢ excitement (n), exciting, excited (adj) ❖ συναρπάζω, ενθουσιάζω

Listening Page 116

9.98 **mermaid** (n) /ˈmɜːmeɪd/
a creature that is like a woman with a long fish tail instead of legs • *She swam under the water like a mermaid with feet inside her large flipper.* ❖ γοργόνα

9.99 **trapezing** (n) /trəˈpiːzɪŋ/
the sport of swinging on a trapeze (a swing hanging on ropes high above the ground)
• *We watched the team of acrobats trapezing in the circus.* ➢ trapeze (n) ❖ σπορ σε ακροβατική κούνια

9.100 **zorbing** (n) /ˈzɔːbɪŋ/
the sport of running inside a large ball filled with air that rolls around • *Zorbing looks like fun, but never do it on a windy day or the zorb ball will blow away.* ➢ zorb (v, n) ❖ zorbing, άθλημα που τρέχει κάποιος μέσα σε μεγάλη φουσκωτή μπάλα που κυλάει

9.101 **wide** (adj) /waɪd/
(the distance) from one side of sth to the other
• *The river is three metres wide.* ➢ widen (v), width (n) ❖ πλατύς, φαρδύς

Activities

banana boat riding	paragliding
biking	scuba diving
bungee jumping	skydiving
carousel	soapbox racing
hand cycling	trapezing
kitesurfing	zorbing
marathon	

Speaking Page 117

9.102 **high life** (n) /ˈhaɪ laɪf/
a way of life that includes spending a lot of money on food, new things and entertainment
• *The family aren't exactly living the high life since Dad lost his job.* ❖ πολυτελής ζωή, η μεγάλη ζωή

9.103 **trapeze** (n) /trəˈpiːz/
a swing hanging on ropes high above the ground usually in a circus • *Armando jumped from the top of the high ladder and caught the trapeze in the air.* ➢ trapezing (n) ❖ ακροβατική κούνια

9.104 **fee** (n) /fiː/
the money you pay to do sth or join a club, class, etc. • *I pay a small fee every month to use the sports centre.* ❖ συνδρομή, χρέωση

9.105 **online** (adv) /ˌɒnˈlaɪn/
on the Internet • *Silvia booked her plane tickets online.* ➢ online (adj) ❖ στο διαδίκτυο

9.106 **Switzerland** (n) /'swɪtsələnd/
➤ Swiss (n, adj) ❖ Ελβετία

9.107 **glove** (n) /glʌv/
an item of clothing to keep your hand warm
• *Put on your gloves to keep your hands warm on the ski slope.* ❖ γάντι

Writing   Pages 118–119

9.108 **heading** (n) /'hedɪŋ/
a title for a piece of writing • *He gave his blog an interesting heading.* ➤ head (v), head (n)
❖ τίτλος, επικεφαλίδα

9.109 **subheading** (n) /ˌsʌb'hedɪŋ/
a title for small parts of a long piece of writing that has a main heading • *Each paragraph in her report had a subheading to show the subject it was about.* ❖ υπότιτλος, κεφαλίδα

9.110 **link** (v) /lɪŋk/
connect • *Remember to link your sentences with words like 'but' or 'so'.* ➤ link (n)
❖ συνδέω

9.111 **call** (n) /kɔːl/
an order or request • *The blog includes a call to make sport free for everyone.* ➤ call (v), caller (n) ❖ κλήση, έκκληση

9.112 **action** (n) /'ækʃn/
what sb does to make sth happen • *There's lots of action on the island in summer. You won't get bored!* ➤ act (v), active (adj), actively (adv) ❖ δράση

9.113 **image** (n) /'ɪmɪdʒ/
a picture; the idea that sb/sth gives others about them • *The image above Tim's article was a photo of him scuba diving.* ❖ εικόνα

9.114 **emotion** (n) /ɪ'məʊʃn/
a feeling • *She photographed the children laughing happily to show their emotions.*
➤ emotional (adj) ❖ συναίσθημα

9.115 **characteristic** (n) /ˌkærəktə'rɪstɪk/
a feature, e.g. describing age, personality, appearance • *He gave a description of his personal characteristics, including his age and appearance.* ➤ characteristic (adj)
❖ χαρακτηριστικό

9.116 **shocking** (adj) /'ʃɒkɪŋ/
surprising in a bad way; very bad • *Yesterday on TV, there was a shocking story about the rubbish in the sea.* ➤ shock (v, n), shocked (adj) ❖ συγκλονιστικός, σοκαριστικός

9.117 **surprising** (adj) /sə'praɪzɪŋ/
not expected to happen • *A surprising number of people want to try bungee jumping.*
➤ surprise (v, n), surprised (adj)
❖ απροσδόκητος, εκπληκτικός

9.118 **route** (n) /ruːt/
the way from one place to another
• *Ken takes the shortest route home from school every day.* ❖ διαδρομή

9.119 **map** (n) /mæp/
a plan that shows the surface of the earth and all the roads, etc., to go somewhere • *I looked at the map to find the way to the village.*
❖ χάρτης

9.120 **graffiti** (n) /grə'fiːti/
things painted or written on walls in public places • *The walls in the city centre are covered with graffiti.* ❖ τοιχογραφία, γκραφίτι

9.121 **streetlight** (n) /'striːtlaɪt/
a light on top of a tall pole at the side of a road or another public place • *There aren't many streetlights near the station, so I don't like walking there at night.* ❖ λάμπα δρόμου

9.122 **statue** (n) /'stætʃuː/
a figure of a person, animal or object that sb makes from stone or metal • *There's a statue of Lord Byron in the park.* ❖ άγαλμα

9.123 **urban** (adj) /'ɜːbən/
related to or in a town or city • *You can travel by urban railway from the airport to the city centre.* ❖ αστικός

9.124 **confusing** (adj) /kən'fjuːzɪŋ/
not easy to understand • *The streets all looked the same, which was confusing for visitors.* ➤ confuse (v), confusion (n), confused (adj) ❖ πολύπλοκος, που μπερδεύει

Adjectives

amazed	dizzy	paralysed
brave	elastic	sandy
careful	exhausting	shocking
confusing	extreme	spectacular
disappointed	frightened	surprising
disappointing	frightening	urban
diverse	gentle	wide

Adverbs

bravely	mentally	quietly
dangerously	noisily	slowly
extremely	physically	unique

9.125 **realise** (v) /'riːəlaɪz/
understand that sth is happening • *I didn't realise your parents were Italian.*
➤ realisation (n) ❖ διαπιστώνω, αντιλαμβάνομαι

9.126 **step** (n) /step/
a stair, usually outdoors or on a ladder; the movement of lifting up your foot then putting it down when you walk • *They sat on the steps ouside the library, waiting for it to open.* ➣ step (v) ❖ σκαλί, σκαλοπάτι, βήμα

9.127 **exist** (v) /ɪɡ'zɪst/
live; be • *Smartphones didn't exist until a few years ago.* ➣ existence (n) ❖ υπάρχω

9.128 **encourage** (v) /ɪn'kʌrɪdʒ/
talk to sb to make them do sth by saying it is a good thing to do • *My friends encouraged me to go climbing with them.* ➣ encouragement (n), encouraging (adj) ❖ ενθαρρύνω

9.129 **certificate** (n) /sə'tɪfɪkət/
a piece of paper which says you have finished a course • *At the end of the weekend, everyone got a certificate to show that they attended the training course.* ➣ certify (v) ❖ πιστοποιητικό

9.130 **prove** (v) /pruːv/
use evidence to show that sth is true or that sth really happened • *Matthew studied French for eight years, but he hasn't got a paper to prove it.* ➣ proof (n) ❖ αποδεικνύω

9.131 **certify** (v) /'sɜːtɪfaɪ/
write or say that sth is true or that sb has done sth • *The doctor wrote a note to certify that Kim wasn't too ill to go to school.* ➣ certificate (n), certify (adj) ❖ πιστοποιώ, επιβεβαιώνω

Video 9
Extremely Spectacular

Page 120

9.132 **extremely** (adv) /ɪk'striːmli/
very much • *Mum was extremely worried when I went bungee jumping.* ➣ extreme (adj, n) ❖ ακραία, υπερβολικά

9.133 **spectacular** (adj) /spek'tækjʊlə(r)/
exciting to see • *There was a spectacular fireworks display at the end of the event.* ❖ θεαματικός, εντυπωσιακός

9.134 **diverse** (adj) /daɪ'vɜːs/
including many different kinds of things or people • *Our walking club is a diverse group of people of many nationalities.* ➣ diversity (n) ❖ ποικίλος

9.135 **landscape** (n) /'lændskeɪp/
the things you can see across a large area of land • *The typical Dutch landscape has canals and fields of flowers.* ❖ τοπίο

9.136 **formation** (n) /fɔː'meɪʃn/
sth that has been formed; a particular pattern • *Jake is studying geology to learn about the formation of our planet.* ➣ form (v, n), formative (adj) ❖ σχηματισμός

9.137 **erosion** (n) /ɪ'rəʊʒn/
the natural process that slowly destroys sth or makes it weaker because of water, or the weather, etc. • *A large rock broke off the clif and fell onto the beach because of erosion by the sea.* ➣ erode (v) ❖ διάβρωση

9.138 **inspire** (v) /ɪn'spaɪə(r)/
to give somebody an idea to do something • *His journey to India inspired him to write the blog.* ➣ inspiration (n), inspiring (adj) ❖ εμπνέω

9.139 **climber** (n) /'klaɪmə(r)/
sb who climbs mountains or rocks • *The group of climbers used ropes to help them down from the hilltop.* ➣ climb (v, n), climbing (n) ❖ ορειβάτης

9.140 **physically** (adv) /'fɪzɪkli/
related to the body • *We were physically exhausted by the end of the marathon.* ➣ physical (adj) ❖ σωματικά

9.141 **unique** (adj) /ju'niːk/
the only one of a kind • *Every child is unique because no two people can be exactly the same.* ❖ μοναδικός

9.142 **adventurer** (n) /əd'ventʃərə(r)/
sb who enjoys doing exciting new things and travelling to strange places • *Sue's family think she's an adventurer because she's always travelling to different places and doing dangerous activities.* ➣ adventure (n), adventurous (adj) ❖ τυχοδιώκτης, εξερευνητής

9.143 **interact** (v) /ɪntə'rækt/
communicate and act with sb/sth • *It's interesting how animals interact when they meet each other for the first time.* ➣ interaction (n), interactive (adj) ❖ αλληλεπιδρώ

9.144 **mentally** (adv) /'mentəli/
related to the mind • *Are you mentally prepared for the cycling race?* ➣ mental (adj) ❖ διανοητικά, πνευματικά

9.145 **affect** (v) /ə'fekt/
cause a change to sb/sth • *The weather affected our plan to go camping because it was too cold and wet.* ❖ επηρεάζω, επιδρώ

Vocabulary Exercises

A Circle the odd one out.

1 bend	motor	slope
2 coral	trapeze	earth
3 derby	blog	article
4 crampon	ski	mermaid
5 fee	knee	joint
6 carousel	offer	soapbox
7 vertically	mentally	horizontally

B Choose the correct words (A, B or C).

1 After winning the competition, Angela's dreams have ___ true.

   A be　　　　　　**B** come　　　　　**C** give

2 Why don't you ___ along with us to the climbing wall? It's fun!

   A come　　　　　**B** carry　　　　　**C** get

3 Jerry has decided to take ___ a new hobby, so he's joined a diving club.

   A care　　　　　**B** off　　　　　　**C** up

4 Paragliding was a ___ experience.

   A frighten　　　**B** frightening　　**C** frightened

5 You're getting better at snowboarding. Don't ___ up now!

   A carry　　　　　**B** take　　　　　**C** give

6 Did you ___ a place on the skydiving course?

   A book　　　　　**B** compete　　　**C** time

C Complete the sentences with these words.

ankle　chest　elbow　kit　map　medal　rope　wave

1 Rania's new tennis racket was very heavy, so her _____ hurt after playing for hours.

2 The _____ has everything you need to build a model plane.

3 Hold onto the _____ to climb up the rock.

4 He stood up on his surfboard and rode along the high _____.

5 He won a silver _____ for skiing in the Winter Olympics.

6 Dad felt pains in his _____ because he had a problem with his heart.

7 When I felt the pain in my foot, I realised that my _____ was broken.

8 Have you got the _____? I think we're on the wrong path.

D Complete the sentences with words formed from the words in bold.

1 Racing down the hill in the soapbox was so _____!　　　**EXCITE**

2 We felt _____ about the score at the end of the match.　　**DISAPPOINT**

3 The cars raced _____ round the track.　　　　　　　　　**NOISE**

4 Tony felt a sharp _____ in his left leg when he fell off the bike.　**SENSE**

5 Charlie is a sportsman with _____ who never gives up.　　**DETERMINE**

6 The runners were _____ at the end of the marathon.　　　**EXHAUST**

E Do the crossword.

Across

4   the sport of swinging on a trapeze high above the ground
6   swimming underwater using a container of air from a container that you have on your back to breathe
8   a sport in which you jump off a high place, like a bridge or a cliff, with a kind of rope tied on your feet
9   a sport in which you make a bike move with your hands instead of your legs
10 a sport in which you wear a kind of parachute and jump from a high place, then get moved by the wind until
    you reach the ground

Down

1   a long distance race, usually about 42 kilometres
2   the sport of riding on a board on water and holding a large kite that gets pushed by the wind
3   a sport in which sb jumps out of a plane and falls without opening a parachute for as long as possible
5   the sport of running inside a large ball filled with air that rolls around
7   the sport of riding a bicycle or motorbike

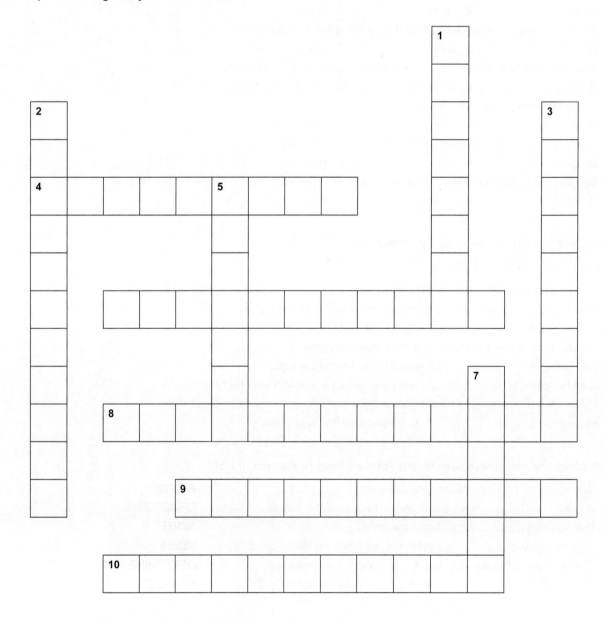

9.1 Present Perfect (1)

Ο Present Perfect σχηματίζεται με το ρήμα *have* + past participle (παθητική μετοχή).

Κατάφαση
I/we/you/they **have ('ve)** walk**ed**.
He/she/it **has ('s)** walk**ed**.

Άρνηση
I/we/you/they **have not (haven't)** walk**ed**.
He/she/it **has not (hasn't)** walk**ed**.

Ερώτηση
Have I/we/you/they walk**ed**?
Has he/she/it walk**ed**?

Σύντομες απαντήσεις	
Yes, I/we/you/they **have**.	**No**, I/we/you/they **haven't**.
Yes, he/she/it **has**.	**No**, he/she/it **hasn't**.

Ορθογραφία:
walk → walk**ed**   play → play**ed**   dance → danc**ed**   study → stud**ied**   travel → travel**led**

Σημείωση: Τα ανώμαλα ρήματα δεν ακολουθούν αυτούς τους ορθογραφικούς κανόνες.
Δες τη λίστα των ανώμαλων ρημάτων στις σελίδες 185–186 του Student's Book.

Χρησιμοποιούμε τον Present Perfect:
για κάτι που έγινε στο παρελθόν αλλά δεν αναφέρουμε πότε ακριβώς.
→ *We **have been** to South America once.*
για εμπειρίες.
→ *They **have climbed** Everest.*
με *ever* για να ρωτήσουμε για εμπειρίες.
→ *Have you **ever** flown in a helicopter?*
με *never* για να πούμε ότι δεν έχουμε κάνει κάτι ποτέ.
→ *I have **never** flown in a helicopter.*

Σημείωση: Όταν θέλουμε να μιλήσουμε για ένα συγκεκριμένο χρόνο στο παρελθόν, χρησιμοποιούμε τον Past Simple.
→ *They **went** to New York **in 2015**.*

9.2 First Conditional

If clause	Main clause
Present Simple	*will* + bare infinitive

Χρησιμοποιούμε τον First Conditional για να μιλήσουμε για τα αποτελέσματα μιας πιθανής κατάστασης τώρα ή στο μέλλον.
→ *If you **like** skating, you**'ll love** snowboarding!*
→ *I**'ll get** better at swimming if I **join** a club.*
→ *If it **rains** tomorrow, we **won't go** climbing.*

9 Grammar

Grammar Exercises

A Circle the correct words.

1 He **hasn't** / **didn't** joined the walking group.
2 Steven has never **ran** / **run** in a marathon.
3 My sister **has gone** / **went** to university in 2016.
4 I have never **travel** / **travelled** in a hot air balloon.
5 Last year, we **climbed** / **have climbed** to the top of Mount Olympus.
6 **Have** / **Did** you ever been to Australia?
7 They **haven't** / **didn't** like zorbing. It was scary and felt dangerous.
8 **Have** / **Did** you enjoy the scuba diving course?

B Complete the sentences with the Present Perfect form of these verbs.

| eat   fly   never swim   not break   not jump   see   try   win |

1 Dennis _____ his arm, but it hurts a lot.
2 My parents _____ in a helicopter.
3 I _____ out of a plane with a parachute. And I don't want to!
4 _____ you ever _____ bungee jumping?
5 Gina _____ the whole pizza.
6 _____ you ever _____ a competition?
7 My dog _____ in the sea. He's afraid of water!
8 _____ Francesca ever _____ a hand cycling race?

C Complete the sentences with the correct form of the verbs in brackets.

1 If you practise often, you _____ (get) better at cycling.
2 We won't get into the stadium if there _____ (not be) any tickets left.
3 If you don't wear a helmet, you _____ (not feel) safe.
4 If it _____ (rain), we won't go rock climbing.
5 She _____ (have) great fun if she goes sailing.
6 He _____ (not do) well in the swimming competition if he doesn't do any training.
7 If she _____ (not lose) this match, she'll win the whole tournament.
8 We won't get to the top if we _____ (not stop) to rest on the way up.

10 Eat Your Greens!

Page 121

10.1 **greens** (n) /griːnz/
green vegetables • *Have some fresh greens with your meal. They're good for you.*
➣ green (adj) ❖ (πράσινα) λαχανικά

10.2 **beaver** (n) /ˈbiːvə(r)/
an animal with a flat tail which lives in rivers or lakes • *Beavers cut wood with their strong teeth to build their homes on the lake.*
❖ κάστορας

10.3 **willow** (n) /ˈwɪləʊ/
a kind of tree with long thin leaves and branches • *There are some willow trees next to the river.* ❖ ιτιά

10.4 **branch** (n) /brɑːntʃ/
the part of a tree that leaves and flowers grow out of • *The monkey was swinging on the branches of a tree.* ❖ κλαδί

10.5 **pond** (n) /pɒnd/
a small lake or pool, usually in a park or garden • *I saw some frogs in a pond in the park.* ❖ λιμνούλα

Reading   Page 122

10.6 **dislike** (v) /dɪsˈlaɪk/
not like • *Lena dislikes cauliflower and she doesn't want to eat it.* ➣ dislike (n) ❖ δεν μου αρέσει, απεχθάνομαι

10.7 **result** (n) /rɪˈzʌlt/
the information or mark from a test or research; sth caused or made by sth else
• *Lorna was surprised when she got her exam results that showed a good pass.* ➣ result (v)
❖ αποτέλεσμα

10.8 **habit** (n) /ˈhæbɪt/
sth that you do as part of your usual routine
• *Andreas looks much healthier now that he's changed his eating habits.* ❖ συνήθεια

10.9 **questionnaire** (n) /ˌkwestʃəˈneə(r)/
a set of questions for people to answer so that sb can collect information about the answers
• *Our class made a questionnaire about sleeping habits and the result showed that nobody sleeps enough!* ❖ ερωτηματολόγιο

10.10 **portion** (n) /ˈpɔːʃn/
an amount of food for one person • *Henry has a large portion of salad with his dinner every day.* ❖ μερίδα

10.11 **congratulations** (excl) /kənˌɡrætʃuˈleɪʃnz/
sth you say to sb when you are happy about an event or when they do well at sth
• *Congratulations! You came first in the race.*
➣ congratulate (v) ❖ Συγχαρητήρια!

10.12 **fit** (adj) /ˈfɪt/
ealthy and strong • *Rhona keeps fit by running in the park.* ➣ fitness (n) ❖ σε καλή φυσική κατάσταση

Word Focus   Page 122

10.13 **headache** (n) /ˈhedeɪk/
a pain in the head • *I need an aspirin to stop my headache.* ❖ πονοκέφαλος

10.14 **hydrated** (adj) /ˈhaɪdreɪtɪd/
with enough water; not thirsty • *It's important to keep your body hydrated when you're doing sports. So take some water to the gym.*
➣ hydrate (v), hydration (n)
❖ που ενυδατώνεται

10.15 **thirsty** (adj) /ˈθɜːsti/
needing to drink water • *We were hot and thirsty after an hour on the beach.* ➣ thirst (n)
❖ διψασμένος

10.16 **freezer** (n) /ˈfriːzə(r)/
a large piece of equipment where food can stay frozen for a long time • *Johanne cooked the pies and then put them in the freezer when they were cool.* ➣ freeze (v) ❖ κατάψυξη

10.17 **can** (n) /kən/
a metal container for food or drink • *They brought some cans of lemonade for the party.*
➣ canned (adj) ❖ μεταλλικό κουτί, κουτάκι (κυρίως για αναψυκτικό)

10.18 **decay** (n) /dɪˈkeɪ/
the process of being destroyed slowly, often by not being cared for • *Cleaning your teeth can protect them from tooth decay.* ➣ decay (v)
❖ σάπισμα, σήψη
✎ tooth decay = τερηδόνα

10.19 **weak** (adj) /wiːk/
not strong • *Edmund's legs felt weak and tired after the climb.* ➣ weaken (v), weakness (n)
❖ αδύναμος

Reading   Pages 122–123

10.20 **per cent** (n) /pə ˈsent/
one part of every hundred • *I got 85 per cent of the answers right, so I passed the test.*
➣ percentage (n) ❖ τοις εκατό
✎ Also: percent

10.21 **properly** (adv) /ˈprɒpəli/
correctly; in the right way for the situation
● *Our freezer isn't working properly, so the ice cream is melting.* ➢ proper (adj) ❖ σωστά, όπως πρέπει

10.22 **concentration** (n) /ˌkɒnsnˈtreɪʃn/
the act of focussing all your thoughts and attention on one thing ● *You need total concentration on running to win the race.* ➢ concentrate (v) ❖ συγκέντρωση

10.23 **contain** (v) /kənˈteɪn/
have inside ● *These biscuits contain a lot of sugar.* ➢ container, content (n) ❖ περιέχω

10.24 **sugar** (n) /ˈʃʊgə(r)/
a sweet white or brown substance used to make food or drinks sweet ● *I put honey in my tea instead of sugar.* ➢ sugary (adj) ❖ ζάχαρη

10.25 **cause** (v) /kɔːz/
make sth happen ● *The rain caused the drivers to stop the race.* ➢ cause (v) ❖ προκαλώ

10.26 **taste** (n) /ˈteɪst/
flavour ● *Lemons don't have a sweet taste.* ➢ taste (v) ❖ γεύση

10.27 **pear** (n) /peə(r)/
a fruit that is shaped wide at the bottom and thinner at the top ● *Aunt Jess bought apples and ears at the market.* ❖ αχλάδι

10.28 **spoon** (n) /spuːn/
a metal item with a handle and a small bowl shape on the end, used for serving or eating food; a small amount of sth served from a spoon ● *I used a big spoon to put the soup into bowls.* ❖ κουτάλι

10.29 **cereal** (n) /ˈsɪəriəl/
food made from grain, often eaten for breakfast ● *I usually eat cereal with banana and milk in the morning.* ❖ δημητριακά

10.30 **grape** (n) /greɪp/
a small purple or green fruit that grows on a climbing plant ● *The farmer picked some nice juicy green grapes for us.* ❖ σταφύλι

10.31 **snack** (n) /snæk/
a small meal ● *Dina usually takes a snack to school for lunchtime.* ➢ snack (v) ❖ κολατσιό, σνακ

10.32 **strawberry** (n) /ˈstrɔːbəri/
a small, juicy, red, summer fruit ● *We're having ice cream with strawberries for dessert.* ❖ φράουλα

10.33 **yoghurt** (n) /ˈjɒgət/
creamy food made from milk ● *Let's have some yoghurt and honey with nuts.* ❖ γιαούρτι

10.34 **dried fruit** (n) /ˌdraɪd ˈfruːt/
fruit that has been dried to keep it for a longer time ● *You can take some dried fruit and nuts for a snack at the beach.* ❖ αποξηραμένα φρούτα

10.35 **spoonful** (n) /ˈspuːnfʊl/ /
an amount served from one spoon ● *Dad takes one spoonful of sugar in his coffee.* ❖ κουταλιά

10.36 **teaspoon** (n) /ˈtiːspuːn/
a small spoon used to put sugar in drinks or to eat small amounts of sth, e.g. desserts; an amount served from a teaspoon ● *Nancy used a teaspoon to eat her yoghurt.* ❖ κουταλάκι του γλυκού

10.37 **toast** (n) /təʊst/
slices of bread that are heated to make them brown on the outside ● *Can I have a piece of toast and honey?* ➢ toast (v), toasted (adj) ❖ φρυγανιά, φρυγανισμένο ψωμί

10.38 **jam** (n) /dʒæm/
a sweet food made by boiling fruit with sugar ● *One spoonful of strawberry jam in yoghurt gives it a nice sweet taste.* ❖ μαρμελάδα

10.39 **bowl** (n) /bəʊl/
a deep round dish used for food or liquid ● *She had a bowl of vegetable soup.* ❖ μπολ

10.40 **put on (weight)** (phr v) /pʊt ɒn weɪt/
become heavier ● *Bessie got very thin when she was ill, but she's put on some weight now.* ❖ παίρνω βάρος
✎ Opp: lose weight ❖ χάνω βάρος

10.41 **stomach ache** (n) /ˈstʌmək eɪk/
a pain in your stomach ● *Don't eat too quickly or you'll get a stomach ache.* ❖ πόνος στο στομάχι

10.42 **reserve** (v) /rɪˈzɜːv/
ask for sth to be kept for you to use ● *Did you reserve your tickets for the theatre?* ➢ reservation (n) ❖ κελίνω (τραπέζι, δωμάτιο κτλ.)
✎ Syn: book

10.43 **reuse** (v) /riːˈjuːz/
use again ● *We can clean glass jars and reuse them to keep things in.* ➢ reusable (adj) ❖ ξαναχρησιμοποιώ

10.44 **permit** (v) /pəˈmɪt/
allow; give permission for sth ● *They don't permit people to eat or drink on the bus.* ➢ permission (n) ❖ επιτρέπω

10.45 **sugar-free** (adj) /ˌʃʊgə ˈfriː/
without sugar ● *Fresh orange juice is a sugar-free drink.* ❖ χωρίς ζάχαρη

10.46 **refreshing** (adj) /rɪˈfreʃɪŋ/
making you feel less hot or thirsty ● *We had a refreshing drink of lemonade.* ➢ refresh (v), refreshment (n) ❖ αναζωογονητικός

Food

aubergine	grape
avocado	greens
cauliflower	jam
cereal	pear
crisp	strawberry
dried fruit	sugar
garlic	yoghurt

Vocabulary   Pages 124–125

10.47 **rough** (adj) /rʌf/
not smooth or flat on the surface ● *Cut the rough skin off the pineapple.* ➤ roughen (v), roughness (n), roughly (adv) ❖ τραχύς

10.48 **avocado** (n) /ˌævəˈkɑːdəʊ/
a tropical fruit with a hard dark green skin and soft creamy fruit with a large stone inside ● *Louise is trying to grow an avocado tree from the stone that was inside the fruit.* ❖ αβοκάντο

10.49 **aubergine** (n) /ˈəʊbəʒiːn/
a large oval vegetable that has purple skin outside and soft and white inside ● *We're having stuffed aubergines for dinner.* ❖ μελιτζάνα
✎ Also: eggplant (US Eng)

10.50 **cauliflower** (n) /ˈkɒliflaʊə(r)/
a vegetable with a big white head that looks like a hard flower ● *Do you prefer cauliflower or carrots?* ❖ κουνουπίδι

10.51 **carbohydrate** (n) /ˌkɑːbəʊˈhaɪdreɪt/
a substance in food that gives the body energy and heat ● *Rice and pasta have a lot of carbohydrates.* ❖ υδατάνθρακας

10.52 **calcium** (n) /ˈkælsiəm/
a chemical substance that is in teeth and bones ● *We need calcium from our food to have healthy bones and teeth.* ❖ ασβέστιο

10.53 **fat** (n) /fæt/
the oily substance from animals or plants that we can eat or use in cooking ● *Ice cream has a lot of fat and sugar, so don't eat big portions.* ➤ fatty, fat (adj) ❖ λίπος

10.54 **bone** (n) /bəʊn/
the hard parts of the body that form the skeleton ● *Gary fell off his horse and broke two bones in his arm.* ➤ boney (adj) ❖ κόκκαλο

10.55 **unhealthy** (adj) /ʌnˈhelθi/
bad for your health; not in good health ● *You need to change your unhealthy eating habits or you'll get sick.* ➤ unhealthily (adv) ❖ ανθυγιεινός

10.56 **crisp** (n) /krɪsp/
a thin slice of potato that is fried, then dried ● *We shared a packet of crisps for a snack.* ➤ crispy (adj) ❖ πατατάκι

10.57 **salty** (adj) /ˈsɔːlti/
with salt on or with a taste like salt ● *This salad is really salty. I can't eat it!* ➤ salt (v, n) ❖ αλατισμένος, αλμυρός

10.58 **cooked** (adj) /kʊkt/
that has been made by cooking ● *You can put cooked food in the freezer to keep it frozen and use days later.* ➤ cook (v), cook, cooker, cookery, cooking (n) ❖ μαγειρεμένος

10.59 **raw** (adj) /rɔː/
not cooked ● *Raw carrots taste good in salad.* ❖ ωμός, άψητος

10.60 **disgusting** (adj) /dɪsˈɡʌstɪŋ/
horrible ● *Eating insects sounds disgusting!* ➤ disgust (v, n) ❖ αηδιαστικός

10.61 **cold** (n) /kəʊld/
a common illness that makes you cough and sneeze, etc. ● *Maya's got a cold, so she doesn't want to go out.* ➤ cold (adj) ❖ κρυολόγημα

10.62 **fever** (n) /ˈfiːvə(r)/
a feeling of being hot with a temperature higher than normal ● *Mum was worried and called the doctor when I had a fever.* ➤ feverish (adj) ❖ πυρετός

10.63 **toothache** (n) /ˈtuːθeɪk/
a pain in your teeth ● *I went to the dentist because I had toothache.* ❖ πονόδοντος

10.64 **temperature** (n) /ˈtemprətʃə(r)/
how hot or cold sth/sb is; a body temperature higher than usual ● *The nurse checked my temperature, but I didn't have a fever.* ❖ θερμοκρασία, πυρετός

10.65 **brush** (v) /brʌʃ/
clean sth by using a brush ● *Don't forget to brush your teeth.* ➤ brush (n) ❖ βουρτσίζω

10.66 **medicine** (n) /ˈmedsn/
sth you drink or eat to make you well when you're ill ● *The doctor told Sophie to take her medicine twice a day.* ❖ φάρμακο

10.67 **rest** (v) /rest/
relax and not do anything tiring ● *You worked hard all day, so go and rest now.* ➤ rest (v), restful (adj), restless (adj) ❖ ξεκουράζομαι

10.68 **protein** (n) /ˈprəʊtiːn/
sth in meat and fish that helps sb grow ● *You can eat more fish if your body needs more protein.* ❖ πρωτεΐνη

10.69 **juicy** (adj) /ˈdʒuːsi/
sth that has a lot of juice inside ● *The grapes were sweet and juicy.* ➤ juice (v, n) ❖ ζουμερός

10.70 **lifestyle** (n) /ˈlaɪfstaɪl/
the way that you choose to live • *People living in cities have a very busy lifestyle.* ❖ τρόπος ζωής

10.71 **vegetarian** (n) /ˌvedʒɪˈteəriən/
sb who doesn't eat meat or fish • *Katie and Bob don't eat any meat because they're vegetarians.* ➣ vegetarian (adj) ❖ χορτοφάγος

Other Food-related Nouns

bowl	protein
calcium	snack
can	spoon
carbohydrate	spoonful
chopstick	taste
fat	teaspoon
honey pot	toast
portion	vegetarian

Grammar

Pages 126–127

10.72 **trampoline** (n) /ˈtræmpəliːn/
a piece of equipment in a gym that sb can bounce up and down on • *Follow the instructions when you're using the trampoline so you don't hurt yourself.* ❖ τραμπολίνο

10.73 **aspirin** (n) /ˈæsprɪn/
a medicine used to help headaches and other pains • *Angus took and aspirin and soon felt a bit better.* ❖ ασπιρίνη

10.74 **excuse** (n) /ɪkˈskjuːs/
a reason that you give to explain why you do or don't do sth • *Alan is always making excuses for being late for school.* ➣ excuse (v) ❖ δικαιολογία

10.75 **hungry** (adj) /ˈhʌŋgri/
needing or wanting to eat sth • *Are you hungry? Let's have lunch.* ➣ hunger (n), hungrily (adv) ❖ πεινασμένος (I'm hungry = πεινάω)

10.76 **warm-up** (adj) /wɔːm ʌp/
preparing for an exercise session by doing exercises to stretch the muscles • *The players did some warm-up exercises before the match began.* ➣ warm up (phr v), warm-up (n) ❖ προθέρμανση, ζέσταμα

10.77 **nephew** (n) /ˈnefjuː/
the son of your sister or brother • *My nephew George is six years old, so my sister and her husband are taking him to school next week.* ❖ ανηψιός

10.78 **terrible** (adj) /ˈterəbl/
really bad • *I don't want to go back to that restaurant. The food was terrible!* ❖ απαίσιος, φριχτός

Food-related Adjectives

cooked	rough
crispy	salty
disgusting	sugar-free
hungry	terrible
juicy	thirsty
raw	unhealthy
refreshing	

10.79 **design** (v) /dɪˈzaɪn/
draw lines and shapes to make sth • *Who designed the posters for the concert? They look good.* ➣ design, designer (n) ❖ σχεδιάζω

10.80 **print** (v) /ˈprɪnt/
use a machine for putting words or pictures on paper • *The teacher printed the lines for the school play.* ➣ print, printing (n), printed (adj), ❖ εκτυπώνω

10.81 **programme** (n) /ˈprəʊgræm/
a leaflet or piece of paper with information about an event • *Tom's art teacher helped him make the programmes for the concert.* ➣ programme (v) ❖ πρόγραμμα

Listening

Page 128

10.82 **chopstick** (n) /ˈtʃɒpstɪk/
a thin wooden stick used to pick up food for eating in some Asian countries • *Can you really eat food using chopsticks? It looks difficult.* ❖ ξυλάκι (για κινέζικο φαγητό)

10.83 **garlic** (n) /ˈgaːlɪk/
a small vegetable with a very strong taste and smell • *French people sometimes eat snails with garlic sauce.* ❖ σκόρδο

10.84 **sauna** (n) /ˈsɔːnə/
a small room with a very high temperature inside, where you go to clean your skin and relax • *In really hot weather, our house feels like a sauna!* ❖ σάουνα

10.85 **Bulgaria** (n) /bʌlˈgeəriə/
➣ Bulgarian (n, adj) ❖ Βουλγαρία

10.86 **Sweden** (n) /ˈswiːdn/
➣ Swedish (n, adj) ❖ Σουηδία

10.87 **Colombia** (n) /kəˈlɒmbiə/
➣ Colombian (n, adj) ❖ Κολομβία

10.88 **decision** (n) /dɪˈsɪʒn/
a choice you make after thinking about sth • *My aunt made a decision to change her job.* ➣ decide (v), decisive (adj), decisively (adv) ❖ απόφαση

Health

Nouns
aspirin
bone
cold
concentration
decay
fever
habit
headache
injection
lifestyle
medicine

muscle
sauna
stomach ache
temperature
toothache

Adjectives
fit
hydrated
warm-up
weak

Speaking

Page 129

10.89 injection (n) /ɪnˈdʒekʃn/
an act of putting medicine into sb through a
needle • *Dave is taking his dog to the vet to
have an injection.* ➢ inject (v) ❖ ένεση

10.90 What's the matter? (expr) /wɒts ðə ˈmætə(r)/
What's wrong? • *What's the matter? Have you
got a headache?* ❖ Τι τρέχει; Τι έχεις;

10.91 stretch (v) /stretʃ/
put your arms or legs straight and tighten your
muscles • *Jack stretched his arm to reach the
book on the top shelf.* ➢ stretch (n) ❖ τεντώνω

10.92 muscle (n) /mʌsl/
a part of the body that holds bones together
and makes them move • *Fleur does a lot of
running and cycling, so she's got strong leg
muscles.* ➢ muscular (adj) ❖ μυς

10.93 not at all (expr) /nɒt ət ˈɔːl/
a polite way to reply when sb says 'thanks'
• *'Thanks very much for your advice.' 'Not at
all. I'm happy to help.'* ❖ (δεν κάνει) τίποτα

10.94 government (n) /ˈgʌvənmənt/
the group of people chosen to be in control of
a country • *The government doesn't spend
enough money on hospitals.* ➢ govern (v),
governor (n) ❖ κυβέρνηση

Expressions

congratulations
I'm afraid
not at all

put on (weight)
What's the matter?

Writing

Pages 130–131

10.95 apologise (v) /əˈpɒlədʒaɪz/
say you are sorry for doing sth wrong
• *Fran apologised for arriving late.* ➢ apology
(n), apologetic (adj) ❖ ζητώ συγγνώμη,
απολογούμαι

10.96 I'm afraid (expr) /aɪm əˈfreɪd/
a polite way to say you're sorry about sth
• *I'm afraid I can't come to your party because
I'm going on holiday.* ❖ φοβάμαι πως, λυπάμαι
αλλά, δυστυχώς

10.97 cancel (v) /ˈkænsl/
say that sth planned will not happen • *We
cancelled the barbecue because of the rain.*
➢ cancellation (adj) ❖ ακυρώνω

10.98 apology (n) /əˈpɒlədʒi/
sth you say or write to apologise for sth
• *The shop assistant made an apology for his
mistake.* ➢ apology (v), apologetic (adj)
❖ συγγνώμη

10.99 interview (n) /ˈɪntəvjuː/
a meeting where one person (or more) asks
questions and another gives answers
• *My brother has an interview for a new job
tomorrow, so he's a bit nervous.* ➢ interview
(v), interviewer (n) ❖ συνέντευξη

10.100 last (v) /lɑːst/
to keep going for a certain amount of time
• *How long did the interview last?* ➢ lasting
(adj) ❖ διαρκώ

10.101 approximately (adv) /əˈprɒksɪmətli/
almost exactly • *We've been friends for
approximately five years.* ➢ approximate (adj)
❖ περίπου

10.102 confirm (v) /kənˈfɜːm/
say that sth is true; show sth to be true
• *I sent an email to confirm that I was going to
the meeting.* ➢ confirmation (n)
❖ επιβεβαιώνω

10.103 attendance (n) /əˈtendəns/
the act of being present at a place or event
• *Our teacher keeps a note of our attendance
at class every day.* ➢ attend (v) ❖ παρουσία

10.104 sincere (adj) /sɪnˈsɪə(r)/
showing your real feelings • *He sent his
sincere apologies for missing his brother's
wedding.* ➢ sincerity (n), sincerely (adv)
❖ ειλικρινής

10.105 unfortunately (adv) /ʌnˈfɔːtʃənətli/
sadly; unluckily; used to show that you're
unhappy about sth that happens or doesn't
happen • *Unfortunately, he didn't win the
competition.* ➢ unfortunate (adj) ❖ δυστυχώς

10.106 **following** (adj) /ˈfɒləʊɪŋ/
next in time; that will be mentioned next
• *Judy went for an interview and started work at the company the following day.* ➢ follow (v), follower (n) ❖ επόμενος, ακόλουθος

10.107 **reschedule** (v) /ˌriːˈʃedjuːl/
change the time of an event • *The weather was terrible, so we rescheduled the trip for the following week.* ➢ schedule (v, n) ❖ επαναπρογραμματίζω, αναβάλλω

10.108 **explain** (v) /ɪkˈspleɪn/
give details or describe sth for sb to understand • *Malcolm explained how to get to the restaurant.* ➢ explanation (n) ❖ εξηγώ

Verbs

apologise	last
brush	permit
cancel	reschedule
cause	reserve
confirm	rest
dislike	reuse
explain	stretch

Video 10
Tasty Snacks!   **Page 132**

10.109 **honey pot** (n) /ˈhʌni pɒt/
a container for honey • *There's a honey pot in the bottom of the cupboard.* ❖ βάζο για μέλι

10.110 **ant** (n) /ænt/
a very small insect that makes holes under the ground and lives in large groups • *We've got lots of ants in our garden.* ❖ μυρμήγκι

10.111 **grub** (n) /ɡrʌb/
a young insect when it comes out of its egg and looks like a kind of worm • *A group of beetle grubs were walking in a line across the grass.* ❖ σκουλήκι, προνύμφη

10.112 **tree bark** (n) /triː bɑːk/
the thick skin on the outside of a tree • *The insects made their home in the tree bark.* ❖ φλοιός δέντρου

10.113 **cicada** (n) /sɪˈkɑːdə/
a large insect that makes a noise with its legs when it's hot • *The sound of cicadas filled the evening air outside our hotel balcony.* ❖ είδος μεγάλου τζίτζικα

10.114 **underground** (adv) /ˌʌndəˈɡraʊnd/
under surface of the ground • *Can you imagine living in a house that's underground?* ➢ underground (adj) ❖ κάτω από το έδαφος, υπόγεια

10.115 **fear** (n) /fɪə(r)/
the feeling of being frightened of/by sth • *Harry has a fear of snakes and he won't go near them.* ➢ fear (v), fearful, fearless (adj) ❖ φόβος

10.116 **nest** (n) /nest/
a place that an animal, especially a bird, builds to have its babies • *The eagle's nest was on the rocks high up on the side of the mountain.* ➢ nest (v) ❖ φωλιά

10.117 **treetop** (n) /ˈtriːtɒp/
the top part of a tree • *The birds flew down and landed on the treetop.* ❖ κορυφή δέντρου

10.118 **crispy** (adj) /ˈkrɪspi/
describing food that has a thin hard surface that is tasty • *We ate some crispy biscuits and cheese.* ➢ crisp (n) ❖ τραγανός

10.119 **past** (n) /pɑːst/
the time before now • *Village life was very difficult in the past.* ➢ past (adj) ❖ παρελθόν

10.120 **local** (n) /ˈləʊkl/
sb who lives in an area • *Brian is a local, so he knows the streets very well.* ➢ local (adj), locally (adv) ❖ ντόπιος

Vocabulary Exercises

A Match to make short dialogues.

1 I'm thirsty. ☐
2 You look hungry. ☐
3 I'm really tired. ☐
4 I've got toothache. ☐
5 Why have you got stomach ache? ☐
6 I've got a high temperature. ☐

a I need a snack.
b Go to the dentist.
c Take your medicine.
d Have a glass of water.
e You need to rest.
f I ate too many greens.

B Put these words under the correct heading.

aubergine   avocado   bowl   can   cauliflower   freezer   garlic   grape   per cent   portion   spoonful   strawberry

Vegetable	Fruit	Amount	Container
_____	_____	_____	_____
_____	_____	_____	_____
_____	_____	_____	_____

C Circle the correct words.

1 It's important to drink enough water to keep your body **dried** / **hydrated**.
2 Remember to **brush** / **stretch** your teeth before you go to bed.
3 Natural yogurt is **sugar-free** / **salty**, so it's a healthy snack.
4 Healthy eating **results** / **habits** can help you stay fit.
5 Did you call to **reuse** / **reserve** a table at the restaurant?
6 I can't possibly eat cicadas. The idea is **disgusting** / **juicy**!
7 Please come along **unfortunately** / **approximately** 15 minutes before your interview.
8 Does Tim's **nephew** / **ant** have a fever?

D Complete the sentences with the words you did not circle in C.

1 A tiny _____ was carrying a small piece of toast on its back.
2 It's unhealthy to eat a lot of _____ crisps.
3 Mum got the _____ of her blood test and she's very healthy.
4 Always do warm-up exercises to _____ your muscles before and after running.
5 Let's have a slice of _____ watermelon for dessert.
6 I took some _____ fruit and nuts to eat on the walk.
7 _____, they have cancelled the outdoor performance.
8 You can _____ glass jars to keep things in.

E Unjumble the words to complete the sentences.

1 What's the _____? You look very tired? (TRAMET)
2 Kevin made a silly _____ for not doing his homework. He said the cat ate it! (CUXESE)
3 Marjory sent her _____ for forgetting her friend's birthday. (GYOLAPO)
4 What time is your job _____ tomorrow? (WERVINTIE)
5 Did your arm hurt when the nurse gave you the _____? (ONJEINCTI)
6 Ilona has made the _____ to become a vegetarian. (SIDECINO)
7 Add a _____ of honey to your yoghurt. (POTESONA)
8 Exercise and rest will improve your _____. (CENTONCONRATI)

10 Grammar

10.1 Past Continuous

Κατάφαση
I/he/she/it **was** drink**ing**. We/you/they **were** drink**ing**.

Άρνηση
I/he/she/it **was nor (wasn't)** drink**ing**. We/you/they **were not (weren't)** drink**ing**.

Ερώτηση
Was I/he/she/it drink**ing**? **Were** we/you/they drink**ing**?

Σύντομες απαντήσεις	
Yes, I/he/she/it **was**. **Yes**, we/you/they **were**.	**No**, I/he/she/it **wasn't**. **No**, we/you/they **weren't**.

Ορθογραφία:

rid**e** → rid**ing**   cut → cut**ting**   tr**y** → tr**ying**

Χρησιμοποιούμε τον Past Continuous για:

πράξεις που ήταν σε εξέλιξη σε συγκεκριμένη χρονική στιγμή στο παρελθόν.

→ *Danny **was eating** his lunch at two o'clock.*

δύο ή περισσότερες πράξεις που ήταν σε εξέλιξη την ίδια χρονική στιγμή στο παρελθόν.

→ *Mary **was cooking** dinner and I **was helping** her.*

να δώσουμε το σκηνικό μιας ιστορίας.

→ *The sun **was shining** and they **were going** for a picnic.*

μια πράξη που ενώ ήταν σε εξέλιξη στο παρελθόν, διακόπηκε από μια άλλη.

→ *We **were walking** home from school when it **began** to rain.*

Σημείωση: Κάποιες συνηθισμένες χρονικές εκφράσεις που χρησιμοποιούνται συχνά με τον Past Continuous είναι: *while, as, all day/week/month/year, at eight o'clock in the morning, last night, last Monday/week/month/year, this afternoon*, κλπ.

10.2 Present Perfect (2)

Ο Present Perfect σχηματίζεται με το ρήμα *have* + past participle (παθητική μετοχή).

Μπορούμε να χρησιμοποιήσουμε τον Present Perfect με:

το *just* για κάτι που έγινε πολύ πρόσφατα στο παρελθόν, πριν από λίγα λεπτά.

→ *I have **just** finished my lunch.*

το *already* για να εξηγήσουμε ότι έχουμε ολοκληρώσει κάτι (που αναμενόταν να κάνουμε).

→ *We have **already** eaten everything.*

→ *We have eaten everything **already**.*

το *yet* για να μιλήσουμε για κάτι που δεν έχουμε κάνει ακόμη, αλλά πρέπει να το κάνουμε. Το χρησιμοποιούμε στο τέλος μιας ερώτησης ή μιας αρνητικής πρότασης.

→ *I haven't finished my homework **yet**.*

→ *'Have you had dinner **yet**?' 'No, not **yet**.'*

Σημείωση: Μπορούμε να χρησιμοποιήσουμε το *just* μόνο μεταξύ του auxiliary (βοηθητικό ρήμα) και του past participle (παθητική μετοχή). Το *already* μπορεί να χρησιμοποιηθεί μεταξύ του auxiliary και του past participle ή στο τέλος μιας πρότασης. Το *yet* πρέπει να χρησιμοποιηθεί στο τέλος μιας ερώτησης ή μιας αρνητικής πρότασης.

10.3 Reflexive Verbs

Subject	Pronoun
I	myself
you	yourself
he	himself
she	herself
it	itself
we	ourselves
you	yourselves
they	themselves

Μερικά ρήματα απαιτούν μια αυτοπαθή αντωνυμία. Μπορούμε να τα χρησιμοποιήσουμε όταν το αντικείμενο είναι το ίδιο με το υποκείμενο.
→ The boy **hurt himself** when fell off the wall.
→ We **enjoyed ourselves** at the party.
→ I **cut myself** when I was making a sandwich.
→ The kitten is very young and it can't **look after itself**.

Grammar Exercises

A Complete the sentences with the Past Continuous form of the verbs in brackets.

1 We were making food for the party and my aunt _____ (help) us.

2 _____ (they / have) dinner when you arrived.

3 I _____ (feel) thirsty, so I drank some refreshing fruit juice.

4 Dad _____ (put) the food on the plates.

5 The boys _____ (not study) for their test when their mum came home.

6 The nurse _____ (give) the man an injection on his arm.

7 She took her cat to the vet because it _____ (not eat) its food.

8 _____ (he / run) to catch a bus when he fell?

B **Write the words in the correct order to make sentences and questions.**

1 my / haven't / I / yet / had / lunch

_____

2 has / himself / just / Michael / cut

_____

3 already / grapes / all / we / have / the / eaten

_____

4 ? / has / medicine / her / taken / the / yet / girl

_____

5 done / he / any / exercises / hasn't / stretching / yet

_____

6 ? / yet / finished / have / your / you / project

_____

7 have / cycled / around / park / the / they / already / twice

_____

8 photos / haven't / the / you / yet / printed

_____

C **Choose the correct answers (A, B or C).**

1 Jeanette has ___ come home from work.
   A ago   **B** just   **C** yet

2 What was she doing when she cut ___?
   A herself   **B** himself   **C** yourself

3 They were living in Spain ___ year.
   A for   **B** next   **C** last

4 Was it raining ___ day yesterday?
   A at   **B** all   **C** in

5 When I get a job, I can look after ___.
   A yourselves   **B** ourselves   **C** myself

6 Our teacher ___ feeling well, so we didn't have our maths lesson.
   A didn't   **B** wasn't   **C** weren't

7 The girls were enjoying ___ in the park.
   A herself   **B** ourselves   **C** themselves

8 Was it snowing when you hurt ___?
   A yourself   **B** myself   **C** itself

11 Be Creative!

Page 135

11.1 **chalk** (n) /tʃɔːk/
a very soft kind of white stone used for writing or drawing • *The teacher cleaned the chalk from the board and then wrote some new examples.* ➤ chalk (v, adj), chalky (adj)
❖ κιμωλία

11.2 **pavement** (n) /ˈpeɪvmənt/
the path made on the side of a street for pedestrians to walk on • *A lot of people were standing waiting on the pavement next to the bus stop.* ➤ pave (v), paved (adj)
❖ πεζοδρόμιο

Word Focus — Page 136

11.3 **canvas** (n) /ˈkænvəs/
a strong cloth used for painting on; a cloth for making sails, tents, etc. • *Martha did a quick drawing on paper first, then began to paint her picture on the canvas.* ❖ καμβάς

11.4 **cloth** (n) /klɒθ/
material made from cotton or wool, etc. • *Her beach bag is made of blue and white cloth that looks like canvas.* ❖ ύφασμα, πανί

11.5 **warrior** (n) /ˈwɒriə(r)/
sb who fights in a war • *The brave warriors fought to save their city.* ➤ war (v, n)
❖ πολεμιστής, μαχητής

11.6 **fighter** (n) /ˈfaɪtə(r)/
sb who fights • *We watched the fighter in the judo tournament.* ➤ fight (v, n) ❖ πολεμιστής, μαχητής, πυγμάχος

11.7 **villain** (n) /ˈvɪlən/
a bad or evil character in a story • *Sherlock had a clever plan to catch the villain who killed the old man.* ➤ villainous (adj) ❖ κακός, κακούργος

11.8 **evil** (adj) /ˈiːvl/
very bad to others • *The evil king killed his wife and children.* ➤ evil (n) ❖ κακός, διαβολικός

11.9 **character** (n) /ˈkærəktə(r)/
a person or animal in a story • *Hamlet was a strange and confused character in the famous Shakespeare play.* ❖ χαρακτήρας

11.10 **enemy** (n) /ˈenəmi/
people who hate you, who want to harm you or who are fighting against you • *They built a high wall around the city to protect it from their enemies.* ❖ εχθρός

11.11 **dye** (n) /daɪ/
a substance used to colour material or hair • *Bess bought some purple dye and changed the colour of her bag.* ➤ dye (v), dyed (adj)
❖ βαφή

Reading — Pages 136–137

11.12 **culture** (n) /ˈkʌltʃə/
the beliefs, art and way of life in a country • *I learnt about Spanish food and culture on my trip to Barcelona.* ➤ cultural (adj)
❖ κουλτούρα

11.13 **cave** (n) /keɪv/
a large hole in the side of a mountain or under the ground • *There were paintings of animals on the walls of the cave.* ❖ σπηλιά, σπήλαιο

11.14 **tribal** (adj) /ˈtraɪbl/
connected with people in tribes • *Anna designs T-shirts using traditional Australian tribal art.* ➤ tribe, tribespeople, tribesman, tribeswoman (n) ❖ φυλετικός

11.15 **frighten** (v) /ˈfraɪtn/
scare; make sb feel frightened • *The villagers told the story about a giant to frighten their enemies.* ➤ fright (n), frightening, frightened (adj) ❖ τρομάζω

11.16 **ceremony** (n) /ˈserəməni/
a traditional event where people do things in a special way • *After the wedding ceremony, they had their reception in a big tent in the park.* ➤ ceremonial (adj) ❖ τελετή

11.17 **transform** (v) /trænsˈfɔːm/
change sth/sb into sth else • *We tranformed our playground into a theatre for the school play.* ➤ transformation (n) ❖ μεταμορφώνω

11.18 **dramatic** (adj) /drəˈmætɪk/
connected with drama; exciting and surprising • *The paintings on the back of the stage made the whole scene look dramatic.* ➤ drama (n), dramatically (adv) ❖ δραματικός

11.19 **root** (n) /ruːt/
the part of a plant that grows under the ground • *Make sure the roots of the plant have enough water.* ❖ ρίζα

11.20 **berry** (n) /ˈberi/
a small fruit that grows on trees or bushes • *Sheila picked some juicy berries to make jam.* ❖ μούρο

11.21 **ingredient** (n) /ɪnˈɡriːdiənt/
one of the things needed to make particular food or to put in a meal • *Have you got all the ingredients you need to make chocolate biscuits?* ❖ συστατικό

11.22 **crush** (v) /krʌʃ/
press sth hard so that it breaks • *Farmers use a special machine to crush grain to make flour.* ❖ σπάω, συνθλίβω

11.23 **powder** (n) /ˈpaʊdə(r)/
very small pieces of soft dry material • *The actors put coloured powder on their faces before the performance.* ➣ powder (v), powdery (adj) ❖ σκόνη, πούδρα

11.24 **dust** (n) /dʌst/
very small pieces of dirt that move in the air and land on things • *The bookshelves are covered in dust. I need to clean the room.* ➣ dust (v), duster (n), dusty (adj) ❖ σκόνη

11.25 **feather** (n) /ˈfeðə(r)/
a soft light part from a bird's body • *The baby chickens looked very cute with their soft yellow feathers.* ❖ φτερό, πούπουλο

11.26 **special effects** (n) /ˌspeʃl ɪˈfekts/
unusual pieces of action in a film or play, with sounds or lights, etc. made by special machines • *The special effects in the film were amazing. It looked so real and scary!* ❖ ειδικά εφέ, σπέσιαλ εφέ

11.27 **scare** (v) /skeə/
make sb feel afraid • *The cat scared the birds in the garden and they flew away.* ➣ scare (n), scary (adj) ❖ τρομάζω, φοβίζω
✎ Syn: frighten

11.28 **a bit** (adv) /ə bɪt/
a little • *You looked a bit frightened when the villain came on stage.* ❖ λιγάκι

11.29 **custom** (n) /ˈkʌstəm/
a traditional way of doing sth; • *It's a custom to give visitors flowers when they arrive in Hawaii.* ➣ customary (adj) ❖ έθιμο, παράδοση

Vocabulary   Pages 138–139

11.30 **aisle** (n) /aɪl/
a passage between the rows of seats in a plane, train, theatre, etc. or between shelves in a shop • *The milk and yoghurt are in the fridge in the next aisle.* ❖ διάδρομος

11.31 **audience** (n) /ˈɔːdiəns/
the people who watch a performance in a cinema or theatre • *The audience was excited when the villain came on stage.* ❖ ακροατήριο, κοινό

11.32 **author** (n) /ˈɔːθə(r)/
sb who writes books, articles, etc. • *Who is your favourite author? Mine is Roald Dahl.* ❖ συγγραφέας

11.33 **back cover** (n) /bæk ˈkʌvə(r)/
the hard outside page on the back of a book or magazine • *There was a short description of the characters on the back cover of the book.* ❖ οπισθόφυλλο

11.34 **conductor** (n) /kənˈdʌktə(r)/
sb who stands in front of musicians to lead their performance • *Our music teacher was the conductor for the school orchestra.* ➣ conduct (v) ❖ μαέστρος

11.35 **front cover** (n) /frʌnt ˈkʌvə(r)/
the hard outside page on the front of a book or magazine • *Katrina was so happy to see her name on the front cover of the book.* ❖ εξώφυλλο

11.36 **orchestra** (n) /ˈɔːkɪstrə/
a large group of people who play musical instruments together • *Marinos plays the violin in the school orchestra.* ❖ ορχήστρα

11.37 **musician** (n) /mjuˈzɪʃn/
sb who plays or writes music • *Phil Lynott was a great singer and musician.* ➣ music (n), musical (n, adj) ❖ μουσικός

11.38 **row** (n) /rəʊ/
a group of people or things in a straight line next to each other • *We sat in the front row at the theatre.* ❖ σειρά

11.39 **seat** (n) /siːt/
sth for sitting on • *I had a seat next to the aisle on the plane.* ➣ seat (v), seating (n) ❖ θέση

Theatre

aisle	row
audience	seat
balcony	silence
curtain	special effects

11.40 **title** (n) /ˈtaɪtl/
the name of a book or story • *The title of the book is Fantastic Mr Fox.* ❖ τίτλος

11.41 **clap** (v) /klæp/
hit your hands together to show you like sth • *The audience clapped loudly at the end of the play.* ➣ clap (n) ❖ χειροκροτώ

11.42 **novel** (n) /ˈnɒvl/
a long story in a book • *The Twits is my favourite Roald Dahl novel.* ➣ novelist (n) ❖ μυθιστόρημα

11.43 **curtain** (n) /ˈkɜːtn/
a piece of cloth to cover a stage • *When the curtains opened, the two main actors were on the stage.* ❖ αυλαία

11.44 **heroine** (n) /ˈherəʊɪn/
a female hero • *Kate Winslet played the heroine in the film.* ➣ hero, heroism (n), heroic (adj) ❖ ηρωίδα, πρωταγωνίστρια

11.45 **energetically** (adv) /ˌenəˈdʒetɪkli/
with a lot of energy or showing excitement
● *They sang and danced energetically until the end of the night.* ➣ energy (n), energetic (adj)
❖ με ενέργεια

11.46 **brilliantly** (adv) /ˈbrɪliəntli/
very well ● *The guitarist played brilliantly.*
➣ brilliance (n), brilliant (adj) ❖ εξαιρετικά, λαμπρά

11.47 **beautifully** (adv) /ˈbjuːtɪfli/
in a beautiful way ● *Miranda sings beautifully.*
➣ beauty (n), beautiful (adj) ❖ όμορφα

11.48 **creatively** (adv) /kriˈeɪtɪvli/
in a creative way ● *She writes music creatively.* ➣ create (v), creation, creator (n), creative (adj) ❖ δημιουργικά

11.49 **sadly** (adv) /ˈsædli/
in a sad way; unfortunately ● *Sadly, we couldn't get tickets for the concert.* ➣ sadden (v), sadness (n), sad (adj) ❖ δυστυχώς

11.50 **quickly** (adv) /ˈkwɪkli/
fast ● *The actors left the theatre quickly after the performance.* ➣ quick (adj) ❖ γρήγορα

Adverbs

beautifully	energetically
brilliantly	meanwhile
creatively	quickly
downstairs	sadly

11.51 **keen on sth/sb** (adj) /kiːn ɒn ˈsʌmθɪŋ ˈsʌmbədi/
interested in sth/sb ● *Hilda isn't very keen on jazz. She prefers rock music.*
❖ ενθουσιασμένος με κάτι/κάποιον, το να μου αρέσει πολύ κάτι

11.52 **tired of sth/sb** (adj) /ˈtaɪəd əv ˈsʌmθɪŋ ˈsʌmbədi/
bored with sth/sb ● *I'm tired of watching the same kind of films on TV every week.*
❖ βαρέθηκα με κάτι/κάποιον

11.53 **obvious** (adj) /ˈɒbviəs/
clear to see ● *It was obvious that the audience enjoyed the play very much.* ➣ obviously (adv)
❖ φανερός

Grammar   Pages 140–141

11.54 **marvellous** (adj) /ˈmaːvələs/
wonderful ● *The dancers were marvellous!*
➣ marvel (v, n), marvellously (adv)
❖ υπέροχος

11.55 **twit** (n) /twɪt/
a silly person ● *Don't call your brother a twit! Apologise to him.* ❖ ζωντόβολο, βλάκας

11.56 **sunflower** (n) /ˈsʌnflaʊə(r)/
a tall plant with big yellow flowers ● *Grandma usually puts sunflower seeds on salads.*
❖ ηλιοτρόπιο

11.57 **thief** (n) /θiːf/
sb who steals sth ● *A thief stole the musical instruments and the orchestra couldn't play.*
➣ theft (n) ❖ κλέφτης
✎ Plural: thieves

11.58 **actress** (n) /ˈæktrəs/
a female actor ● *Who was the actress who played Mary Poppins?* ➣ act (v), actor, acting (n) ❖ ηθοποιός (γυναίκα)

11.59 **recycled** (adj) /ˌriːˈsaɪkld/
made from sth that was used before ● *These programmes were made from recycled paper.*
➣ recycling (n), recycle (v) ❖ ανακυκλωμένος

11.60 **bottom** (n) /ˈbɒtəm/
the lowest part of sth ● *The vegetables are in the bottom of the fridge.* ❖ κάτω μέρος

11.61 **wizard** (n) /ˈwɪzəd/
a male who does magic ● *In the story, Harry goes to Hogwarts, the school for wizards and witches.* ❖ μάγος

11.62 **dragon** (n) /ˈdrægən/
a large animal in stories, like a giant lizard that breathes fire and has wings ● *She wrote a lovely children's book about friendly dragons.*
❖ δράκος

11.63 **all of a sudden** (expr) /ɔːl əv ə ˈsʌdn/
suddenly ● *All of a sudden, the frog became a wizard!* ❖ ξαφνικά

11.64 **scream** (v) /skriːm/
shout because you are scared ● *The boy screamed when he saw the snake.* ➣ scream (n) ❖ ουρλιάζω

11.65 **bar** (n) /baː(r)/
a long flat piece of sth with straight sides, e.g. chocolate, soap ● *Don't eat a whole bar of chocolate before your dinner.* ❖ μπάρα, πλάκα

11.66 **expensive** (adj) /ɪkˈspensɪv/
costing a lot of money ● *Theatre tickets are expensive, so we don't go very often.*
❖ ακριβός

11.67 **violin** (n) /ˌvaɪəˈlɪn/
a musical stringed instrument that you hold on your shoulder to play ● *Marinos played a ζωντόβολο, ζωντόβολο, beautiful tune on his violin.* ❖ βιολί

Music

conductor	rock
musician	violin
orchestra	

11.68 **rubbish** (n) /ˈrʌbɪʃ/
things that sb throws away • *The bins were full of rubbish.* ❖ σκουπίδια

11.69 **practise** (v) /ˈpræktɪs/
do sth often to get better at it • *We practised our songs for weeks before the concert.* ➤ practice (n) ❖ εξασκώ, κάνω πρόβα

Listening
Page 142

11.70 **present** (v) /prɪˈzent/
show sth to sb • *We presented our school magazine to the class.* ➤ presentation, presenter (n) ❖ παρουσιάζω

11.71 **detective** (n) /dɪˈtektɪv/
sb who looks for information about crimes to find criminals • *Diane likes reading detective stories to guess what happens in the end.* ➤ detect (v) ❖ ντετέκτιβ, αστυνομικός

11.72 **rock** (n) /rɒk/
a kind of music usually played with electric guitars and drums, etc. • *I think rock music is better than rap.* ❖ ροκ μουσική

11.73 **comic** (n) /ˈkɒmɪk/
a magazine that tells stories with pictures, usually for children • *Do you like reading comics like Superman?* ➤ comic, comical (adj) ❖ κόμικ

11.74 **presenter** (n) /prɪˈzentə(r)/
sb who presents a TV or radio show • *The presenter welcomed the actress to the talk show.* ➤ present (v), presentation (n) ❖ παρουσιαστής

11.75 **writer** (n) /ˈraɪtə(r)/
sb who writes things for others to read • *Anna Sewell was an unusual writer who wrote only one book – Black Beauty.* ➤ write (v), writing (n) ❖ συγγραφέας

11.76 **maximum** (n) /ˈmæksɪməm/
the most that is possible or needed • *The maximum time allowed to do the writing exam is one hour.* ❖ μέγιστο

11.77 **announce** (v) /əˈnaʊns/
to tell people an important plan or decision • *Julia and Hugh announced that they're getting married.* ➤ announcement (n), announcer (n) ❖ ανακοινώνω

People

actress	presenter
author	thief
character	twit
detective	villain
enemy	warrior
fighter	wizard
heroine	writer

Speaking
Page 143

11.78 **portrait** (n) /ˈpɔːtreɪt/
a picture of a person, often just the head and shoulders • *The art gallery was full of portraits of kings and queens from the past.* ❖ πορτρέτο

11.79 **abstract** (adj) /ˈæbstrækt/
generally from the imagination, not based on real things or events • *He did an abstract painting with a beautiful pattern using the colours of fire.* ❖ αφηρημένος (για τέχνη)

11.80 **adventure** (n) /ədˈventʃə(r)/
a journey or experience that is exciting and may be dangerous • *The story about pirates was full of action and adventure.* ➤ adventurous (adj) ❖ περιπέτεια

11.81 **fantasy** (n) /ˈfæntəsi/
a story often with magic and things that are different from real life • *Alice fell down the rabbit hole into a fantasy world of talking animals.* ❖ φαντασία

11.82 **romance** (n) /rəʊˈmæns/
a story about people in love • *Jane writes novels about love and romance.* ➤ romantic (adj) ❖ ρομάντζο

11.83 **mystery** (n) /ˈmɪstri/
sth that is difficult to understand or explain • *The clever detective solved the mystery at the end of the story.* ➤ mysterious (adj) ❖ μυστήριο

11.84 **balcony** (n) /ˈbælkəni/
the seats upstairs in a theatre; an area on the outside wall of a building that you can walk out on to • *We had a great view of the stage from the front row on the balcony.* ❖ μπαλκόνι

11.85 **silence** (n) /ˈsaɪləns/
a state of having no noise or sounds • *Tania sat down to relax and enjoy the silence in her room.* ➤ silent (adj), silently (adv) ❖ ησυχία

11.86 **relax** (v) /rɪˈlæks/
rest and do something you enjoy • *After finishing the difficult project, Mike took a few days off work to relax.* ➤ relaxed (adj), relaxing (adj) ❖ χαλαρώνω

11.87 **preference** (n) /ˈprefrəns/
liking one thing or person more than another • *Maria has a preference for detective stories. She has read all the Inspector Rebus books.* ➤ prefer (v) ❖ προτίμηση

11.88 **respect** (v) /rɪˈspekt/
take care not to say/do sth sb else thinks is wrong • *Visitors have to respect the local people on the island.* ➤ respect (n) ❖ σέβομαι, εκτιμώ

Writing

11.89 **narrative** (n) /ˈnærətɪv/
a story; an account of sth • *It was an interesting narrative with colourful descriptions.* ➢ narrate (v), narrator (n) ❖ αφήγηση/-ημα, διήγηση/-ημα

11.90 **calm** (adj) /kɑːm/
quiet; without wind • *The sea was calm when we sailed out of the port.* ➢ calm (v, n) ❖ ήρεμος, ψύχραιμος

11.91 **as soon as** (expr) /əz suːn əz/
in a short time; the moment when • *As soon as I heard about the earthquake, I called my family to make sure they were okay.* ❖ μόλις

11.92 **meanwhile** (adv) /ˈmiːnwaɪl/
while sth else is happening • *Mum and Dad were putting the tent up. Meanwhile, I was exploring the campsite.* ❖ εν τω μεταξύ, την ίδια ώρα

11.93 **firewood** (n) /ˈfaɪəwʊd/
wood cut into pieces for making a fire • *Outside the house, there was enough firewood to last for the winter.* ❖ καυσόξυλο

11.94 **rubber** (n) /ˈrʌbə(r)/
a small piece of soft material to remove pencil marks • *Take a pencil and rubber with you for the test.* ➢ rub (v), rubber (adj) ❖ γόμα, σβήστρα ✎ Syn: eraser

11.95 **erase** (v) /ɪˈreɪz/
make a pencil mark disappear • *This pen has special ink that you can erase easily.* ➢ eraser (n) ❖ σβήνω

11.96 **sketchbook** (n) /ˈsketʃbʊk/
a book with paper for drawing on • *Rosemary sat under a tree with her sketchbook to draw some pictures.* ➢ sketch (v, n) ❖ τετράδιο για σκίτσο

11.97 **wherever** (adv, conj) /weərˈevə(r)/
in all places • *Wherever she went, her dog followed her.* ❖ όπου, οπουδήποτε

11.98 **find** (n) /faɪnd/
sth that sb has found • *They made some interesting historical finds when they dug in the fields near the castle.* ➢ find (v) ❖ ανακάλυψη

11.99 **scream** (n) /skriːm/
a loud cry made by sb who is scared or hurt • *She heard a scream outside and looked out of the window.* ➢ scream (v) ❖ κραυγή

11.100 **downstairs** (adv) /ˌdaʊnˈsteəz/
the lower floor of a building below the one where you are • *Our bedrooms are upstairs and the kitchen and living room are downstairs.* ➢ downstairs (adj) ❖ στον κάτω όροφο

11.101 **crab** (n) /kræb/
a small animal that has a hard shell, eight legs and two sharp arms and lives in the sea • *The crabs ran between the rocks into the sea.* ❖ καβούρι

11.102 **hermit crab** (n) /ˈhɜːmɪt kræb/
a type of crab that lives in the shells of other sea creatures • *When a hermit crab gets too big for its shell, it moves out and find another one.* ❖ πάγουρος (είδος κάβουρα που ζει μέσα σε άδειο όστρακο)

11.103 **setting** (n) /ˈsetɪŋ/
where sth happens • *The island of Corfu was the setting for Gerald Durrell's novels.* ➢ set (v) ❖ τοποθεσία ✎ Syn: location

11.104 **solution** (n) /səˈluːʃn/
a way of solving a problem or doing sth • *Let's talk and try to find a solution to our money problems.* ➢ solve (v) ❖ λύση

11.105 **all at once** (expr) /ɔːl ət wʌns/
suddenly • *All at once, I realised that he was the thief.* ❖ ξαφνικά

11.106 **stuck** (adj) /stʌk/
not able to move out of a position • *When the boat engine stopped, we were stuck in the middle of the sea.* ➢ stick (v) ❖ κολλημένος

11.107 **improve** (v) /ɪmˈpruːv/
make sth better • *Your drawing has improved since you started taking art classes.* ➢ improvement (n) ❖ βελτιώνω

11.108 **punctuation** (n) /ˌpʌŋktʃuˈeɪʃn/
the system of marks used to separate sentences, phrases or questions • *Correct punctuation helps to make the meaning of the sentence clear.* ➢ punctuate (v) ❖ στίξη

Books

adventure	novel
back cover	punctuation
comic	romance
fantasy	setting
front cover	solution
mystery	title
narrative	

Video 11
Creative Recycling

Page 146

11.109 **recycling** (n) /ˌriːˈsaɪklɪŋ/
using things again that were used before
● *Recycling is important for our environment so we don't throw so many things away.*
➣ recycle (v) ❖ ανακύκλωση

11.110 **label** (n) /ˈleɪbl/
a piece of paper on the side of a container, etc. to give information about what is inside
● *Always read the labels on cans or packets to check what's in the food you're buying.*
➣ label (v) ❖ ετικέτα

11.111 **pane** (n) /peɪn/
a piece of glass that is part of a window
● *The thief broke the pane of glass on the door to open it.* ❖ τζάμι

11.112 **stained-glass** (adj) /ˌsteɪnd ˈɡlɑːs/
pieces of coloured glass used to make windows ● *The neighbours have a lovely stained-glass window on their front door.*
❖ βιτρό

11.113 **lorry** (n) /ˈlɒri/
a large vehicle for transporting heavy things by road ● *There was a big lorry driving in front of us, but we couldn't pass it on the country road.*
❖ φορτηγό

11.114 **melt** (v) /melt/
heat sth, e.g. ice, to turn it into liquid ● *Put the ice cream in the freezer so that it doesn't melt.*
❖ λιώνω

11.115 **vase** (n) /vɑːz/
a container for putting flowers in or as a decoration ● *We saw a display of beautifully painted old vases in the museum.* ❖ βάζο

11.116 **recycle** (v) /ˌriːˈsaɪkl/
use sth again that was used before ● *In our neighbourhood, you can put papers into the special bins to recycle them.* ➣ recycling (n), recycled (adj) ❖ ανακυκλώνω

11.117 **craftsperson** (n) /ˈkrɑːftspɜːsn/
sb who makes artistic things by hand
● *Tourists often stop in the village to buy carpets made by the local craftspeople.*
❖ τεχνίτης ✎ Plural: craftspeople
✎ Also: craftsman, craftswoman

11.118 **turn (sth/sb) into (sth/sb)** (phr v) /tuːn ˈsʌmθɪŋ ˈsʌmbədi ˈɪntə ˈsʌmθɪŋ ˈsʌmbədi/
change sth/sb to make them become sth/sb else ● *The weekend course has turned Jim into an expert photographer.* ❖ μετατρέπω

11.119 **warehouse** (n) /ˈweəhaʊs/
a large store where a company keeps things to send to shops or customers ● *The building was a clothes warehouse before it was turned into flats.* ❖ αποθήκη

11.120 **oven** (n) /ˈʌvn/
a machine that sth is baked in; the inside part of a cooker where food is cooked ● *The craftsperson took the vases out of the oven, then left them to cool before painting them.*
❖ φούρνος

Art

abstract	pavement
canvas	portrait
cave	powder
chalk	rubber
cloth	sketchbook
craftsperson	stained-glass
dye	sunflower
feather	vase
oven	

Vocabulary Exercises

A Circle the odd one out.

1	berry	root	cave
2	title	row	seat
3	chalk	feather	dye
4	adventure	comic	novel
5	romance	fantasy	portrait
6	canvas	culture	sketchbook

B Match the synonyms.

1	scare	☐	a	material
2	relax	☐	b	rest
3	warrior	☐	c	powder
4	dust	☐	d	tradition
5	author	☐	e	turn into
6	custom	☐	f	frighten
7	cloth	☐	g	fighter
8	transform	☐	h	writer

C Complete the sentences with words formed from the words in bold.

1 Which row do you want to sit in? Do you have any _____?   **PREFER**
2 Is there a special bin to put rubbish in for _____ at your school?   **RECYCLE**
3 They decorated the stage _____ for the dance performance.   **BEAUTIFUL**
4 The special effects made the film more _____.   **DRAMA**
5 I'm taking violin lessons because I want to become a _____.   **MUSIC**
6 The conductor waved his arms _____ to lead the orchestra.   **ENERGETIC**
7 The _____ found a solution to the mystery.   **DETECT**
8 She spends her free time _____ painting pictures of landscapes.   **CREATE**

E Find the eight people words. Then complete the sentences with these words.

C	O	N	D	C	P	R	E	Z	A	R	D
W	I	Z	A	R	D	O	I	N	E	Z	Y
A	T	O	R	A	R	M	T	H	I	E	F
P	T	H	E	F	D	Y	W	I	T	O	R
E	S	E	M	T	N	E	I	C	O	N	T
R	P	R	E	S	E	N	T	E	R	P	R
P	R	O	A	P	I	E	F	N	O	E	A
T	E	I	F	E	P	R	E	E	I	R	F
W	R	N	T	R	C	O	N	M	N	S	E
I	A	E	M	S	D	E	T	Y	E	O	N
Z	F	T	S	O	I	V	E	I	E	F	M
A	T	C	O	N	D	U	C	T	O	R	Y

1 We watched carefully as the _____ made the vase.
2 Don't be such a _____! The answer is obvious.
3 Did the _____ escape with all the money?
4 The orchestra began to play as soon as the _____ waved his stick.
5 The warrior waited until the _____ came close enough to attack.
6 The evil _____ turned the lion into a statue.
7 The audience clapped when the _____ announced the results.
8 In the end, the clever _____ caught the villain and everyone was happy.

11 Grammar

11.1 The Passive Voice: Present Simple

Σχηματίζουμε την Passive Voice με τον Present Simple του ρήματος *be* + past participle (παθητική μετοχή).

Tense	Active	Passive
Present Simple	take/takes	**am/are/is** taken

11.2 The Passive Voice: Past Simple

Σχηματίζουμε την Passive Voice με τον Past Simple του ρήματος *be* + past participle (παθητική μετοχή).

Tense	Active	Passive
Past Simple	took	**was/were** taken

Χρησιμοποιούμε Passive Voice (παθητική φωνή) όταν:
μας ενδιαφέρει η πράξη ή το γεγονός.
→ The library **is used** by lots of people.
→ The bridge **was painted** green.
δεν γνωρίζουμε ή δεν μας ενδιαφέρει ποιός έκανε την πράξη.
→ The paintings **were found** on the walls of the cave.

Μετατρέπουμε μια ενεργητική πρόταση σε παθητική με τον παρακάτω τρόπο:
Το αντικείμενο του ρήματος της ενεργητικής πρότασης γίνεται υποκείμενο του ρήματος της παθητικής πρότασης. Το ρήμα *to be* χρησιμοποιείται στον ίδιο χρόνο με το κύριο ρήμα της ενεργητικής πρότασης, μαζί με την παθητική μετοχή (past participle) του κυρίου ρήματος της ενεργητικής πρότασης.
→ Artists **paint pictures** here. Pictures **are painted** here.
→ Children **wrote** these poems. These poems **were written** by children.

Σημείωση: Όταν είναι σημαντικό να αναφέρουμε ποιός έκανε την πράξη ή αλλιώς το ποιητικό αίτιο (agent) στην παθητική πρόταση, χρησιμοποιούμε τη λέξη *by*.
→ Roald Dahl **wrote** 'Matilda'. 'Matilda' **was written** by Roald Dahl.

11.3 Narrative Tenses

Χρησιμοποιούμε Narrative Tenses (αφηγηματικούς χρόνους) για να αφηγηθούμε γεγονότα, ανέκδοτα και ιστορίες.
Μπορούμε να χρησιμοποιήσουμε τον Past Continuous για να:
περιγράψουμε την τοποθεσία ή να δώσουμε πληροφορίες για το σκηνικό.
→ It **was snowing** when the children **were playing** football.
περιγράψουμε μια πράξη που διακόπηκε από μια άλλη πράξη.
→ We **were watching** a film when the lights **went** out.
Μπορούμε να χρησιμοποιήσουμε τον Past Simple για:
πράξεις που έγιναν σε συγκεκριμένο χρόνο στο παρελθόν.
→ **Last Monday** I went on the stage for the first time.
πράξεις που έγιναν η μία μετά την άλλη.
→ **First**, we went on a boat trip to the island, and **then** we walked along the beach. **Eventually**, we found the cave.

Σημείωση: Οι λέξεις και εκφράσεις *while, first, then, after that, as soon as, at first, until, eventually, in the end*, χρησιμοποιούνται συχνά με Narrative Tenses.

11 Grammar

Grammar Exercises

A Circle the correct words.

1 These sunflowers were **paint / painted** by Vincent van Gogh.
2 People **buy / are bought** tickets inside the cinema.
3 Her costume **makes / is made** of recycled plastic.
4 Where was this photo **taken / took**?
5 The feathers **collect / are collected** from ducks.
6 His last book **was / were** written in 1927.
7 The book **wasn't printed / didn't print** until the author died.
8 **Were / Did** the children given free tickets to the show?

B Complete the sentences using the passive voice. Use the word *by* if necessary.

1 Many tourists visit the island every summer.
The island _____.
2 They opened the new museum in 2008.
The new museum _____.
3 Rihanna sings that song.
That song _____.
4 Did they find the missing painting?
Was _____.
5 They paint these vases with bright colours.
These vases _____.
6 Sir Arthur Conan Doyle wrote the Sherlock Holmes books.
The Sherlock Holmes books _____.
7 Do they make these clothes with natural materials?
Are _____.
8 They played rock music at the wedding.
Rock music _____.

C Complete the sentences with the Past Simple or Past Continuous form of the verbs in brackets.

1 First we _____ (buy) tickets, then we went into the theatre.
2 They _____ (dance) on the stage when the earthquake happened.
3 It was a beautiful day and the sun _____ (shine).
4 The children were playing while their parents _____ (sit) by the lake.
5 As soon as the villain _____ (see) the detective, he started to run.
6 I _____ (not read) a comic when the teacher arrived. I was studying.
7 Eventually, the heroine _____ (save) the child.
8 Last week, Tom _____ (go) to the theatre for the first time.

12 School's Out!

Page 147

12.1   **cobbled** (adj) /ˈkɒbld/
having a surface made of small stones
• *Eric's feet hurt after walking for hours in the cobbled streets of the old town.* ❖ καλντερίμι, με βότσαλα

Reading   Page 148

12.2   **caravan** (n) /ˈkærəvæn/
a vehicle which you can live inside and you can pull with a car • *The Smiths decided to go on a caravan holiday instead of camping in a tent.* ❖ τροχόσπιτο

12.3   **floating** (adj) /ˈfləʊtɪŋ/
moving freely in water • *People were selling vegetables from boats at the floating market in the harbour.* ➢ float (v, n) ❖ που επιπλέει

Word Focus   Page 148

12.4   **deck** (n) /dek/
a floor on a ship • *We stood on the deck and waved goodbye to our friends on the harbour as our ship sailed.* ❖ κατάστρωμα

12.5   **neighbourhood** (n) /ˈneɪbəhʊd/
part of a town • *William has just moved to the neighbourhood, so he doesn't know many people here yet.* ➢ neighbour (n) ❖ γειτονιά

12.6   **community** (n) /kəˈmjuːnəti/
all the people that live in one area; a group of people wo share sth in common, e.g. work, nationality, etc. • *Everyone in the local community came to help the families affected by the fire.* ❖ κοινότητα

12.7   **promenade** (n) /ˌprɒməˈnɑːd/
a public walkway, often by the sea • *In the evening, we walked along the promenade and watched the sun setting over the sea.* ❖ παραλιακός πεζόδρομος

12.8   **walkway** (n) /ˈwɔːkweɪ/
a path for walking on, usually built higher than the ground • *A covered walkway goes through the aquarium.* ❖ δρομάκι, πεζόδρομος

12.9   **on board** (expr) /ɒn bɔːd/
on a plane, ship or train • *The captain welcomed everyone on board the plane and gave us some information about the route.* ❖ πάνω σε αεροπλάνο, πλοίο ή τρένο

12.10   **cabin** (n) /ˈkæbɪn/
a small room where you sleep on a ship
• *There was no window in our cabin, but instead there was a screen with a view of the sea!* ❖ καμπίνα

Reading   Pages 148–149

12.11   **the Mediterranean** (n) /ðə ˌmedɪtəˈreɪniən/
➢ Mediterranean (adj) ❖ η Μεσόγειος

12.12   **man-hour** (n) /ˈmæn aʊə(r)/
the amount of work that one person can do in one hour • *How many man-hours did it take to build the new bridge?* ❖ ποσότητα εργασίας που μπορεί να κάνει κάποιος μέσα σε μια ώρα

12.13   **zone** (n) /zəʊn/
an area used for something in particular
• *There's a parking zone next to the shopping centre.* ❖ χώρος, περιοχή

12.14   **full-size** (adj) /ˌfʊl ˈsaɪz/
of the usual size, not smaller • *The camping site has a full-size Olympic swimming pool.* ❖ κανονικού μεγέθους

12.15   **court** (n) /kɔːt/
the area where a game is played in tennis, badminton, basketball or volleyball • *Vanessa hit the ball across the net to the other side of the court.* ❖ γήπεδο

12.16   **golf course** (n) /ˈgɒlf kɔːs/
a large area of land where golf is played
• *A storm began when we got to the ninth hole of the golf course, so we had to stop the game.* ❖ γήπεδο του γκολφ

12.17   **passenger** (n) /ˈpæsɪndʒə(r)/
sb who is travelling on a type of transport, e.g. bus, car, boat, plane, train • *The ship waited for all the passengers to return, and then set sail for the next port.* ❖ επιβάτης

12.18   **crowded** (adj) /ˈkraʊdɪd/
with a lot of people • *The harbour was crowded with people waiting to board the ships.* ➢ crowd (n) ❖ πολυσύχναστος, γεμάτος με κόσμο

12.19   **cafeteria** (n) /ˌkæfəˈtɪəriə/
a café or self-service restaurant, often in a public building • *You can buy snacks from the school cafeteria.* ❖ κυλικείο

12.20   **pad** (n) /pæd/
a small tablet • *Instead of calling a waiter, passengers use an electronic pad to order drinks.* ❖ τάμπλετ, ηλεκτρονικό σημειωματάριο

12.21 **in advance** (expr) /ɪn ədˈvɑːns/
before the time sth happens • *The cruise is very popular, so you need to book tickets months in advance.* ❖ προκαταβολικά, πιο μπροστά

12.22 **sun cream** (n) /ˈsʌnkriːm/
cream to protect your skin from the sun • *Don't forget to put on your suncream before you go out.* ❖ αντιηλιακό

12.23 **passport** (n) /ˈpɑːspɔːt/
a small official book that shows who you are and where you come from when you travel to another country • *Make sure you've got your passport before you go to the airport.* ❖ διαβατήριο

Vocabulary
Pages 150–151

12.24 **board** (v) /bɔːd/
get into a plane, boat, etc., to start travelling • *We waited for three hours to board the ship that arrived late.* ➤ boarding (adj, n) ❖ επιβιβάζομαι

12.25 **departure** (n) /dɪˈpɑːtʃə(r)/
leaving a place at a particular time • *All the flight departures from London were late because of bad weather.* ➤ depart (v) ❖ αναχώρηση

12.26 **passport control** (n) /ˈpɑːspɔːt kənˈtrəʊl/
the part of an airport or port, etc. where sb checks your passport • *The passengers had to wait for half an hour to go through passport control before collecting their bags.* ❖ έλεγχος διαβατηρίου

12.27 **security** (n) /sɪˈkjʊərəti/
the part of an airport where your bags are checked to make sure you aren't carrying anything illegal • *They took everything out of Daniel's bag to check it when he went through security.* ➤ secure (v, adj), securely (adv) ❖ ασφάλεια

12.28 **platform** (n) /ˈplætfɔːm/
the part of a train station where you get on or off a train • *The train to Dundee is leaving from Platform 6.* ❖ πλατφόρμα

12.29 **seatbelt** (n) /ˈsiːtbelt/
a belt on a seat in a plane, car, coach, etc. that you put around you to keep you safe • *The passenger was hurt in the car crash because he wasn't wearing a seatbelt.* ❖ ζώνη ασφαλείας

12.30 **motorway** (n) /ˈməʊtəweɪ/
a wide road where cars can travel very fast between cities • *You can drive across the country very quickly now on the new motorway from Thessalonika.* ❖ αυτοκινητόδρομος

12.31 **cloudy** (adj) /ˈklaʊdi/
with lots of clouds and not bright • *Cloudy weather makes some people feel sad.* ➤ cloud (n) ❖ συννεφιασμένος

12.32 **rainy** (adj) /ˈreɪni/
with a lot of rain • *The city has lots of museums and other places to visit on a rainy day.* ➤ rain (v, n) ❖ βροχερός

12.33 **snowy** (adj) /ˈsnəʊi/
with a lot of snow • *The snowy mountains looked perfect for skiing.* ➤ snow (v, n) (adv) ❖ χιονισμένος

12.34 **stormy** (adj) /stɔːmi/
with very bad weather with strong wind and usually rain or snow • *We cancelled the sailing trip because of the stormy weather.* ➤ storm (n) ❖ θυελλώδης

12.35 **sunny** (adj) /ˈsʌni/
with a lot of sunshine • *It was a sunny morning when we started our journey, but it got cloudy later.* ➤ sun (n) ❖ ηλιόλουστος

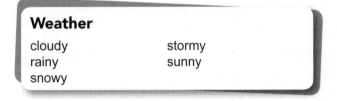

Weather

cloudy	stormy
rainy	sunny
snowy	

Directions

north	east
south	west

12.36 **Sicily** (n) /ˈsɪsəli/
➤ Sicilian (adj, n) ❖ Σικελία

12.37 **south** (n) /saʊθ/
the south part of a country; the direction that is on your right when you watch the sun rising • *Cornwall is a beautiful place in the south of England.* ➤ south, southern, southerly (adj) ❖ νότος

12.38 **east** (n) /iːst/
the direction you look at to see the sun rising • *Turkey is a country to the east of Greece.* ➤ east, eastern, easterly (adj) ❖ ανατολή

12.39 **west** (n) /west/
the direction you look at to see the sun setting • *The rain was coming across the sea from the west.* ➤ west, western, westerly (adj), ❖ δύση

12.40 **postcard** (n) /ˈpəʊstkɑːd/
a card with a picture on one side and a space to write a message on the back • *My aunt always sends me a postcard with a nice view when she goes on holiday.* ❖ καρτ-ποστάλ

12.41 sunbathe (v) /ˈsʌnbeɪð/
stay outside in the sunshine to make your skin go brown • *Tracy's skin was bright red after she was sunbathing on her first day in Spain.*
➢ sunbathing (n) ❖ κάνω ηλιοθεραπεία

12.42 pack (v) /pæk/
put things into a bag or box • *Sotiria was packing her suitcase to prepare for her holidays.* ❖ φτιάχνω τη βαλίτσα, πακετάρω

12.43 creamy (adj) /ˈkriːmi/
with a lot of cream; that feels or tastes thick and smooth like cream • *We had creamy yoghurt with fruit and honey for dessert.*
➢ cream (n) ❖ κρεμώδης

12.44 abroad (adv) /əˈbrɔːd/
in or to a foreign country • *Georgia has been to lots of countries because she travels abroad for her work.* ❖ στο εξωτερικό

Grammar   Pages 152–153

12.45 schedule (n) /ˈʃedjuːl/
a list of events or jobs and when they will happen or when you must do them • *Jane's got an appointment at the hairdresser's on her schedule.* ❖ πρόγραμμα

12.46 set sail (expr) /set ˈseɪl/
start a journey by boat • *The sea was calm when we set sail for the island.* ❖ σαλπάρω, ξεκινώ ταξίδι (με βάρκα/πλοίο)

12.47 historical (adj) /hɪˈstɒrɪkl/
about events or people in the past • *He wrote historical novels set in the sixteenth century.*
➢ history (n), historic (adj) ❖ ιστορικός

12.48 cathedral (n) /kəˈθiːdrəl/
the largest and most important church of a city • *The tourists stopped to watch a wedding at St Giles Cathedral after visiting the castle in Edinburgh.* ❖ καθεδρικός ναός

12.49 the Vatican (n) /ˈvætɪkən/
❖ Βατικανό

12.50 evidence (n) /ˈevɪdəns/
information, proof • *The police are looking for evidence to help them find the killer.*
❖ απόδειξη, αποδεικτικό στοιχείο

12.51 delay (v) /dɪˈleɪ/
make sth happen later than planned • *The ship was delayed because of the stormy weather.* ➢ delayed (adj), delay (n)
❖ καθυστερώ

12.52 couch potato (n) /ˈkaʊtʃ pəteɪtəʊ/
a lazy person who sits and watches TV all the time • *Don't be such a couch potato! Let's go for a walk in the hills.* ❖ αργός, αδρανής

Expressions

couch potato   set sail
on board   what a shame
in advance

Listening   Page 154

12.53 accommodation (n) /əˌkɒməˈdeɪʃn/
a place to stay in • *We looked for accommodation in Geneva on the Internet and found a really nice hotel.* ➢ accommodate (v)
❖ κατάλυμα

12.54 excursion (n) /ɪkˈskɜːʃn/
a short journey to a place and back for fun
• *We're going on a school excursion to Nafplion next week.* ❖ εκδρομή
✎ Syn: trip

12.55 luggage (n) /ˈlʌɡɪdʒ/
all the bags you're carrying when you're travelling • *Joan put her luggage in the back of the car and drove to the campsite.*
❖ αποσκευές, βαλίτσα

12.56 raincoat (n) /ˈreɪnkəʊt/
a coat that protects you from the rain
• *Take your raincoat because the weather will be wet this afternoon.* ❖ αδιάβροχο

Travel

Nouns	seatbelt
accommodation	security
cabin	sun cream
canoeing	walkway
caravan	
deck	**Adjectives**
departure	alone
excursion	cobbled
luggage	crowded
motorway	deep
passenger	floating
passport	helpful
passport control	historical
platform	safe
postcard	serious
schedule	stressful

Speaking   Page 155

12.57 countryside (n) /ˈkʌntrisaɪd/
land with fields, woods, etc. • *I like living in the city, but it's nice to go out for walks in the countryside at weekends.* ❖ εξοχή

12.58 **cottage** (n) /ˈkɒtɪdʒ/
a small house, especially in the countryside
• *Helen's grandparents live in a lovely little cottage in a mountain village.* ❖ μικρό εξοχικό σπίτι

12.59 **alone** (adj, adv) /əˈləʊn/
without any other person • *My brother lives alone in a flat near his university and he visits us during the holidays.* ❖ μόνος

12.60 **canoeing** (n) /kəˈnuːɪŋ/
the hobby or sport of travelling across water in a canoe • *We hired boats and went canoeing on the lake.* ➢ canoe (v, n), canoeist (n) ❖ κανό (το άθλημα)

12.61 **deep** (adj) /diːp/
going a long way down between the top and the bottom of sth, especially water • *The pool is two metres deep at one end and one metre at the other.* ➢ deepen (v), depth (n), deeply (adv) ❖ βαθύς

12.62 **helpful** (adj) /ˈhelpfl/
able to help others • *The Browns got some helpful leaflets about tours from the tourist information office.* ➢ help (v, n) ❖ χρήσιμος

12.63 **serious** (adj) /ˈsɪəriəs/
careful and thoughtful; not silly • *Are you serious about going to Antarctica? Do you know how cold it is?* ➢ seriousness (n), seriously (adv) ❖ σοβαρός

12.64 **stressful** (adj) /ˈstresfɔːl/
worrying; not relaxing • *Studying for exams can be so stressful.* ➢ stress (v, n), stressed (adj) ❖ αγχωτικός, έντονος

Writing

Pages 156–157

12.65 **occasion** (n) /əˈkeɪʒn/
a special time or event • *My grandparent's 50th wedding anniversary was a very important occasion for them.* ❖ περίσταση, περίπτωση

12.66 **term** (n) /tɜːm/
a period of time that is part of the school year • *We have tests at the end of each term at school.* ❖ τρίμηνο

12.67 **prom** (n) /prɒm/
a dance, usually at the end of the school year at high school • *My sister can't decide what to wear to the school prom. She's been in front of the mirror for hours!* ❖ χορός αποφοίτησης

12.68 **dress code** (n) /ˈdres kəʊd/
the rules about what sb is allowed to wear at a place • *Passengers need to follow the dress code in the cruise ship's restaurant. No swimwear allowed.* ❖ κανόνας ένδυσης

12.69 **tie** (n) /taɪ/
an item of clothing usually worn by men, which hangs down from the neck of a shirt • *Frank wore a shirt and tie for the first time at his cousin's wedding.* ❖ γραβάτα

12.70 **what a shame** (expr) /wɒt ə ʃeɪm/
used to say you feel sad or disappointed about sth • *What a shame you lost your camera before you could put your photos on the laptop.* ❖ κρίμα
✎ Syn: what a pity

12.71 **graduation** (n) /ˌɡrædʒuˈeɪʃn/
the time when sb completes a university course and gets their degree; the ceremony where certificates, etc. are given to students at the end of a course • *My mum has just finished her teaching course and we're going to her graduation next month.* ➢ graduate (v, n) ❖ αποφοίτηση

Places

cafeteria	zone
cathedral	Arctic Ocean
community	Atlantic Ocean
cottage	Greenland
countryside	Sicily
court	the Mediterranean
golf course	the Northwest
neighbourhood	Passage
promenade	the Vatican

Video 12
Best Summer Job

Page 158

12.72 **Arctic Ocean** (n) /ˌɑːktɪk ˈəʊʃn/
❖ Αρκτικός Ωκεανός

12.73 **Atlantic Ocean** (n) /ətˌlæntɪk ˈəʊʃn/
❖ Ατλαντικός Ωκεανός

12.74 **Greenland** (n) /ˈɡriːnˌlænd/
❖ Γροινλανδία

12.75 **identify** (v) /aɪˈdentɪfaɪ/
find or discover sb/sth • *It was difficult to identify the woman in the old photo at first. Then I realised she was my great-grandmother.* ➢ identity, identification (n) ❖ αναγνωρίζω

12.76 **moult** (v) /məʊlt/
lose skin, hair or feathers before the new skin/hair/feathers grow in • *Our dog only moults once a year – for 52 weeks!* ❖ αλλάζω δέρμα/πτέρωμα/τρίχωμα, μαδάω

12.77 **socialise** (v) /ˈsəʊʃəlaɪz/
meet others and spend time with them
• *Children can learn to socialise with others at school.* ➤ socialisation (n), social (adj), socially (adv) ❖ κοινωνικοποιούμαι

12.78 **behaviour** (n) /bɪˈheɪvjə(r)/
the way sb does things • *Tina was confused at her cat's strange behaviour before the earthquake.* ➤ behave (v) ❖ συμπεριφορά

12.79 **the Northwest Passage** (n) /ðəˌnɔːθ ˈwest ˈpæsɪdʒ/
❖ το Βορειοδυτικά Πέρασμα (το πέρασμα μεταξύ τον Ατλαντικό και τον Ειρηνικό Ωκεανό)

12.80 **safe** (adj) /seɪf/
not in danger or dangerous • *Is the water safe to drink on the island?* ➤ save (v), safety (n), safely (adv) ❖ ασφαλής

Vocabulary Exercises

A **Match to make sentences.**

1 She found her seat number after getting on ☐
2 We waited for hours at passport ☐
3 You can play a game on the golf ☐
4 It's better to book tickets in ☐
5 My brother is a real couch ☐
6 Oh, no. What a ☐

a advance if you want to visit the Vatican.
b board the plane.
c potato who isn't interested in going anywhere.
d shame you can't come with us.
e control and nearly missed the flight.
f course near the beach.

B **Unjumble the words to find the places.**

1 yesidcountr _____
2 tagotec _____
3 rahedlcat _____
4 turco _____
5 noze _____
6 fetaerica _____
7 rompedena _____
8 hboodouneigrh _____

C **Match the meanings a–h to the words 1–8 from B.**

☐ a the area where a game is played in tennis, basketball or volleyball
☐ b land with fields, woods, etc. not in a city
☐ c an area used for something in particular
☐ d a public walkway, often by the sea
☐ e the largest and most important church of a city
☐ f part of a town
☐ g a café or self-service restaurant, often in a public building
☐ h a small house, especially in the countryside

D **Complete the sentences with words formed from the words in bold.**

1 The travel guide was really _____ and took us on a tour of the city.   HELP
2 Tourists can _____ with each other around the pool area.   SOCIAL
3 People's _____ changes when they relax on holiday.   BEHAVE
4 Travelling a long distance with young children is _____ for parents.   STRESS
5 I like reading _____ novels when I'm travelling by plane.   HISTORY
6 The _____ weather destroyed the roof of the old cottage.   STORM
7 We were waiting for the _____ of our plane when the storm began.   DEPART
8 We often go to the west coast on _____ days in summer.   SUN

E Do the crossword.

Across

3 a person who is travelling on a type of transport, e.g. bus, car, boat, plane
5 a small official book that shows who you are and where you come from when you travel to another country
7 all the bags you're carrying when you're travelling
9 a place to stay in
10 a coat that protects you from the rain

Down

1 a wide road where cars can travel very fast between cities
2 a card with a picture on one side and a space to write a message on the back
4 the time when somebody completes a university course and gets their degree
6 a vehicle which you can live inside and you can pull with a car
8 a small room where you sleep on a ship

12 Grammar

12.1 Present Continuous: future plans & arrangements

Σχηματίζουμε τον Present Continuous με *is/are* + το ρήμα + *-ing*.
Μπορούμε να χρησιμοποιήσουμε τον Present Continuous για να:
μιλήσουμε για σχέδια και ό,τι έχουμε κανονίσει για το μέλλον.
→ *Our class **is visiting** the museum next week.*
ρωτήσουμε για μελλοντικά σχέδια και ό,τι έχουμε κανονίσει για το μέλλον.
→ *What time **are** you **visiting** the museum?*

Σημείωση: Όταν χρησιμοποιούμε τον Present Continuous για το μέλλον, αναφερόμαστε συχνά σε συγκεκριμένες ημερομηνίες, μέρες και χρόνο γενικότερα. Χρησιμοποιούμε και χρονικές εκφράσεις όπως *this weekend/week, next summer, in the summer, tomorrow,* κλπ.

2.1 *Be going to*

Κατάφαση
I **am ('m) going to** travel.
He/she/it **is ('s) going to** travel.
We/you/they **are ('re) going to** travel.

Άρνηση
I **am ('m) not going to** travel.
He/she/it **is not (isn't) going to** travel.
We/you/they **are not (aren't) going to** travel.

Ερώτηση
Am I **going to** travel.
Is he/she/it **going to** travel.
Are we/you/they **going to** travel.

Σύντομες απαντήσεις	
Yes, I **am**.	**No**, I'**m not**.
Yes, we/you/they **are**.	**No**, we/you/they **aren't**.
Yes, he/she/it **is**.	**No**, he/she/it **isn't**.

Χρησιμοποιούμε *be going to* για:
μελλοντικά σχέδια και προθέσεις.
→ *They'**re going to visit** their relatives in Poland next month.*
σχέδια που αποφασίσαμε πριν από τη στιγμή που μιλάμε.
→ *It's hot in here. I'**m going to open** the window.*
ένα μελλοντικό γεγονός που βασίζεται σε στοιχεία ή ό,τι γνωρίζουμε.
→ *Neil loves the sea, so he'**s going to have** a great time on the cruise.*

Σημείωση: Χρονικές εκφράσεις που αναφέρονται στο μέλλον χρησιμοποιούνται και με το *will* και το *be going: this week/month/summer, tonight, this evening, tomorrow, tomorrow morning/afternoon/night, next week/month/year, at the weekend, in January, on Thursday, on Wednesday morning,* κλπ.

12 Grammar

Grammar Exercises

A Match to make sentences.

1 Where are you going to go for your holiday? □ a We're taking the plane to Belfast.
2 How are you going to travel there? □ b My parents and Grandad.
3 Who is going with you? □ c We're going to see the Giant's Causeway.
4 Are you staying in a hotel? □ d Yes, we're spending a whole month there.
5 What are you going to see there? □ e We're going to go to Ireland.
6 Are you planning to stay there for a long time? □ f No, we're going to stay with my Irish cousins.

B Look at William's diary and write sentences about his plans for each day. Use the Present Continuous.

MONDAY	TUESDAY	WEDNESDAY	THURSDAY	FRIDAY	SATURDAY	SUNDAY
do English homework	practise playing violin for school concert	school concert 6 o'clock – play in orchestra	play basketball – after school	meet Mark outside cinema – 6.30 p.m.	go to Fred's birthday party – 8 o'clock	visit Uncle George and Aunt May

1 On Monday, he _____
2 _____
3 _____
4 _____
5 _____
6 _____
7 _____

C Complete the sentences using *be going to* with these verbs. Use each verb only once.

carry   go   hang out   miss   not catch   put on   study   take

1 I _____ for my science test.
2 It's raining, so Tracy _____ her raincoat before she goes out.
3 We _____ on a boat tour along the coast.
4 Andrew _____ with his friends this weekend, but they haven't made any special plans.
5 You must hurry up, or you _____ the plane.
6 They _____ warm clothes on the camping trip.
7 I _____ the bus to the airport. I'm going by taxi.
8 How _____ you _____ your suitcase? It looks heavy!

Alphabetical Word List

An alphabetical list of all the words that appear in the companion follows. The number next to the entry shows where the word appears.

A

(I'm) sorry   2.109
a bit   11.28
a.m. (abbrev)   3.47
abroad   12.44
abstract   11.79
accommodation   12.53
action   9.112
active   2.45
activity   1.6
actor   3.80
actress   11.58
actually   1.112
adult   3.50
adventure   11.80
adventurer   9.142
adventurous   2.100
advert   2.111
advertisement   2.112
affect   9.145
afterwards   5.40
again and again   2.33
age   1.9
ago   5.79
agree   1.61
airport   1.163
aisle   11.30
alarm clock   1.60
all at once   11.105
all of a sudden   11.63
allow   3.71
almost   2.147
alone   12.59
amaze   9.85
amazed   9.86
amazing   1.174
ambulance   3.32
amphibian   6.54
amusement park   5.50
ankle   9.89
anniversary   8.53
announce   11.77
ant   10.110
anywhere   7.78
apologise   10.95
apology   10.98
appointment   5.99
approximately   10.101
April   4.107
aquarium   6.129
Arctic Ocean   12.72
Argentina   1.19

armadillo   6.9
arrange   2.95
art gallery   3.150
article   9.16
artist   8.97
as (conj)   5.80
as soon as   11.91
aspirin   10.73
at first   8.63
at least   1.142
Atlantic Ocean   12.73
attach   5.84
attack   6.26
attend   5.59
attendance   10.103
attention   6.32
attraction   7.112
aubergine   10.49
audience   11.31
aunt   1.68
Australia   4.53
Austria   4.109
author   11.32
autumn   4.51
average   6.49
avocado   10.48

B

back cover   11.33
background   3.126
backpack   5.92
backwards   8.42
bakery   3.94
balcony   11.84
banana boat   9.8
bar   11.65
bar   3.151
barbecue   4.70
Battleships™   8.77
be born   4.68
be called   1.101
be good company   6.106
be late   1.88
be slow   1.86
be worth   9.30
beach   2.83
beak   6.58
beautifully   11.47
beaver   10.2
because (conj)   1.5
bedtime   5.77
before   4.10

beginner   2.125
beginning   2.129
behaviour   12.78
believe   5.35
belong to   1.104
bend   9.34
bend   6.45
Berlin   3.156
berry   11.20
best   4.64
best friend   1.96
best wishes   1.146
better   8.27
bhangra   2.14
biker   9.95
biking   9.94
biodegradable   7.15
blanket   2.3
block   8.29
blog   9.15
blood   6.137
blood vessel   5.113
board   9.60
board   12.24
board game   2.68
body   1.165
boil   4.145
Bolivia   6.44
Bolivian   4.112
bone   10.54
bonfire   4.72
book   9.38
booklet   8.69
bookshop   3.91
boot   2.52
bored   8.35
boring   2.36
borrow   3.114
both   1.56
bottom   11.60
bowl   10.39
boyfriend   1.76
brain   1.172
brake   7.109
branch   10.4
brave   9.76
bravely   9.77
Brazil   6.43
Brazilian   1.75
break   8.106
breathe   6.72
bride   4.75
bridesmaid   5.12

bridge   3.28
brilliant   5.44
brilliantly   11.46
British   4.111
broccoli   1.57
brown bear   6.90
brush   10.65
bubble   1.3
Buddhist   8.2
bug   6.139
build   5.5
building   3.15
Bulgaria   10.85
bungee jumping   9.84
burn   8.104
burrow   3.161
bus station   3.139
bus stop   3.118
busy   6.107
butcher   3.92
butterfly   6.8
button   1.159

C

cabin   12.10
cafeteria   12.19
cage   6.128
calcium   10.52
calf   6.67
call   9.111
calm   11.90
Cambodia   8.5
camel   6.103
camera   1.117
camouflage   6.19
camp   1.164
camp   2.104
camping   2.99
can   10.17
cancel   10.97
candle   4.91
canoeing   12.60
canvas   11.3
capital   1.134
caption   1.100
capture   6.141
car park   3.57
caravan   12.2
carbohydrate   10.51
card game   8.6
careful   9.13
carefully   1.110

Ecuador 6.5
edge 9.5
educational 8.57
Egypt 2.149
elastic 9.87
elbow 9.64
elbow pad 9.65
electricity 7.93
electronic 8.34
electronics 8.26
emergency 3.85
emotion 9.114
encourage 9.128
endangered 6.15
ending 2.130
enemy 11.10
energetic 2.38
energetically 11.45
energy 5.110
engineer 7.110
enjoy 1.39
enormous 7.61
enough 3.170
entertainment 8.85
entrance 7.87
environment 7.11
equipment 9.53
erase 11.95
erosion 9.137
especially 4.127
eventually 8.62
everyday 3.34
everywhere 4.38
evidence 12.50
evil 11.8
exam 1.102
excite 9.97
excited 4.63
exciting 4.28
excursion 12.54
excuse 10.74
excuse me 1.103
exercise 6.108
exhausting 9.14
exhibition 7.81
exist 9.127
exotic 5.81
expensive 11.66
experience 5.97
experiment 8.92
expert 8.102
explain 10.108
explode 4.14
explore 3.146
extra 2.40
extreme 9.11
extremely 9.132

F

facilities 3.53

fact 6.111
fair 8.41
fair 3.39
fall 8.108
famous 3.119
fancy dress 4.71
fantastic 1.147
fantasy 11.81
far 3.107
farm 1.26
fat 10.53
fear 10.115
feather 11.25
February 4.120
fee 9.104
feed 3.60
feel 5.96
feeling 5.94
female 6.119
Ferris wheel 5.54
festival 4.89
fever 10.62
fifth 8.45
fight 5.21
fighter 11.6
file 6.112
fill 4.18
fin 6.60
finally 4.131
find 11.98
finger 7.97
fire station 3.26
firefighter 3.37
firewood 11.93
fireworks 4.13
first 1.70
fish 5.3
fisherman 3.42
fishing 5.29
fishmonger 3.93
fit 10.12
fit 7.99
Fitbit 7.104
fizzy drink 4.76
flag 4.117
flap 6.99
flashlight 3.166
flavour 1.98
flight 7.85
flipper 9.57
floating 12.3
floor 7.77
floor 7.82
flour 3.8
follow 8.59
following 10.106
football boots 1.77
footpath 5.62
for example 4.133
for hire 3.58
for sale 2.118

forget 4.157
form 3.17
formal 2.134
formation 9.136
four hundredth 8.51
fourth (number) 4.122
free 2.120
free time 1.128
freezer 10.16
French 1.94
frequency 2.80
frequent 3.56
fresh 7.13
Friday 2.10
fridge 4.86
friendly 2.27
frighten 11.15
frightened 9.73
frightening 9.12
front cover 11.35
frozen 3.122
fry 4.134
full 7.106
full-size 12.14
fun 1.48
fun run 5.61
function 7.80
fur 6.61
furry 6.76

G

garland 4.161
garlic 10.83
gecko 6.12
general 8.91
gentle 9.20
gentleman 3.41
geography 8.84
geologist 9.2
get away 6.37
get dressed 4.101
get married 2.153
get off 3.98
get on 3.99
get on with 2.73
giant 3.44
gift 6.105
giraffe 6.86
girlfriend 2.79
give up 9.21
glass 7.55
glide 9.18
glove 9.107
go 8.18
go out 2.61
goggles 9.59
gold 1.83
goldfish 1.17
golf course 12.16
goose 6.65

government 10.94
GPS 7.70
graduation 12.71
graffiti 9.120
grain 3.7
gram 6.120
gramophone 7.92
grandfather 1.106
grandmother 1.45
grandparent 1.108
grape 10.30
graze 3.64
great 1.47
great-grandmother 5.25
greengrocer 3.90
Greenland 12.74
greens 10.1
grind 3.6
ground 4.165
ground floor 7.86
grow 1.28
grub 10.111
guacamole 4.139
guard 1.153
guard dog 1.154
guess 8.93
guide 1.151
guide dog 1.152
gymnasium 4.114

H

habit 10.8
habitat 6.57
hairdresser's 5.26
half an hour 3.102
Halloween 4.54
hand cycling 9.39
handle 7.45
handloom 1.31
handwriting 2.133
hang 6.41
hang out with 2.72
harbour 3.9
hardly ever 2.78
harm 6.29
hate 1.51
have a go 5.64
Hawaii 9.6
headache 10.13
heading 9.108
healthy 5.111
heart 5.112
heavy 6.80
helmet 5.46
helpful 12.62
herbivore 6.39
hermit crab 11.102
hero 8.65
heroine 11.44
hiccups 7.17